AF541615

Economic Reforms and Employment

ECONOMIC REFORMS AND EMPLOYMENT

Edited by

Dr. M. Soundarapandian

DISCOVERY PUBLISHING HOUSE
NEW DELHI

Published by:
Namit Wasan

DISCOVERY PUBLISHING HOUSE PVT. LTD.
4383/4B, Ansari Road, Darya Ganj
New Delhi-110 002 (India)
Phone : +91-11-23279245; 23253475; 43596065
E-mail : discoverybooksindia@gmail.com
discoverypublishinghouse@gmail.com
namitwasan9@gmail.com
web : www.discoverypublishinggroup.com

***Edition:* 2020**

ISBN: 978-81-7141-979-1

Economic Reforms and Employment

Printed at:
Infinity Imaging Systems
Delhi

Preface

While going through the past literature on the subject, it is also clearly noted that some scholars did attempt examination of the impact of economic reforms on the employment/unemployment situation in India (Visaria, 2002; Sen, 1996; 2002; Sundaram, 2001; Dutt, 2001; Bandyopathyay and Giri 2001; Chadha, 2001; Chandra and Sahu, 2002). An attempt has been made to analyse the objective of understanding the magnitude and growth of rural. unemployment in India during the pre-and post-economic reforms periods. This comparison of rural unemployment levels and their growth rates for the periods would facilitate assessing the effect of the economic reforms on unemployment situation.

In this context, a national level seminar on Economic Reforms and Labour Market has organized in our institute. The selected papers presented in the seminar are edited as a book. This work contains 33 contributions of eminent writers including one write up of the editor. This volume examines the impact of economic reforms on the employment level in rural India and the issues like economic reforms, effects of the New Economic Policy, Employment and Unemployment level, role of the institutions on employment generation, Human Resource Development, Entrepreneurship Development Programme, etc.

Undoubtedly, the book will be immensely beneficial to the administrators, policy-makers, planners and researchers. I am thankful to Dr. N. Thillainayagam, Professor and Head, Department of Rural Industries and Management, Gandhigram Rural Institute for his encouragement for publishing the book. It gives me great pleasure to thank my wife Mrs. S. Indhumathy and my children S. Diwakaran and S. Vidya for their support in completion of this work. Finally, my sincere thanks to Discovery Publishing House for their acceptance in publishing the book.

Dr. M. Soundarapandian

Contents

List of Contributors

Dr. A. Meenakshi Sundara Rajan, Reader in Economics, S.T. Hindu College, Nagercoil, Tamil Nadu.

Jeyalakshmi, Research Scholar, School of Economics, Madurai Kamaraj University, Madurai, 625021, Tamil Nadu.

M. Regina Mary, Selection Grade Lecturer, Department of Economics, Fatima College, Madurai-18, Tamil Nadu.

M. Jeyakani, S.G. Lecturer, Department of Business Administration, S.V.N. College, Madurai-625019, Tamil Nadu.

S. Natchathira Jothi, S.G. Lecturer, P.G. Department of Economics, Lady Doak College, Madurai-625002, Tamil Nadu.

V. Santhanalakshmi, Research Scholar, School of Economics, Madurai Kamaraj Unviersity, Madurai, Tamil Nadu.

Dr. S. David Amitharajan, Head, Post-graduate Department of Commerce, The American College, Madurai-625002, Tamil Nadu.

Dr. R. Seerangarajan, Reader, Department of Rural Industries and Management, Gandhigram Rural Institute, Gandhigram-624302, Tamil Nadu.

Dr. N. Namasivayam, Professor and Head, Department of Commerce, DDE, Madurai Kamaraj University, Madurai, Tamil Nadu.

Dr. S. Vijayakumar, Lecturer, Department of Commerce, M.K.U. College, Madurai, Tamil Nadu.

Dr. P. Jeya Baskaran, Lecturer in Commerce, Aditanar College, Tiruchendur, Tamil Nadu.

K. Sivagami, S.G. Lecturer, Arulmigu Palaniandavar Arts College for Women, Palani-624615, Tamil Nadu.

M. Pushpa, S.G. Lecturer, Arulmigu Palaniandavar Arts College for Women, Palani-624615, Tamil Nadu.

T. Tamilselvi, S.G. Lecturer, Arulmigu Palaniandavar Arts College for Women, Palani-624615, Tamil Nadu.

A. Shahin Sultana, Junior Research Fellow, Department of Social Work, Layola College, Chennai-34, Tamil Nadu.

M. Raju, Lecturer, P.G. and Research, Department of Economics, Gobi Arts and Science College, Gobichettipalayam-638453, Tamil Nadu.

Dr. M. Soundarapandian, Reader in Rural Industries and Management, Gandhigram Rural Institute, Gandhigram-624302, Tamil Nadu.

Dr. S. Jagadeespandi, Department of Rural Industries and Management, Gandhigram Rural Institute, Gandhigram, Tamil Nadu.

Dr. M. Nagesh Kumari, Lecturer in Economics, P.S.G.R. Krishammal College for Women, Coimbatore, Tamil Nadu.

C. Renuka, Head, Department of Economics, P.S.G.R. Krishanammal College for Women, Coimbatore, Tamil Nadu.

Dr. G. Themozhi, Head, Department of Commerce, Arulmigu. Palaniandavar Arts College for Women, Palani, Tamil Nadu.

P. Sorubarani, Research Scholar, Madurai Kamaraj University, Madurai, Tamil Nadu.

Dr. J. Chandrakantha, Principal, Arulmigu Palaniandavar College for Women, Palani, Tamil Nadu.

Dr. C. Sivapragasam, Reader in Statistics, Department of Applied Research, Gandhigram Rural Institute, Gandhigram.

M. Jeganathan, Research Scholar, Department of Applied Research, Gandhigram Rural Institute, Gandhigram, Tamil Nadu.

Dr. N. Markkendayan, Reader in Commerce, G.T.N. Arts College Dindigul, Tamil Nadu.

M. Ponniah, Lecturer (SS) in Commerce G.T.N. Arts College, Dindigul, Tamil Nadu.

Dr. V. Mohanasundaram, Reader, Department of Economics, P.S.G. College of Arts and Science, Coimbatore-14, Tamil Nadu.

Dr. M. Swaminathan, P.G. Professor and Head of the Department of Commerce, A.V.V.M. Sri Pushpam College (Autonomous), Poondi-613503, Thanjavur District, Tamil Nadu.

Dr. A. Venkatachalam, Reader in Commerce, G.T.N. Arts, College Dindigul-624005, Tamil Nadu.

Dr. M. Inbalakshmi, Lecturer (SS) in Commerce, G.T.N. Arts College, Dindigul-624005, Tamil Nadu.

Dr. K. Alamar, Faculty Members, Department of Economics (Centre for Research) Arul Anandar College (Autonomous), Karumathur, Madurai-625514, Tamil Nadu.

Dr. N. Murali, Faculty Member, Department of Economics Arul Anandar College, Karumathur, Madurai-625514, Tamil Nadu.

Dr. R. Shashikumar, Lecturer, Department of Economics, Bangalore University, Bangalore-560056, Tamil Nadu.

Dr. P. Gnana Soundari, Reader in Economics, Lady Dock College, Madurai, Tamil Nadu.

Dr. Vanathi Vembar, S.R. Lecturer, Department of Business Administration, Annamalai University, Tamil Nadu.

Dr. Venkatesh Kumar, Faculty, Thiagarajar School of Management, Madurai, Tamil Nadu.

Dr. R. Shashi Kumar, Lecturer, Department of Economics, Bangalore University, Bangalore-560056, Karnataka State.

Dr. N. Balasubramanian, Prof., Department of Management Studies, University of Madras, Chennai.

Prof. G. Shankar, Department of Management Studies, University of Madras, Chennai.

S. Pravin, Research Scholar, Department of Economics, P.S.G. College of Arts, and Science, Coimbatore, Tamil Nadu.

Dr. Samwel Kakuko Lopoyetum, Senior Post-Doctoral Research Fellow, (PDRF), Department of Co-operation, Gandhigram Rural Institute Gandhigram–624302, Dindigul, Tamil Nadu.

S. Kanagasabai, Senior Scale Lecturer, Post-graduate Department of Economics, Thiagarajar College, Madurai, Tamil Nadu.

Dr. S. Hasan Banu, Reader in Commerce, H.K.R.H. College, Uthamapalyam, Theni District, Tamil Nadu.

Dr. S. Karuppaiyan, SR. Project Officer-cum-Lecturer, Centre for Adult Continuing Education, Bharathidasan University, Tiruchirappalli-24, Tamil Nadu.

A. Chandraprabha, Research Scholar in Rural Industries and Management, Gandhigram, Tamil Nadu.

Economic Reforms and Youth Unemployment in India

Dr. A. Meenakshi Sundara Rajan

Introduction

The problem of youth unemployment is one of the few policy concerns that are common to both the developing and developed economies. It is now well established that unemployment levels are higher among the young than for any other age cohort, in most countries, regardless of their level of development. The problem of youth unemployment is thus global as well as serious. Nonetheless, while the transition of youth from the educational to the work environments poses formidable challenges to public policy analysts in the developed world, it is the switchover from a pre-work/educational environment, under increasing pressure to start earning a livelihood from an early age, constitutes a major area of policy concern in the developing societies. In recent years, the situation has tended to become pretty serious in India, like many other developing societies in Asia and elsewhere.

The definition of the youth, in the ordinary course, varies from country to country. Many countries treat persons in the age group 25-29 years, along with those in the age groups 15-19 and 20-24 years as young; some go even upto 34 years. ILO defines that persons belonging to the age groups, 15-19 and

20-24 years as the youth, although for some problems and issues they might have to look at the age group 10-14 at the lower end and the age group 25-29 at the upper end.[1]

In a country like India, where there is acute unemployment and underemployment problems, the introduction of "right to work" as a fundamental right has great implications. Constitutionally, it would mean that every citizen, who is idle and willing, must be in a position to claim work. In that case, it would become binding on the government to provide jobs or make payments in cash lieu of the same. This would be an effective way of fulfilling the major objectives of eliminating poverty, reducing inequality and sustaining a high rate of economic growth. The Economic Reforms initiated by the Government have failed to promote adequate employment opportunities to the Indian youths. The Table 1.1 gives the details of Employment and Unemployment during Pre-reform and Post-reform period.

Table 1.1 reveals that one of the most daunting challenges facing India is to provide employment not only for the additions to the labour force but also to reduce the backlog of unemployment accumulated from the past. The number of unemployed applicants on the live register of the Employment Exchanges increased from 162 lakh in 1980 to 400.9 lakh in 1998 registering 147.46 per cent increase. The total number of employed increased from 223.1 lakh in 1980 to 279.4 lakh in 1996 an increase of 20.15 per cent. The percentage of the unemployed has been steadily increasing from 12.1 per cent in 1980 to 15.8 per cent in 1996. It is true that not all applicants on the live register are unemployed and that some register for better prospects. Nevertheless, the unemployment problem is a serious problem under reform period.

Unemployment is painful to everybody but the youth are the worst victims of the problem. The potential energies of the youth in the country are often misdirected for socially unproductive activities. There is no doubt about the massive character of the increase that is taking place in educated unemployment. This has obvious consequences in creating

Table 1.1: Employment and Unemployment in India during 1980-1998

Year	*Total Employed (in lakhs)*	*Percentage of unemployed to total employment*	*Number of live register at the end of the year (in lakhs)*
1980	223.1	12.1	162.00
1981	228.8	12.2	178.38
1982	234.9	12.3	197.53
1983	240.1	12.5	219.53
1984	242.1	12.6	235.47
1985	245.8	12.9	262.70
1986	250.6	13.0	301.13
1987	253.9	13.2	302.47
1988	257.1	13.4	300.50
1989	259.6	13.7	327.76
1990	263.5	13.8	346.32
1991	267.3	14.1	363.00
1992	270.6	14.4	367.58
1993	271.8	14.8	362.75
1994	273.7	15.2	366.91
1995	274.1	15.4	367.42
1996	279.4	15.8	374.30
1997	N. A.	N. A.	380.48
1998	N. A.	N. A.	400.90

Source : Selected Socio-economic Statistics, India 1996 and 1997.

social tensions and frustrations among the young and leads to a fall in the quality of life, apart from the economic waste it involves in lowering the returns from the investment in education. As the Indian Government "does not collect or publish annual data on the growth or decline of unemployment, one is forced to rely on the number of job seekers registered with the nation's 300 plus employment exchanges to get an idea of trends in it".

Concern for employment stems from the fact that even with a GDP growth rate exceeding five per cent per annum, employment growth has not kept the growth in labour force that is estimated to be 2.5 per cent per annum.[2] The development process is the only viable way to generate additional employment opportunities on a sufficiently large scale to absorb the increments to the labour force of our young generations and the backlog of the unemployed and the underemployed young labour force.

Table 1.2: State-wise Unemployment in India (1998)

State	*Employment Exchanges*	*Registration*	*Live Register*	*Percentage of live register to total live Register*
Andhra Pradesh	31	346.8	3206.5	8.0
Assam	53	148.4	1489.3	3.7
Bihar	67	411.3	3310.0	8.3
Gujarat	41	218.3	943.3	2.4
Haryana	95	263.7	820.1	2.0
Karnataka	40	326.5	1812.7	4.5
Kerala	78	417.3	3672.1	9.2
Madhya Pradesh	65	547.2	2547.1	6.4
Maharashtra	42	684.6	4103	10.2
Orissa	37	176.9	970.9	2.4
Punjab	44	136.6	578.8	1.4
Rajasthan	38	148.2	891.2	2.2
Tamil Nadu	37	562.5	4175.8	10.4
Uttar Pradesh	102	578.4	2638.5	6.6
West Bengal	74	413.1	5724.7	14.3

Source: Report of Ministry of Labour, 1997-98,

Table 1.2 clearly reveals that unemployment is a basic problem of all states. Punjab shows the least registration and the least number on the live register. It may be because agricultural activities engage people of that state and it is remunerative. Uttar Pradesh, Tamil Nadu and Maharastra show more registration than the other states. West Bengal also shows the highest level in terms of live register. These figures are standing testimony to the defective manpower planning in the country. Moreover, the country's economic growth is not creating enough jobs. The most serious but apparent consequence of the problem of unemployment is abject poverty.

One of the principal ways of linking economic growth and human lives to remove poverty is to invest liberally in the education and health of the people. Whenever India has made adequate investment in education and skill training of its people and in strengthening its human capital, the strategy has paid rich dividends especially in employment. For example, India has already emerged as the second largest exporter of computer software as a result of extensive investment in skill formation in Bengalore in Karnataka State.

Tamil Nadu is also emerging as a forerunner in education and skill training of its people and is taking efforts to improve the health and employment of its people.

Magnitude of Youth Unemployment in India

Statistics regarding the magnitude of educated unemployed is given in Table 1.3.

On the basis of the data collected from the Ministry of Labour, estimates of growth of number of young job seekers on the live register of employment exchanges in the country, classified by Age-group for the 10 years (1987-97), have been prepared. The Table 1.1, reveals the unemployment position of the young generation in India. The number of youths registered in the live register of employment exchanges for

Table 1.3: Number of Job Seekers on the Live Register of Employment Exchanges in the Country Classified by Age-Group (1987-97) (in thousand)

Year	*Age Groups (in years)*									*Total*
	0-14	*15-19*	*20-24*	*25-29*	*30-34*	*35-39*	*40-49*	*50-59*	*60+*	
1987	87.8	5860.7	11111.7	8146.4	3418.4	1303.3	274.3	19.4	2.0	30224.2
	0.3	19.4	36.8	27.0	11.3	4.3	0.9	0.1	0.9	100.0
1988	67.0	5718.7	10943.4	8141.7	3493.1	1333.1	293.1	29.4	1.4	30020.9
	0.2	19.0	36.5	27.1	11.6	4.4	1.0	0.1	0.0	100.0
1991	229.1	7538.8	12481.7	9285.3	4370.9	1883.3	452.1	50.0	8.5	36299.7
	0.6	20.8	34.4	25.6	12.0	5.2	1.2	0.1	0.0	100.0
1994	120.0	7285.8	12003.4	9513.6	4968.3	2137.0	577.8	76.7	8.9	36691.5
	0.3	19.9	32.7	25.9	13.5	5.8	1.6	0.2	0.0	100.0
1997	156.6	7867.1	12759.6	10019.8	5323.0	2309.3	626.2	78.3	0.0	39139.9
	0.4	20.1	32.6	25.6	13.6	5.9	1.6	0.2	0.0	100.0

Note: Total percentage in second line totals may not tally due to rounding.

the 10-year period has fallen from 99 per cent to 98.2 per cent that is a decrease of 0.8 percent.[3]

But, by Age-group-wise, there is an increase on the total number of youths seeking employment at the age group of 0-14. It swells from 87.8 million to 156.6 million, that is an increase of 178 per cent for the 10-year period. In the age group of 15-19, the number of job seekers has risen from 586.07 million (in 1987) to 786.71 million. In the age group of 20-24, and 25-29, the total percentage of job seekers on the live register of employment exchanges shows an increase of 14.83 percentage, 22.99 percentage and 55.73 percentage respectively.[4]

During 1987 the total number of job seekers on the live register of employment exchanges in the country was 3.02 crore and it rose to 3.91 crore during 1997. In that total, the youth unemployment figure was 2.85 crore. But in 1997 the youth unemployment figure went up to 359 crore. At the same time the percentage of the youth seeking jobs in the total live register of employment exchanges in the country fell down from 94.3 per cent (1987) to 91.8 per cent (1997).[5]

Magnitude of the Educated Unemployment

Educated manpower refers to those persons who have obtained at least a matriculation or a Higher Secondary Certificate. The unemployment rate in this category has been relatively high which points to the mismatch between the growth of the educated labour force and employment opportunities. The stock of educated manpower of matriculates and graduates registered in the employment exchanges, rose from 34.74 million in 1987 to 41.86 million during 1996 as per the Table 1.3. The percentage of educated in the total live register went up from 55.3 per cent in 1987 to 67.5 per cent in 1996.[6]

The placement figure for the educated people through employment exchanges shows a downward trend, say 113.58 million in 1987 to 11.13 million in 1996. It clearly tells us the failure of the employment exchanges to find out jobs for educated youth. The percentage of increase in the live register over the previous years goes on fluctuating. It was 1.7 in 1987, and increased to 10.2 in 1990 and decreased to 1.9 in 1996. This figure clearly shows that the educated youth do not have faith in the employment exchanges of our country to find out jobs for them.[7]

The following table gives the details about the educated unemployed who registered in employment exchanges in India during 1987-1996.

Table 1.4: Employment Exchange Statistics—Educated (Matric and Above) All India 1987-1996 (in thousand)

Year	*Registration*	*Placement*	*Educated live $ Register*	*Total live $ Register*	*% of Placement to Registration*	*% Increase in live Register over per various year*	*% of Educated live Register to total live Register*
1	2	3	4	5	6	7	8
1987	3474.4	135.8	16735.4	30247.3	3.9	1.7	55.3
1988	3726.0	147.3	17511.8	30050.2	4.0	4.6	58.3
1989	4052.6	143.9	19147.3	32776.2	3.6	9.3	58.4
1990	4365.7	129.0	21106.8	34631.8	3.0	10.2	60.9
1991	4208.2	125.5	22434.5	36299.7	3.0	6.3	61.8
1992	3874.8	128.4	23006.3	36758.4	3.3	2.5	62.6
1993	3653.6	95.1	23616.8	36275.5	2.6	2.7	65.1
1994	4046.1	101.7	23976.6	36691.5	2.5	1.5	65.3
1995	4166.3	103.6	24795.0	36742.3	2.5	3.4	67.5
1996	4186.5	111.3	25265.3	37429.6	2.7	1.9	67.5

Source: Report of Ministry of Labour, 1997-98.

$ At the end of year

If we look at the number of educated job seekers (matric and above), the total number of matriculates or Xth pass who

Table 1.5: Number of Educated Job-Seekers (Matric and above) by Educational Level as on 31.12.1996

Sl. No.	*Educational Level*		*Number of Live Register*			% of each Stream to Total Graduate & above	*% of each level to Total*
1.	Matriculates or X Pass		11183.1	3346.6	14529.7		57.5
2.	Higher Secondary Intermediate and Undergraduates or XII Pass		4820.5	1422.7	6243.2		24.7
3.	Graduates and Post-graduates						
	I						
	II					41.8	
	III	Arts	1272.6	603.3	1875.9	17.8	
	IV	Science	567.9	232.5	800.4	15.7	
	V	Commerce	561.8	144.7	706.5	3.8	
	VI	Engineering	155.0	16.4	171.4	0.7	
	VII	Medicine	21.8	10.1	31.9	0.0	
	VIII	Veterinary	3.6	0.8	4.4	0.7	
	IX	Agriculture	29.5	3.0	32.0	0.3	
	X	Law	12.5	2.6	15.1	15.1	
		Education	365.8	314.2	680.0	3.9	
		Others	107.7	66.6	174.3		
		Total	3098.2	1394.2	4492.4	100.0	17.8
Grand Total			19101.8	6163.5	25265.3		100.00

Note: The information in collected at Half Yearly Intervals ending June and December each year.

Source: Records of Registrar of Employment Exchanges.

have registered in the employment exchange, was 1452.97 million. Among them 1118.31 millions were men and 334.66 million were women in 1996. The percentage of matriculates seeking employment through employment exchange was 57.5 per cent.

624.32 million Higher Secondary, Intermediate and undergraduates were waiting for appointment order from the employment exchanges of India. Among them 482.05 million were men and 142.27 million were women. Their percentage to the total educated unemployed was 24.7 per cent.

The Graduates and Post-graduates were also in queue for getting employment opportunities through employment exchanges. 449.24 million graduates and post-graduates had registered their names in employment exchanges of India. Among them 309.82 million were men and 139.42 million were women. Their percentage to the total number of educated job seekers was 7.8 per cent.[8] The Table 1.4 reveals above said facts (Refer Table 1.5).

Magnitude of the Women Job Seekers

The employment exchange statistics on women job seekers at all India level from 1989-1998 is given in the Table 1.6.

The number of women job seekers in the employment exchange statistics rose from 127.57 million in 1989 to 151.80 million in 1998. The percentage of women in the live register rose from 18.6 percentage in 1989 to 23.8 percentage in 1998; within 10 years the increase was 5.2 per cent.[9]

Women Job Seekers—State-wise

The Table 1.6 has given the particulars about the employment exchange statistics on women job seekers state-wise, 1998.

Among the 25 states, Kerala stands first among women job seekers that is, 22.78 million, followed by Tamil Nadu

Table 1.6: Employment Exchanges Statistics on Women Job Seekers All India 1989-1998 (in thousand)

Year	*Registration*	*Placement*	*Live and Register*	*Total (Live and Register*	*% of Placement to Registration*	*% increase in Live Register over previous year*	*% of Live Register of women to total live Register*
1	2	3	4	5	6	7	8
1989	1275.7	50.5	6108.6	32776.2	4.0	11.9	18.6
1990	1319.9	50.6	6699.8	34631.8	3.8	9.7	19.3
1991	1326.7	50.9	7307.7	36299.7	3.8	9.1	20.1
1992	1160.9	44.2	7652.9	36758.4	3.8	4.7	20.8
1993	1226.2	42.4	7865.3	36275.5	3.5	2.8	21.7
1994	1316.5	42.1	8044.5	36691.5	3.2	2.3	21.9
1995	1376.0	43.6	8020.3	36742.3	3.2	0.3	21.8
1996	1446.9	50.1	8379.5	37429.6	3.5	4.5	22.4
1997	1609.1	61.5	9032.7	39139.9	3.8	7.8	23.1
1998	1518.1	42.0	9526.1	40089.9	2.7	5.4	23.8

Source: Report of Ministry of Labour.

22.13 million and Maharastra 15.93 million. But the percentage of placement to registration of women job seekers is high in Gujarat that is, 9.2 per cent which is followed by Rajasthan 8.3 per cent and Karnataka 7.9 per cent. The states like Kerala, Tamil Nadu and Maharastra have failed to create job opportunities to women. Kerala provided only 3.4 per cent placement to women job seekers and for Tamil Nadu it was only 3.3 per cent and Maharastra only two percentage. Without creating adequate employment opportunities to women job seekers gender bias could not be solved, and social upliftment of women is not possible.[10]

Table 1.7: Employment Exchange Statistics on Women Job-Seekers State-wise, 1998

Sl. No.	*State/UT*	*Employment Exchanges/UEI GBS$*	*(In Thousand)* Registration	Placement	Live & Register	*% of Placement to Registration*
1	2	3	4	5	6	7
1.	Andhra Pradesh	31	95.6	3.3	650.1	3.5
2.	Arunachal Pradesh	8	1.4	0.0	4.2	0.0
3.	Assam	53	31.7	0.5	335.0	1.6
4.	Bihar	67	67.2	0.3	284.5	0.4
5.	Goa	1	8.5	0.4	37.6	4.7
6.	Gujarat	41	29.7	5.7	139.0	19.2
7.	Haryana	95	43.8	0.4	148.3	0.9
8.	Himachal Pradesh	15	59.7	1.0	239.4	1.7
9.	Jammu & Kashmir	14	4.3	0.0	26.8	0.0
10.	Karnataka	40	92.0	7.3	417.8	7.9
11.	Kerala	78	227.8	7.7	2010.0	3.4
12.	Madya Pradesh	65	122.5	0.9	419.1	0.7
13.	Maharastra	42	159.3	3.2	815.9	2.0
14.	Manipur	10	7.8	0.0	91.3	0.0
15.	Meghalaya	10	2.9	0.0	13.7	0.0
16.	Mizoram	3	4.6	0.0	22.1	0.0
17.	Nagaland	7	3.4	0.1	8.2	2.9
18.	Orissa	37	27.0	0.7	175.1	2.6
19.	Punjab	44	35.1	0.4	144.1	1.1
20.	Rajasthan	38	21.7	1.8	96.8	8.3
21.	Sikkim*					
22.	Tamil Nadu	37	221.3	5.0	1392.1	2.3
23.	Tripura	4	4.7	0.3	91.5	6.4
24.	Uttar Pradesh	102	74.4	0.5	279.5	0.7
25.	West Bengal	74	120.0	0.8	1328.0	0.7
26.	A & N Islands	1	0.9	0.1	9.5	11.1
27.	Chandigarh	2	7.8	0.3	17.7	3.8
28.	D. & N. Haveli	1	0.2	0.1	1.7	50.0

1	2	3	4	5	6	7
29.	Delhi	21	36.7	1.1	277.8	3.0
30.	Damm and Diu	2	0.3	0.0	1.5	0.0
31.	Lakshadweep	1	0.6	0.1	2.5	16.7
32.	Pondicherry	1	5.2	0.1	45.1	1.9
	Total	945	1518	42.0	9526.1	2.8

Source: Registrar of Employment Exchanges.

Note: * No Employment Exchange is Functioning in this state.
@ Figures Less than 50
$ At the end of the year.

Magnitude of Educated Women Job Seekers

Table 1.8: Employment Exchange Statistics on Educated Women Job-Seekers All India 1987-1996 (in thousand)

Year	*Registration*	*Placement*	*Live & Register*	*Total Live $ Register for women*	*% of Placement to Registration*	*% increase in Live Register over previous year*	*% of Educated women to total live Register for Women*
1	2	3	4	5	6	7	8
1987	755.6	32.7	3516.1	5373.2	4.3	5.4	65.4
1988	808.1	37.8	3753.6	5460.5	4.7	1.6	68.7
1989	903.4	34.9	4005.0	6108.6	4.6	11.9	65.6
1990	990.0	35.7	4549.8	6699.8	4.4	9.7	67.9
1991	990.0	34.9	5020.5	7307.7	3.9	9.1	68.7
1992	949.0	35.2	5427.6	7652.9	3.6	4.7	70.9
1993	896.0	32.1	5713.1	7865.3	3.2	2.8	72.6
1994	1045.0	28.4	5873.8	8044.5	2.7	2.3	73.0
1995	1082.9	26.3	5878.6	8020.3	2.4	-0.3	73.3
1996	1129.2	35.9	6163.6	8379.5	3.2	4.5	73.6

Source: Registrar of Employment Exchanges.
$ At the end of the year

The total number of educated women job seekers had been increasing steadily from 1987 to 1996. In 1987, 75.56 million educated women job seekers registered their names in the employment exchanges and it rose to 112.92 million in 1996. The percentage of educated women in the total live register for women had increased from 65.4 per cent in 1987 to 73.6 per cent in 1996. It is due to less placement to the women job seekers by the employment exchanges.

If we refer Table 1.4 we can realize the magnitude of educated women job seekers that is, matric and above in 1996. The total number of educated women job seekers was 616.35 million that is, 24.39 per cent of total educated job seekers.

What Should India Do for Wiping Out Unemployment Among Young Generations?

The present state of unemployment in the country clearly shows that the economic reform has failed to have proper manpower planning. The presence of surplus manpower shows that all is not well with our manpower planning under economic reform. So it is suggested that Economic reforms with proper manpower planning should be made on the basis of past experience. The success of economic reforms depends on the correct estimates of shortages and surpluses of manpower and to concentrate to formulate proper manpower planning which will solve unemployment problems among youth in India.

The problem of educated unemployment requires urgent attention. The unemployment of graduates, post-graduates, engineers and medical graduates is unfortunate in view of the growing need for their services in the country. Keeping in view of the requirements of the economy, the whole system of education has to be reformed by making it employment oriented. This requires perfect co-ordination among the areas of economic planning, manpower planning, educational planning and Economic Reforms. A new wage structure reflecting the needs of the economy will have to be evolved. In effect realistic educational planning combined with a rational wage structure would be an essential step towards solving the problem of educated unemployment.

REFERENCES

1. Government of India, Ministry of Labour and Employment, Selected Socio-economic Statistics, 1996 and 1997, Controller of Publications, New Delhi, 1998.
2. Government of India, Ministry of Labour and Employment, Report of Ministry of Labour 1997-98, Controller of Publications, New Delhi, 1999.
3. Records of Registrar of Employment Exchanges, 1998.
4. Ibid.
5. Ibid.
6. Reports of Ministry of Labour, op. cit.
7. Ibid.
8. Records of Registrar of Employment Exchanges, op. cit.
9. Reports of Ministry of Labour, op. cit.
10. Records of Registrar of Employment Exchanges.

2

New Economic Policy and Service Sector

M. Regina Mary

"The performance of service sector has been impressive in the reform era. However, Services can grow faster only if there is an Industrial revival."

C.R.L. Narasimhan

Introduction

The occupational pattern of a country refers to the division of its working population according to different occupations or industries. All these industries are divided into three groups viz (1) Primary sector—it included cultivation and allied agricultural activities. (2) Secondary sector—Primarily based on capital and (3) Tertiary or service sector—The services which help the primary and secondary sectors come under this category. These are telecommunications, transportation, tourism, banking insurance, construction, computers related services and other governmental and non-governmental services.

The New Economic Policy (NEP)—Structural Adjustment Policy (SAP) envisages rapid industrialisation with modernisation for attaining faster growth of GDP. The basic logic of the NEP is that industrialisation will set in motion forces that will generate growth impulses in other sectors of the economy. The NEP finds its origin in the growth of neo-liberalism during the decades of the eighties and the nineties. The neo-liberalism affirms the role of market in economic decision-making correspondingly, it limits the role of the state to rule-setting and contract upholding. This type of growth aims at establishing a global market based system which in turn would lead to the development of UDCS.

It was the early nineties, when India was passing through an unprecedented economic crisis, following political instability that was further aggravated by the impact of the Gulf-War. Our country was trapped in galloping inflation, stress on balance of payment, frustrating position of foreign exchange reserves, and other micro-economic imbalances. To overcome this situation, Dr. Manmohan Singh the then Finance Minister, introduced the New Economic Policy in the 1991-92 Union Budget. Several Policy measures, popularly known as Economic Reforms, were initiated to revive the Indian Economy. Economic reforms set the stage for gradual liberalisation and globalisation to reinvigorate the economy and to reap the benefits of worldwide moves in these directions. These reforms were introduced, first as a part of stabilisation policy and later to bring in structural adjustment. This new economic policy certainly has direct and indirect impact on agriculture, industry and service sectors of the economy.

The subject of the services sector and its role in the Indian economy have become topical for many reasons: One, since the 1980 the robust performance of the services sector has underpinned economic growth.

Two, although in some respects the Indian experience is similar to the experiences of some developed economies, what has been unique here is that the impressive growth in services (leading to a sectoral shift in its favour) has occurred at a time when the shares of industry and agriculture were either stagnant or showed a decline. Three, the momentum in favour of services continued during the 1990s. In fact, as the RBT puts it, "it was the growth performance of the service sector that provided a modicum of resilience to the overall growth of the Economy, particularly in times of adverse agricultural shocks and Industrial slowdown" four, the services sector has come to occupy a dominant position in the composition of the GDP, since the 1980s.

Impact of Economic Reforms on Indian Agriculture

The economic reforms largely focused on fiscal adjustment, foreign trade and investment, industry and financial sectors. Some of the measures, notably reduction of subsidies, reduction of bank lending for priority sector, tariff reductions and trade liberalisation do have some impact on agriculture. Agricultural subsidies, which had been provided for agricultural input that includes fertilizers, electricity, irrigation and for output in the form of minimum support price (MSP) to give favourable and reasonable price to the farmers, have been either reduced or withdrawn completely. Due to total decontrol of potash and phosphate fertilizers, the price of these two fertilizers have been almost doubled. Moreover, there is a 30 per cent price hike of nitrogenous fertilizers, which is the result of partial reduction of subsidy a nitrogenous fertilizers. In India, where more than 70 per cent farmers have small and marginal landholding, cannot afford to buy potash and phosphate fertilizers in required amount that resulted in imbalanced fertilizer application. It has a deleterious effect on soil structure and composition that ultimately hampers sustainable agricultural production (Raju and Chowdhry; 1997).

Table 2.1: Average compound Growth Rates of GDP and by Sectors During 1980s and 1990s

Year	*GDP*	*Agriculture*	*Industry*	*Manufacturing*	*Services*	*Per capita GNP*
1980-91	5.4	3.9	6.3	6.1	6.4	3.4
1992-00	6.4	3.3	6.5	7.4	8.2	4.9

Source: Economic Survey, Govt. of India, 2001-02.

Indian agriculture was characterised by low and stagnant growth performance till the mid-sixties. However, after Green Revolution, the performance improved till the end of eighties (Table 2.1). Though the other sectors have recorded high growth rate in the 80s as well as the 90s, in their case

Table 2.2: Macro Economic Indicators Relating to Indian Agriculture

Year	*GDP Growth (%)*	*Ag. GDP Growth (%)*	*Share of Ag. in GDP (%)*	*Capital Formation in AG. (% of GDP)*	*% age of Expenditure Total outlay*
1990-91	5.4	4.1	32.9	27.7	5.5
1991-92	0.8	-1.9	32.0	23.4	6.2
1993-94	5.9	4.1	32.8	22.4	4.8
1995-96	7.3	-0.9	30.2	25.8	4.7
1997-98	6.5	-2.4	28.7	24.8	4.5
1999-00	6.1	1.3	27.3	23.6	4.4
2000-02	4.0	-0.2	-	-	4.1

Source: Economic Survey, GOI, Various issues.

also, there was no significant difference in performance over two decades. A distinguishing feature in the case of agricultural output is sharp—year-to-year fluctuations. These high variations imply unpredictable nature of agriculture in India and the precariousness of our food security position. The share of agriculture in GDP is declining steadily; still it continues to contribute nearly one-fourth of the country's GDP (Table 2.2).

Nevertheless, it is interesting to note that agriculture's share in workforce, particularly, in rural areas, is not declining despite its declining importance in the country's GDP. This indicates that more and more people are depending on agricultural activities. It also suggests low absorption capacity of the secondary and tertiary sectors.

Impact of Economic Reform on the Manufacturing Sector

The compound annual rate of growth of gross value added by the registered manufacturing sector was 5.91 per cent between 1990-91 and 1998-99. The corresponding rates between 1950-51 and 1965-66 and between 1980-81 and 1990-91 were 7.30 per cent and 7.66 per cent, respectively (Table 2.3). Proponents of economic reforms, such as Jagdish Bhagwati, have been arguing for radical changes in economic policies on the ground that the growth record in the past has been dismal. Table 2.3 shows that the growth achieved in the eighty-year period since 1991 has not been able to surpass that achieved during the first 15 years of Indian planning. It has also not been able to surpass the 7.47 per cent compound annual rate of growth achieved during the 10-year period of the Second and Third Five-Year plans (between 1955-56 and 1965-66). When planning with a conscious strategy for the development of basic and heavy industries was attempted. It also shows that the growth record during the reforms of the 1990s has been worse than that during the reforms of the 1980s.

Table 2.3: Compound Annual Rate of Growth of Manufacturing

Year	*CARG of Gross Value Added of Registered Manufacturing Sector at constant prices (per cent)*
1950-51 to 1965-66	7.03
1955-56 to 1965-66	7.47
1980-81 to 1990-91	7.66
1990-91 to 1998-99	5.91

Source: CSO, National Accounts Statistics (Various issues).

Impact of Economic Reforms on the Service Sector

A notable feature of the dynamics of structural transformation of the economy in recent years has been the rising contribution of the services sector which includes substantial value-added and skill intensive services, such as software, to the overall output in the economy. It is important to note that the growth of the services sector has imparted much of the resilience to the overall growth of the economy, particularly in times of adverse agricultural shocks and industrial slowdown. But more importantly, the sector has emerged as the fasts expanding sector, with implications for productivity, employment, trade and fiscal prospects of the economy. Between 1990-91 and 1998-99, the share of services (inclusive of construction) in real GDP increased from 43.7 per cent to 51.2 per cent. The contribution of growth of the services sector to the overall growth of GDP has also increased significantly from 47.5 per cent in 1990-91 to 49.8 per cent in 1998-99. The bulk of the increase in shares has taken place in trade, communications and banking and insurance segments. There are areas where there has been a spurt of technical progress and also increased competition, mainly induced but economic reforms. On the other hand, there are other areas like construction, hotels and railways where the shows have moved up in fractional terms.

The recent trends in the services sector point to several implications. First, a relatively high growth of the services sector would be generally suggestive of gains in productivity in agricultural and industrial sectors, induced by technological progress and other innovations, which result in moving employment away from the non-services sector to the services producing sector. It also indicates a shift of real expenditure from manufacturing to value-added services, which is generally associated with the process of economic development Secondly, while the rising share of the services sector in GDP is an encouraging sign of greater degree of diversification of the Indian economy, a corresponding decline in the share of Industry and Agriculture implies that the overall product gains economy will depend increasingly on what happens in the services sector. A large part of the services output continues to be non-tradable in nature. This along with the shift of employment would point to the need for policy initiatives towards introducing greater competition and efficiency in the serviced sector for ensuring its sustained contribution to high long-term growth. Thirdly, the relative prices of the services sector have been moving at a faster pace than those of the industrial sector.

Reforms paved the way for faster manufacturing growth, which in turn boosted the demand for certain types of producer services. Second, the financial sector reform resulted in a rapid growth of financial services. Three, reforms in certain infrastructure areas also contributed to a growth in services. Four, all these factors contributed to the sterling performance of the services sector during the reform period, with its share almost touching the 50 per cent mark. Five, the rapid growth in services is also attributable to external demand, spectacularly seen in software and other computer related services. Finally, the decelerating trend in manufacturing and the overall GDP seems less pronounced in the case of services. The performance of all sub-sectors improved during the reform period barring "financing, insurance, real estate and business services,"—a phenomenon attributable to the poor performance of the non-banking sector. The rate of growth during the 1990s was 7.9 per cent compared to 9.9 per cent earlier. However, the share of this sub-segment moved up substantially (to 26 per cent from 21 per cent earlier). The share of "trade, hotels and restaurants" was slightly lower at 30.7 per cent during the reform period compared to 32.1 per cent for the preceding decade. However, in percentage terms its growth during the reform period at 8.1 per cent was higher than the 5.9 per cent recorded earlier.

Can the impressive growth in services be sustained? According to the RBI, the growth of services stemming from capital productivity is a welcome sign. The gross value added from services registered a higher growth in the reform period. The recent surge in services has been contributed among others by "the skill intensive and high productivity activities" such as IT services, which have emerged as one of the fastest growing segments in the 1990s. Economic liberalisation and the encouragement shown to private capital in industry and infrastructure have also contributed to a surge in services. Finally, increased expenditure on administration and defiance, social services and rural extension services also impacted the services sector growth positively during the 1990.

The Important findings of the study are:

- The services sector's growth has provided an element of stability to the growth process.
- The service sector's growth in the reform period had been sustained by an increasing demand for

producer and consumer services coupled with external demand.

- The role of public administration and defence appears to be limited.
- Producer services have emerged as strong drivers of growth and that indicates a strong interlinkage with commodity producing sector of the economy. Among other things, this means that for services to grow even faster there must be an industrial revival.
- Services growth could be sustained if adequate demand impulses are generated in agriculture and industry.
- India's comparative advantage in the IT sector ought to be exploited to maintain the growth momentum.
- New opportunities in international trade in services can be profitably tapped, especially in the areas of communication and information services, technology transfer and software.
- For the economy as a whole to grow at an accelerated pace over the term, there must be a distinct improvement in the growth performance of the commodity producing sectors.

Conclusion

The services sector has emerged as the growth engine of the Indian economy. It's share in the economy is now around 46 per cent—generating a 4 per cent rise in GDP every year. New areas are emerging in finance and information technology and India could emerge as a major global resource centre. In recent years, there has been greater recognition of India's growing stature in the world economy by the international financial community and independent agencies. Its rate of economic growth makes India one of the fastest growing nations of the world. The world accept that India's integration with the global economy will necessarily by in stages, and that it can not give up all capital movement controls or open up its market to unbridled international competition. But the point is well taken that India continues to make credible progress towards globalisation.

REFERENCES

1. RBI bulletin Sep. Supplementary Issue 1999. pp. 141-151.
2. *India Today* Feb. 13-19, 2001 pp. 46-50.
3. R.C. Nandrajog *"Indian Economic Environment"* The Management Accountant, Feb. 2001 (42nd National Convention Papers) pp. 102-103.
4. Malik "Economic Reforms and Effect on Poverty" *Yojana,* Vol. 44, No. 7 July, 2000, pp. 10 to 18.
5. C.R.L. Narasimhan "The Services Sector in the Reform Era" *The Hindu*. 18th July 2003.
6. Ishwar Dhingra *"Indian Economy Environment and Policy"* Sultan Chand & Sons Publications 2002, pp. 750-51.
7. B.L. Mathur *"Economic Policy and Performance"* Discovery Publishing House, New Delhi, 2001, pp. 245-246.
8. Sethuraman "India's Economic Stability Gains Wider Recognition" *Yojana*, Sep. 2001, pp. 24-29.
9. Aminur Rashid Khan and Sabyasachi Das "Economic Reforms and Rural Development" *Kurukshetra*, January 2003, pp. 31-35.
10. Sudip Chaudhuri "Economic Reforms and Industrial Structure in India" *Economic and Political Weekly* Jan 12, 2002, pp. 155-161.
11. I. Satya Sundaram "Economic Reforms: Retrospect and Prospect" *Southern Economist* Vol. 41, No: 20, Feb. 15, 2003 p. 26.

3

Employment Implications of Economic Reforms

Jeyalakshmi

Introduction

Indian Government introduced many reform measures in the form of globalisation, liberalisation and privatisation in July, 1991. As a result of these measures subsidies to agriculture were reduced, fiscal deficit was controlled, economy was opened up to the global market, restrictions and controls were reduced, private sector had to grow and public sector had to shrink. In the wake of reform measures rural sector of our country has faced uncertain future. Given the predominance of the agricultural sector in the national economy both in terms of its contribution to the gross domestic product and more so in terms of employment provided by it, a meaningful employment strategy for rural India must give high priority to the development of agriculture and allied rural sectors. This chapter is to analyze the implications and effect of reform measures on the rural poor in particular and rural development in general.

Implications of Reform Measures

The above reform measures have many far-reaching implications for rural development. The important of them being the following:

- Irrigation requires huge public investment. Due to fiscal crunch, the government is withdrawing its investments on irrigation and groundwater. Private sector cannot afford to make such investment because it involves long gestation periods and political risks in the recovery of costs through levies and water rates;
- The relative share of the rural producers in consumer's rupee is showing a declining trend over many years. Will reform measures reverse the trend? Opening up of the trade in agricultural commodities will require good marketing facilities including storage, transport and processing;
- Reform measures try to bring free export and import of agricultural commodities so that the level and structure of product prices can be brought in line with international prices. This will benefit only the agriculturally developed areas was irrigation, technology and credit at the cost of backward areas. This will accentuate regional disparities and conflicts;
- The growth of agri-business will help only the large capitalist farmers not the small resource-poor farmers;
- The changes in cropping patterns due to the entry of agri-business firms will lead to decline in the production of cereals which are the main food for the rural poor. So the rural masses become dependent on the market for their food which may not be available at reasonable prices;
- Agri-business leads to the differentiation of peasantry. This leads to increasing inequalities in rural areas. Agri-business sector does not offer much scope for employment of the poor because the production processes are generally mechanised and they need very little labour;

- The proposed privatisation of common property resources also will affect rural people. Under common property resources even the landless labour has to maintain some animals which is possible only by landed families.

Over the past three decades, the employment scene in India has undergone some important changes. First, although agriculture continues to occupy a predominant position in the Indian economy, its share in GDP has declined from 44.8 per cent in 1977-78 to only 27.6 per cent in 1999-2000 at constant 1993-94 prices. However, there has been very little decline in agriculture's share in employment. The share of employment in agriculture (UPSS) declined only from 73.9 per cent in 1972-73 to 60.2 per cent by 1999-2000.

Second, as per the definitions used by the National Sample Survey Organisation (NSSO) in India, the incidence of open unemployment remains relatively low. During the entire period 1973-74 to 1999-2000 for which NSS data are available, employment (defined in terms of UPSS) grew at annual rate of 1.94 per cent. According to NSS, there were 3.98 million unemployed in India in 1973-74 and their number had increased to 7.49 million by 1993-94 and to as much as 9.15 million by 1993-94 and to as much as 9.15 million by 1999-2000. In the meantime, the incidence of unemployment (defined as the ratio of unemployed persons to the labour force) increased from 1.64 per cent in 1973-74 to 1.96 per cent in 1993-94 and to 2.25 per cent in 1991-2000.

Third, deceleration in the growth of employment during the post-liberalisation period 1993-94 to 1999-2000 has not been uniform across sectors of the economy, and a significant development has been a sharp decline in employment growth in agriculture during the 1990s. Thus, while the growth rates in the secondary and tertiary sectors decelerated from 3.62 per cent and 4.02 per cent pa during 1972-73 to 1993-94 to 2.43 per cent and 3.01 per cent pa, respectively during 1993-94 to 1999-2000, the growth rate in agricultural employment decelerated from 1.49 per cent pa to only 0.01 per cent pa.

Rural Credit

As a result of Economic Reforms rural credit became costlier and difficult which has made the rural finance system inefficient. To tone up the rural credit system and to improve its viability, the Government of India, Reserve Bank of India and National Bank for Agricultural and Rural Development have introduced several liberalised policy measures on Commercial Banks and Regional Rural Banks.

Commercial banks are mandated by the RBI to earmark 18 per cent of total annual lending to agricultural sector as part of priority sector lending, with a view to ensuring that flow of credit to agriculture increases substantially. The RBI in recent years has evolved a scheme in which banks have to prepare an annual action plan for disbursement of credit to agriculture under different heads. Accordingly, each bank is preparing Special Agricultural Credit Plan (SACP), segregated into quarterly targets, which is being monitored by the RBI.

The National Bank for Agriculture and Rural Development (NABARD), which is the apex bank in the field of rural credit, has taken several initiatives for facilitating flow of credit to the agricultural sector. These include strengthening of cooperative credit institutions, setting up Rural infrastructure Development Fund, formation of Self-help groups which are provided micro-finance, and the introduction of Kisan Credit Card Scheme (1998-99). The Kisan Credit Card Scheme is regarded as an innovative scheme to facilitate short-term rural lending.

The NABARD acts as a refinancing institution for all kinds of production and investment credit to agriculture, small-scale industries, cottage and village industries, handicrafts and rural artisans with a view to promoting integrated rural development. It also provides short term, medium term and long term credit to State Cooperative Banks, regional rural banks, land development banks and other financial institutions approved by the RBI. NABARD also maintains a Research and Development Fund to promote research in agriculture and rural development, to formulate and design projects and programmes to suit the requirements of different areas and to cover special activities.

Rural Employment Programmes

To generate employment opportunities to the rural masses with a view to generate rural assets and eradicate poverty, the Government of India and State Governments have launched a number of rural employment programmes and allocated massive public investments in various plan period. Following are the more important of them:

- Rural Works Programme (1961)
- Crash Scheme for Rural Employment Projects (1971)
- Pilot Intensive Rural Employment Projects (1972)
- Food for Work Programme (1977)
- National Rural Employment Programme (1980)
- Rural Landless Employment Guarantee Programme (1983)
- Jawahar Rozgar Yojana (1989)
- Employment Assurance Scheme (1993)

An in-depth analysis of the above rural employment programmes reveals the following weaknesses of the schemes:

- Lack of manpower planning
- Undertaking non-productive works
- Selection of schemes without proper examination
- Lack of technical and administrative supervision
- Erratic distribution of foodgrains
- Supply of poor quality of foodgrains
- Undertaking the works on political considerations on ad hoc basis
- Undertaking expenditure oriented programmes

- Lack of serious efforts to provide continuous employment to the beneficiaries
- Undertaking the schemes near the residence of rich farmers
- Frequent changes in the guidelines
- Undertaking schemes which are useful to the industrial class and absentee landlords
- Lack of provision for the maintenance of assets
- Delay in undertaking the schemes and the consequent non-completion of works
- Payment of low wages to the beneficiaries
- Employing the labourers from outside the village concerned
- Lack of committed administrative officers
- Corruption, wastage of money and resources
- Emergence of regional political parties
- Lack of political will.

These factors collectively rendered the rural employment programmes ineffective. Thus, these programmes were not able to generate adequate employment to the poor, increase their nutritional levels to the target levels and create sufficient durable assets. Recent Economic reform measures are not able to cope with the socio-economic conditions of the rural poor. The New Economic Policy with its emphasis on growth, modern technology, mechanisation and capital formation do not have any concern for the rural poor. While it is true that anti-poverty programmes could not be properly implemented and did not realize the targets, but the strategy of liberalisation, privatisation and globalisation comes not as correction but negation of the earlier policies.

Conclusion

Economic reforms with their emphasis on growth, modern technology, and mechanisation and capital formation indeed have no concern for the rural poor. The study emphasis will be on raising the capabilities of small peasants and promoting sustainable agricultural systems. Infrastructure development will be given the highest importance. Therefore, economic reforms can cope with the socio-economic conditions of the rural poor and generate accelerated rural development.

REFERENCES

1. G.S. Bhalla, Peter Hazell, "Rural Employment and Poverty", *Economic and Political Weekly,* Vol. XXXVIII, No. 33, 2003, pp. 3473-3483.
2. S. Mhendra Dev, "Economic Reforms and the Rural Poor", *Economic and Political Weekly*, Vol. XXX, No. 33, 1995, pp. 2085-2088.
3. Abijit Sen, "Economic Reforms, Employment and Poverty—Trends and Options", *National Bank News Review*, 1999, pp. 48-66.
4. Jaivir Singh, "Terms of Employment", *Economic and Political Weekly*, Vol. XXXVIII, No. 2, 2003.
5. T.T. Krishnamachari (Ed.), Arul Anandar *Journal of Economics*, Vol. 7, 1999.

4

Emerging Problems of Employment Generation in the Era of Economic Reforms

M. Jeyakani
S. Natchathira Jothi

Unemployment is one of the major hindrances for the economic development of our country. Unemployment results in poverty since without job people may not have sufficient income to buy even necessaries. Hence, employment generation is essential for improving the standard of living of the people, removal of poverty and for achieving a reasonable rate of economic growth. Economic reforms introduced in India during early 1990, include stabilisation programmes and structural adjustment. That is, measure to stabilize the balance of payment and the programmes to make adjustment in the economic structure to ensure reasonable economic growth.

According to Dr. Manmohan Singh, economic reforms attempts to create a macro-economic environment in which industry spreads ahead with growth rate of 12 per cent or more, generates more jobs and higher levels of wages and income through increased productivity, more than a decade is paved after the introduction of reforms. But, now many economists expressed their opinion that through the reform process resulted in an increase in GDP growth, there was no significant increase in employment. Economists who oppose economic reforms describe liberalisation and reforms as *"jobless growth"*. According to them, reforms leads to reduction of employment since, many public sector units started the process of downsizing and getting rid of excess labour. To compete with foreign companies, private companies in our country also reduce their manpower in the name of introducing new technology. Generation of viable employment in any economy is a necessary condition for its growth and development. This chapter attempts to analyse the employment generation in the era of economic reforms. *Semi-log growth equation* has been used to estimate the growth rates of employment in organised sector during the reform period (1991-1999).

GDP and Employment Generation

There is a general opinion that when compared to annual GDP growth rate, growth rate of employment is very low. Especially during the reform era there is an increase in annual GDP growth rate at the same time rate of growth in employment is declining.

Table 4.1: Growth of GDP and Employment during the Five Year Plans in India

Plans	*Annual GDP Growth Rate at Constant Price*	*Growth of Employment*
I	3.7	0.39
II	4.2	0.85
III	-3.8	2.03
IV	3.4	1.99
V	5.0	1.84
VI	5.5	1.89
VIII	6.7	1.38
IX	6.5	1.13
X	7.7	1.14

Source: P.K. Chatterjee and others, Economic Reforms and Employment Generation—IEA Conference Volume, 2001, p. 520.

Table 4.1 shows that annual GDP growth rate increased from 5.5 per cent during Sixth Plan to 6.7 and 6.5 per cent during Eighth and Ninth plan respectively. But, rate of

Table 4.2: Growth of Employment by Sectors

Industry	*Employed Workers (Million)*			*Annual Growth Rate %*	
	1983	*1993-94*	*1999-00*	*1993-94*	*1999-00*
Primary	208.99 (69.0)	245.16 (65.5)	239.83 (60.4)	1.60	-0.34
1. Agriculture	207.23 (68.4)	242.46 (64.8)	237.56 (59.8)	1.51	-0.34
2. Mining & Quarrying	1.76 (0.6)	2.70 (0.7)	2.27 (0.6)	4.16	-2.85
Secondary	41.66 (13.8)	55.53 (14.8)	66.91 (16.8)	2.90	3.14
3. Manufacturing	34.03 (11.2)	42.50 (11.3)	48.01 (12.1)	2.14	2.05
4. Electricity, Gas & Water Supply	0.85 (0.3)	1.35 (0.4)	1.28 (0.3)	4.50	-0.88
5. Construction	6.78 (2.2)	11.68 (3.1)	17.62 (4.4)	5.32	7.09
Tertiary	52.11 (17.2)	73.76 (19.7)	90.26 (22.7)	3.5	2.42
6. Trade	19.22 (6.3)	27.78 (7.4)	37.32 (9.4)	3.57	5.04
7. Transport, Storage & Communication	7.39 (2.4)	10.33 (2.8)	14.69 (3.7)	3.24	6.04
8. Financial Sector	1.70 (0.6)	3.52 (0.9)	5.08 (1.3)	7.18	6.20
9. Community, Social & Personal Service	23.92 (7.9)	32.2 (8.6)	33.2 (8.4)	2.90	0.55
Total Employment	302.76 (100.00)	374.45 (100.00)	397.00 (100.00)	2.04	0.98

Source: Ruddar Datt, Eco. Liberalisation and its implications for employment in India, IEA Conference Volume 2001, p. 464.

Figures in parenthesis denote the % of the Sector in the Total Employment.

growth in employment declined from 1.38 per cent to 1.13 and 1.14 during the same periods. Moreover according to an estimate made by P.K. Chatterjee and others, the *Correlation Coefficient* between annual GDP growth rate and growth of employment (actual and projected till X Plan) is only –0.36, i.e. there is only low level of negative correlation between these two variables.

Sector-wise Growth of Employment

Growth rates of employment in different sectors are exhibited in Table 4.2. This table depicts acceleration in the growth rate of employment only in three sectors.

Employment growth rate increased sharply to 6.04 per cent during 1993-94 to 1999-2000 when compared to 3.24 per cent during 1983-84 to 1993-94, in transport, storage and communication. Trade and construction sector also experienced acceleration in the growth rate of employment. Except the above-mentioned sectors, all other sectors recorded a deceleration in employment growth rate. The decline in employment growth rate is very high in community, social and personal services sectors. In those sectors the growth was 2.9 per cent during 1983-84 to 1993-94. But during the period 1993-94 to 1999-2000, it was only 0.55 per cent. According to experts, this decline is due to continuous ban on recruitment in Government department, Government companies and reduction of staff through various measures like VRS in Public sector enterprises and in government offices.

Employment in Organised Sector

Decline in employment opportunities in organised sector will affect employment generation. Table 4.3 portrays the figures related to the changes in employment in organised sector over the years and shows the percentage of organised sector employment in total employment.

Figures exhibited in Table 4.3 shows that annual growth rate of population has declined to 1.93 per cent during 1999-2000 from 2.12 per cent during 1983-94. But during the same period there is nearly 50 per cent decrease in annual growth rate of total labour force and total employment. Annual

Table 4.3: Total Employment and Organised Sector Employment

Sector	Employment (Million)				Growth Rate (% per annum)	
	1983	*1988*	*1994*	*1999-00*	*1983-94*	*1994-00*
1. Total Population	718.21	790.0	895.05	1004.1	2.12	1.93
2. Total L. Force	308.64	333.49	318.94	406.05	2.05	1.03
3. Total Employ.	302.75	324.29	374.45	397.00	2.04	0.98
4. Organised sector employment	24.01 (100.00)	25.71 (100.00)	27.37 (100.00)	28.11 (100.00)	1.2	0.53
(a) Public Sector	16.46 (68.6)	18.32 (71.3)	19.44 (71.0)	19.41 (69.1)	1.52	-0.03
(b) Private Sector	7.55 (31.4)	7.39 (28.7)	7.93 (29.0)	8.7 (30.9)	0.45	1.87
5. Share of organised sector employment in total population	7.93	7.93	7.3	7.08		
6. Share of total Labour force in total population	43.0	42.2	42.7	40.4		

Source: Ruddar Datt, Eco. Liberalisation and its implications for employment in India, IEA Conference Volume 2001, p. 464.

growth rate of labour force decreased from 2.05 per cent to 1.03 per cent and annual growth rate of employment declined from 2.04 per cent during 1983-84 to a meager 0.98 per cent during 1994-2000.

Annual growth rate of employment in organised sector was only 0.53 per cent during 1994-2000 when compared to 1.2 per cent during 1983-94. In the organised sector, public sector recorded a deceleration in annual employment growth rate. In public sector, the percentage annual growth rate decreased to the level of –0.03 per cent during 1994-2000 from 1.52 during 1983-94. But private sector recorded an improvement. The growth rate became 1.87 per cent during 1994-2000 when compared to 0.45 per cent during 1983-94. This may be due to an increase in foreign investment.

The share of organised sector employment in total employment was 7.93 during 1988. It declined during the reform era and reached the level of 7.08 during 1999-2000. Share of total labour force to total population decreased to 40.14 during 1999-2000 from 42.2 per cent during 1988.

Analysis of Growth Rates of Employment in Organised Sector

Table 4.4 depicts the data related to the number of persons employed in private sector, public sector and in the total organised sector during the various years in the reform era. Table 4.4 reveals that there exist fluctuations in the employment in private sector as well as in public sector.

Table 4.4: Employment in Organised Sector *(Lakh of Persons)*

Year	*Public Sector*	*Private Sector*	*Total*
1990	187.72	75.82	263.54
1991	190.57 (1.52)	76.76 (1.24)	263.53 (1.44)
1992	192.10 (0.8)	78.46 (2.21)	270.56 (1.21)
1993	193.26 (0.6)	78.51 (0.06)	271.77 (0.45)
1994	194.45 (0.62)	79.30 (0.01)	273.75 (0.73)
1995	194.66 (0.11)	80.59 (1.63)	275.25 (0.55)
1996	194.29 (-0.19)	85.12 (5.62)	279.41 (1.51)
1997	195.59 (0.67)	86.86 (2.04)	282.45 (1.09)
1998	194.18 (-0.072)	87.48 (1.72)	281.66(-0.28)
1999	194.15 (-0.02)	87.58 (0.11)	281.73 (0.04)

Source: Economic Survey, 2000-2001, p. 53.

Figures in parentheses represent the percentage change in employment over the previous period.

The estimated growth rates of employment in organised sector based on semi-log growth model are shown in Table 4.5. The value of the Goodness of Fit (R^2) ranges between 0.664 and 0.947, which indicates the fitted regression, is the best fit. From the perusal of the estimated results, it is understood that, the compound growth rate in private sector is 1.796, which is four times greater than the compound growth rate in the public sector.

Table 4.5: The Estimated Compound Growth Rates of Employment in Organised Sector based on Semi-Log Growth Equation $LnY = a + bt + u$

	Public Sector	*Private Sector*	*Total*
Constant	5.242	4.301	5.571
Regression Coefficient	0.003818 (3.98)*	0.0148 (11.146)*	0.0078 (12.015)*
CGR	0.383	1.796	0.779
R^2	0.664	0.94	0.947

Source: Computed by the researcher CGR denotes Compound Growth Rate.

The above analysis shows that there was deceleration in employment generation during the reform era (1991-2000). Even in agriculture sector and in rural India, the employment generation is declining. According to Nilakantha Rath, the average number of days in unemployment increased from 15 to 19 for rural males, from 11 to 15 for rural females, no change at 10 days for urban male and decreased from 9 to 8 for urban female during 1999-2000. According to Bhalla and Peter Hazel the share of employment in agriculture declined from 73.9 per cent in 1972-73 to 60.2 per cent during 1999-2000. They further add that with 60 per cent of the national workforce producing a little more than a quarter of GDP, the relative productivity of workers in agriculture is less than one fourth that in non-agricultural occupations.

Some of the reasons identified for increase in unemployment during reform era include reduction in the strength of public sector enterprises, government offices; adoption of new technology like computerisation in both private and public sector organisations; ban on recruitment; failure of monsoon etc. According Dr. Mukta S. Adi, the declining trend in employment particularly in the organised industrial sector of the economy may be due to the rise in the growth rate of population and labour force, use of more and more capital intensive techniques of production, use of labour saving, devices, periodical industrial recession etc.

Conclusion

Providing employment to all is necessary for economic growth and development. If it is not planned properly the benefits of reforms may not reach people. Government must evolve suitable policies and measures to generate employment. For example, development of rural infrastructure may enhance the employment of rural people. Promotion of small scale and informal sector, housing for poor, vocational education, promotion of entrepreneurship, restrictions on retrenchment etc. may lead to generation of employment. Hence, it may be concluded that the economic reforms have negative impact on employment generation and it is the appropriate time to take necessary steps to generate employment, especially for unemployed-educated-youth of this country and for the rural people who suffer due to both failure of monsoon and liberalisation.

REFERENCES

1. Chaddha G.K. and A.N. Sharma (1997): *Growth, Employment and Poverty in Rural India*, Vikas Publishing House, New Delhi.
2. Raj Kumar Sen and Biswajit Chatterjee (2002) (ed): *Indian Economy—Agenda for the 21st Century*, Deep and Deep Publications Pvt. Ltd.
3. Nillakantha Rath, Data on Employment, Unemployment and Education, *Economic and Political Weekly*, Vol. XXXVI No.23, January 9, 2001, p. 2083.
4. Bhalla and Peter Hazel, Rural Employment and Poverty, *Economic and Political Weekly*, Vol. XXXVIII No. 33, August 16, 2003, p. 3473.
5. Ruddar Datt, *Economic Liberalisation and Its Implications for Employment in India* (2001), IEA, Conference Volume, Vellore.

5

Impact of New Economic Policy on Service Sector

V. Santhanalakshmi

Introduction

A prominent feature of the growing economic development of Indian economy is an emergence of service sector which involve a very heterogeneous spectrum of economic activities. Today services cover wide range of activities such as management, banking insurance, hospitality, communication, entertainment, wholesale distribution and developmental activities. The share of service sector in the real GDP in India has surpassed that of agriculture and industry at a relatively faster phase as compared top other industrialised nations. Services sector plays an important role in the Indian economy.

The expansion of the services sector has always been seen as a necessary concomitant of economic growth, to the point where it is often listed as one on the indicators of the economic development process. The theory underlying such an assumption [which was elaborated by economists like Kuznets, Clark and Fisher] was one which viewed development as a three-stage process, with the primary, secondary and then tertiary [or services) sectors becoming more dominant in successive phases. Typically, therefore, a rise in the share of services in national income was viewed as being positively associated with both economic growth and quality of life.

The three decades from 1950-51 to 1980-81 saw economic growth average around 3.5 per cent per year which is called "Iron or Hindu rate of growth". There was a welcoming acceleration of economic growth in the 1980s to 5.6 per cent a year, based on a clear acceleration of growth performance in all the three constituent sectors of agriculture, industry and services. Unfortunately, the growth acceleration of the eighties was accompanied by the emergence of unsustainable fiscal deficits, continuation of widespread economic control and a costly anti-export bias in trade policy and growing reliance on external borrowing to fund a widening current account deficit in the balance of payments. A sharp decline in remittances from overseas Indian workers in the wake of the Gulf War (1990) led to outflows of short-term capital and surge in oil prices, putting extreme pressure on India's foreign exchange reserves and balance of payment crisis, which brought growth to a grinding halt in 1991-92 and pushed the economy into considerable disarray.

In July 1991, emergency measures were undertaken by the Indian Government to restore external and domestic confidence in the economy and its management. The rupee was devalued; the fiscal deficit was cut and special balance of payments financing mobilised from the IMF and the World Bank. Being crisis induced, the initial phase of reforms had to focus on macro economic stabilisation, simultaneously, and reform of industrial policy, trade and exchange rate policies, and foreign investment policy were initiated along with tax reforms, financial sector reforms and public sector reform.

The economy responded exceptionally well to these initiatives. There was a dramatic change in the professional perception about the Indian economic performance and prospects. One of the most encompassing and growing areas of activity is the service sector which naturally raises questions regarding the significance of the phenomenon. The reform process now has completed eleven years and this can not be considered as too short a period to assess the impact of reforms. It would, therefore, be proper to undertake an appraisal of the achievements and shortcomings of economic reforms particularly on Service Sector to understand as to whether the country is moving in the right direction, or alternatively, is there a need to reform the reform process undertaken during the nineties.

On these lines, the main aim of this chapter is to assess the impact of economic reforms on service sector. More specifically this study tries to test whether the service sector or any of its major components has shown a statistically valid change in its growth rate since 1991. The analysis has been carried out over a period of twenty-two years from 1980-81 to 2001-02 in order to give equal weightage to pre-reform and post-reform period.

This study completely depends on secondary data. The data regarding services sector are collected from National Accounts Statistics of India 1950-51 to 2000-01. This volume contains Central Statistical Organisation's 51 year data series from 1950-51 to 2000-01 based on the revised national income and production statistics with 1993-94 as the base year.

This chapter consists of VI sections. The Section I constitute the importance objective, methodology and data source of the study. Section II and III discusses the impact of new economic policy on service sector by its percentage contribution to GDP its sub-sector's percentage contribution to total services, simple arithmetic method of average annual growth rate and co-efficient of variation. In the section IV an elegant econometric method of dummy variable has been used to estimate the compound growth rate in the pre- and post-reform period. The section V explores the reasons, positive and negative implication for spurt in the service sector growth. And the suggestions and conclusions are presented in the last section.

Percentage Contribution Analysis

Sectoral Contribution to GDP

The Table 5.1 shows the percentage share of three different sectors. Agricultural, Industrial and Services in Gross Product [GDP] at factor cost is at constant (1993-94) prices over the year 1980-81 to 2001-02. The study period (1980-81 to 2001-02) is sub-divided into pre-reform period (1980-81 to 1990-91 and post-reform period (1991-92 to 2001-02).

Table 5.1: Sectoral Contributions to GDP at factor cost (at 1993-94 prices) During 1980-81 to 2001-02

(in Percentage)

Year	*Agriculture Sector*	*Industrial Sector*	*Services Sector*	*Total*
1980-81	39.7	23.7	36.6	100
1981-82	39.5	24.1	36.4	100
1982-83	38.0	24.3	37.7	100
1983-84	38.7	24.4	36.9	100
1984-85	37.6	24.8	37.6	100
1985-86	36.3	24.8	38.9	100
1986-87	34.6	25.4	40.0	100
1987-88	32.8	26.1	41.1	100
1988-89	34.3	25.8	39.9	100
1989-90	32.7	26.6	40.7	100
1990-91	32.2	27.2	40.6	100
Average 1980-81 to 1990-91	36.04	25.20	38.76	100
1991-92	31.3	26.7	42.0	100
1992-93	31.5	26.4	42.1	100
1993-94	31.0	26.2	42.8	100
1994-95	30.3	27.0	42.7	100
1995-96	28.0	28.1	43.9	100
1996-97	28.5	27.8	43.7	100
1997-98	26.5	27.7	45.8	100
1998-99	26.6	26.9	46.5	100
1999-00	25.2	26.9	47.9	100
2000-01*	23.8	27.3	48.9	100
2001-02**	23.9	26.6	49.5	100
Average 1991-92 to 2001-02	27.87	27.05	45.07	100

Source: National Accounts Statistics of India 1950-51 to 2000-01.

*Provisional estimate;

** Quick estimate

Table 5.1 indicates a fall in the share of primary sector, an increase in the share of secondary sector and a small rise in share of service sector which exhibits the structural change occurred during pre-reform period. But the pattern of structural change of post-reform period has been different. A disturbing development has the fall in the share of industrial sector. Another development has a steady increase in the share of tertiary sector. Over the last decade, services have seen their average share of GDP rise from 38.76 per cent to 45.07 per cent. They now make up the largest sector of the economy, contributing almost double of what agriculture and industry do to GDP. Thus, the evidences suggest that the impact of reforms has much greater in services sector compared to the primary and secondary sectors.

The Composition of Service Sector

According to the National Accounts Statistics Total Service Sector has been classified into four sub-sectors such as (1) Trade, Hotels and Restaurant, (2) Transport, Storage and Communication, (3) Financing, Insurance, Real Estate and Business Services and (4) Community, Social and Personal Services. Table 5.2 shows the trend of the relative shares of the sub-sectors in the total service sector during pre-reform period and post-reform period.

The Table 5.2 explains that largest contribution of the sub-sector is the Trade, Hotel and Restaurant followed by Community, Social and Personal Services; Financing, Insurance, Real Estate and Business Services and finally Transport, Storage and Communication during post- and pre-reform period. However, increase in average contribution of the sub-sector occurred only in Financing, Insurance, Real Estate and Business Services from pre-reform period to post-reform period. And for all other sub-sectors, there has been decline in average contribution during post-reform period.

Growth Pattern Investigation

Annual Average Growth Rate

Table 5.3 presents the annual growth rate of service sector and its sub-sector during pre-reform period (1980-81

Table 5.2: Sub-sectors of Services Contribution to total Services sectors at factor cost (at 1993-94 prices) During 1980-81 to 2001-02

(in Percentage)

Year	*Trade Hotels and Restaurant*	*Transport Storage and Communication*	*Financing, Insurance Real Estate and Business Services*	*Community, Social and Personal Services*	*Total*
1980-81	33.31	17.01	17.82	31.86	100
1981-82	33.61	17.06	18.32	31.01	100
1982-83	33.20	16.47	18.94	31.38	100
1983-84	33.12	16.25	19.74	30.90	100
1984-85	32.49	16.32	20.15	31.04	100
1985-86	32.57	16.22	20.57	30.64	100
1986-87	32.09	16.04	21.32	30.55	100
1987-88	31.44	16.12	21.69	30.74	100
1988-89	31.29	15.69	22.53	30.49	100
1989-90	30.98	15.37	23.30	30.35	100
Average 1980-81 to 1990-91	32.27	16.16	20.75	30.82	100
1991-92	29.69	15.47	25.46	29.37	100
1992-93	29.89	15.37	25.59	29.15	100
1993-94	29.73	15.30	26.95	28.02	100
1994-95	30.73	15.69	26.57	27.01	100
1995-96	31.84	15.76	26.02	26.38	100
1996-97	31.97	15.91	25.96	26.16	100
1997-98	31.36	15.62	26.40	26.62	100
1998-99	31.01	15.50	26.46	27.04	100
1999-00	30.53	15.32	26.57	27.58	100
2000-01*	29.87	16.76	25.74	27.62	100
2001-02**	30.45	17.04	25.20	27.31	
Average 1991-92 to 2001-02	30.64	15.80	26.08	27.48	100

Source: National Accounts Statistics of India 1950-51 to 2000-01.

*Provisional estimate;

**Quick estimate

to 1990-91) and post-reform period (1991-92 to 2001-02). The average annual growth rates are also presented in the table.

Table 5.3: Average Annual Growth Rate of Services Sector and its Sub-Sector (at 1993-94 prices) During 1980-81 to 2001-02

(in Percentage)

Year	*Trade, Hotels and Restaurant*	*Transport Storage and Communication*	*Financing, Insurance Real Estate and Business Services*	*Community, Social and Personal Services*	*Total Services*
1	2	3	4	5	6
1980-81	5.2	6.7	1.9	4.1	4.5
1981-82	6.4	5.7	8.3	2.6	5.4
1982-83	5.4	3.0	10.4	8.0	6.7
1983-84	5.3	4.1	10.0	3.9	5.5
1984-85	4.3	6.8	8.5	6.8	6.3
1985-86	8.2	7.3	10.2	6.5	7.9
1986-87	5.8	6.2	11.3	7.0	7.4
1987-88	4.3	7.0	8.4	7.2	6.5
1988-89	6.8	4.4	11.4	6.4	7.3
1989-90	7.8	6.6	12.6	8.3	8.8
1990-91	5.0	4.6	7.7	4.1	5.3
1980-81 to 1990-91					
Average	5.9	5.7	9.1	5.9	6.5
C.V.	20.9	24.0	29.6	30.5	18.8
1991-92	0.7	6.3	12.0	2.6	4.8
1992-93	6.1	4.6	5.9	4.6	5.4
1993-94	7.1	7.2	13.4	3.5	7.7
1994-95	10.7	9.8	5.6	3.2	7.1
1995-96	14.4	11.0	8.2	7.9	10.5

(Contd.)

1	2	3	4	5	6
1996-97	7.7	8.2	7.0	6.3	7.2
1997-98	7.6	7.8	11.6	11.7	9.8
1998-99	7.0	7.3	8.4	9.9	8.2
1999-00	7.9	8.3	10.1	11.8	9.6
2000-01*	4.0	16.3	3.0	6.4	6.3
2001-02**	8.8	8.5	4.5	5.6	6.8
1991-92 to 2001-02					
Average	7.5	8.7	8.1	6.7	7.6
C.V.	44.5	33.4	39.2	47.0	22.9
1992-93 to 2001-02					
Average	8.1	8.9	7.8	7.1	7.8
C.V.	32.7	33.0	39.8	42.2	20.0

Source: National Accounts Statistics of India 1950-51 to 2000-01.
*Provisional estimate;
** Quick estimate
C.V. Co-efficient of Variation.

As in-depth analysis of growth trends during the post-reform period provides interesting insights. It is inferred that average total service sector growth rate has increased from 6.5 per cent in the pre-reform period to 7.6 per cent in the post-reform period. But it is to be noted that service sector growth rate collapsed to 4.8 per cent in 1991-92 as the balance of payments crisis of 1991 took its toll. Thus, if 1991-92 year is excluded, the average service sector growth rate during post-reform will be further increased to 7.8 per cent. This increase in average service sector growth is contributed by all the sub-sector except Financing, Insurance, Real Estate and Business Services, because its average annual growth rate has declined in the post-reform years compared to the pre-reform period even if 1991-92 excluded.

Stability in Growth Rate

Having compared the average growth rates in the pre-reform and post-reform period, the next step is to assess its stability. The stability in growth rate is assessed in terms of co-efficient of variation which is calculated by the formula.

$$CV = \frac{\sigma}{\overline{\chi}} * 100$$

Where, $\sigma = \sqrt{\Sigma(X - \overline{x})^2 / N}$ and $\overline{x} = \Sigma X / N$

This co-efficient of variation is calculated for Service Sector and its major components during pre-and post-reform period and are shown in Table 5.3. Larger the value of co-efficient of variation, greater is the instability in growth rates and vice versa. The comparison of co-efficient of variation for the post-reform with the pre-reform period expresses that growth rate of Service Sector and its sub-sector hold lesser stability than in pre-reform period. Even 1991-92 year is excluded; all the growth rates have lesser stability in the post-reform period than the pre-reform period. Thus, it may be concluded that growth rate of service sector has improved but with lesser stability during post-reform period.

Comparison with Similar Studies

This coincides with the conclusion of Shankar Aacharya (2002) that acceleration in GDP growth is entirely attributable to the services sector in post-crisis decade. However, Nagaraj (2000) arrived at the conclusion that there is no statistically significant acceleration in the growth rate of Service Sector between the 1980s and the 1990s. Hence, it is intended to test the validity of the statement by introducing the dummy variable in the intercept term and slope co-efficient in the Semi-log model.

Semi-log Model and Dummy Variable

The semi-log model is the best suitable and commonly accepted model for measuring the growth over time of the trend variables. The compound growth rate r is worked out from the least square estimate of slope co-efficient *(b)* in the Semi-log equation, using the formula r = (Antilog b-1)* 100.

$$Ln\ Y = a + bt + U_t \quad \text{.................................} (1)$$

The specific aim of this study being the impact of economic reforms on Service Sector and its components which is qualitative in nature, dummy variables are introduced in both intercept and slope co-efficient and the fitted model is

$$Ln\ Y = a + a_1 D + bt + b_1 Dt + U_t \quad \text{.........(2)}$$

Where Y – Service Sector or any of its components, *t*—time period (taking 1, 2, ..., 22), *a*—intercept, *b*—slope co-efficient, *D* = 1 for the post-reform years beginning with 1991, *D* = 0 for pre-reform years, prior to 1991, a_1 – differential intercept which tells how much the value of intercept change as a result of economic reform and b_1 – differential slope co-efficient which tells how much slope co-efficient change as a result of economic reform and U_t – the stochastic error term.

The results of the semi-log model by introducing dummy variable in intercept and slope co-efficient are given in Table 5.4.

Table 5.4: Results of the Semi-log model with Dummy Variables for Service Sector and its Major Components in India During 1980-81 to 2001-02

Sector	*a*	a_1	*b*	b_1	R^2
Trade, Hotels and Restaurant	10.7361 (774.4)+	-0.3236 (-8.5)	0.0574 (28.1)+	0.0231 (8.0)+	0.9978
Transport, Storage and Communication	10.0524 (754.4)+	-0.3942 (-10.8)	0.0561 (28.6)+	0.028 (10.7)+	0.9981
Financing, Insurance, Real Estate and Business Services	10.0627 (798.5)+	0.2305 (6.7)+	0.0954 (51.3)+	-0.0173 (-6.6)	0.9990
Community, Social and Personal Services	10.6631 (532.9)+	-0.2330 (-4.3)	0.0619 (20.1)+	0.0112 (2.7)++	0.9947
Total Services Sector	11.8132 (1500.4)+	-0.1857 (-8.6)	0.0665 (57.3)+	0.0122 (7.4)+	0.9994

Figures in brackets denote *t*-value.

+ - denotes statistical significance at 1% level.

++ - denotes statistical significance at 5% level.

Very high R^2 values in Table 5.4 shows that the dummy variable model (Equation 2) fitted for Service Sector and its components explains around 99 per cent of variation in the dependent variable. Except Financing, Insurance, Real Estate and Business Service Sector, differential intercept are not found to be statistically significant and differential slope co-efficient are found to be statistically significant for all other sector. Thus, there is statistically change in the growth rate of service sector and its sub-sector between the pre-reform and post-reform period. These regressions show that the performance of all sub-sectors significantly improved during the reform period barring "financing, insurance, real estate and business services", a phenomenon attributable to the poor performance of the non-banking sector.

The year 1991-92 being a crisis year, omission of the year from the analysis may provide better results. The model is estimated excluding 1991-92 and the results are presented in Table 5.5.

Table 5.5: Results of the Semi-log model with Dummy Variables for Service Sector and its Major Components in India During 1980-81 to 2001-02 Excluding the year 1991-92

Sector	a	a_1	b	b_1	R^2
Trade, Hotels and Restaurant	10.7361 (752.6)+	-0.3234 (-7.1)	0.0574 (27.3)+	0.0231 (7.2)+	0.9978
Transport, Storage and Communication	10.0524 (826.6)+	-0.4424 (-11.9)	0.0561 (32.7)+	0.0324 (12.3)+	0.9987
Financing, Insurance, Real Estate and Business Services	10.0627 (778.2)+	0.2372 (5.8)+	0.0954 (50.0)+	-0.0176 (-6.0)	0.9990
Community, Social and Personal Services	10.6631 (626.2)+	-0.3102 (-5.7)	0.0619 (24.7)+	0.0152 (3.9705)+	0.9964
Total Services Sector	11.8132 (1693.1)+	-0.2131 (-9.6)	0.0665 (64.6)+	0.0137 (8.7)+	0.9995

Figures in brackets denote *t*-value.

+ - denotes statistical significance at 1% level.

From Table 5.5, it is clear that more or less same results are obtained when the crisis year 1991-92 is excluded. Only difference to be noted here that differential slope co-efficient is statistically significant at 1 per cent level for Community, Social and Personal Services.

Compound growth rate is calculated by [(Anti log b)-1]*100 for the pre-reform period and by [Anti log $(b+b_1)$-1]*100 for the post-reform period.

The Table 5.6 presents the compound growth rate for Service and its main components during pre-reform and post-reform period.

Table 5.6: Compound Growth Rate of Service Sector and its Major Components during pre-reform and post-reform periods in India

(Per cent per year)

Sector	*Pre-reform period CGR*	*Post-reform period CGR*	*Post-reform excluding 1991-92 CGR*	*Significance of the difference*
Trade, Hotels and Restaurant	5.9	8.4	8.4	Significant
Transport, Storage and Communication	5.8	9.0	9.3	Significant
Financing, Insurance, Real Estate and Business Services	10.0	8.1	8.1	Not-Significant
Community, Social and Personal Services	6.4	7.6	8.0	Significant
Total Services Sector	6.9	8.2	8.4	Significant

Table 5.6 depicts that there is statistically valid break in services sector and its sub-sector except Financing, Insurance, Real Estate and Business Services since 1991.

Service sector growth has increased from 6.9 per cent to 8.2 per cent during post-reform period when 1991-92 year is excluded; the growth rate will be 8.4 per cent in post-reform period. The growth rate of Financing, Insurance, Real Estate and Business Services declined from 10 per cent to 8.1 per cent which is the same even if the year 1991-92 is excluded. But this decline in growth rate is insignificant. Indeed, the sub-sector of Trade, Hotel and Restaurant, Transports, Storage and Communication and Community, Social and Personal Services growth rate has significantly increased.

Possible Explanation and Implications

Factors responsible for spurt in services sector during Post-reform period

The spurt in the contribution of service sector to the GDP has been specially marked after New Economic Reforms Dr. Raja J. Chelliah, Chairman of Tax Reforms Committee, Government of India (1991) and also Madras School of Economics, says "As the economy develops, generally the per capita income increases and there is greater specialisation" which "tends to push up the share of the services".

The Indian economy is well-diversified and has reaped the benefits of a decade of reform. As a consequences Indian economy witness increasingly driven by services, as the tertiary sector now accounts for close to one-half of GDP. Therefore, India is perceived as a post-industrial society—a 'knowledge' based economy. Such optimism is perhaps largely based on the recent spurt in software exports and the perceived potential of trade in services such as information technology, communications and entertainment.

During reform period, Indian economy received a great impetus in her expansion of the infrastructure and social and community services. A large part of the service sector consists of infrastructure such as banking, insurance, finance, transport and communication and social and community services such as educational and medical facilities. Consequently, the service sector has grown tremendously throughout the reform period.

Economic liberalisation leads to the operation of the demonstration effect as a consequence of the growing mobility due to expanding foreign trade, tourism and cultural and educational tours. Indeed, urbanisation is closely associated with a rise in demands for infrastructure services such as communications, public utilities and distribution services. A substantial change in the private consumption pattern of the Indian economy is observed with increasing urbanisation. Many new goods and services enter into the consumption basket.

Tourism has expanded rapidly during the reform period, facilitated by progress in the means of transportation and people of ordinary means are participating more and more due to spreading of knowledge through radio and television and also modern technology. Reforms paved the way for faster manufacturing growth, which in turn boosted the demand for certain types of producer services. Further, the process of reform in the Telecom Sector has been dramatic.

The financial sector reform resulted in a larger contribution of financial services. Finally, increased expenditure on administration and defence, social services and rural extension services also imparted the services sector growth positively during the 1990s. All these factors contributed to the sterling performance of the services sector during the reform period.

Implications of Service Sector

Merits

Karnataka chief minister S.M. Krishna, minister of state for IT and Tourism D.B. Inamdar said the service sector was clearly emerging as the new engine of economic growth. The sector needs to be geared up for improving the quality of life and play a greater role in the economic development.

The expansion of the services sector has important implications for productivity, employment, welfare, income distribution, trade and for the design and conduct of macro economic policies. Because, the relatively high growth of services would generally be supported on the supply side by productivity gains in agriculture and industry due to diffusion of technical progress and innovations.

As a result of the addition of more and more services every year during reform period, service tax was introduced in 1994-95. The number of tax payers has also increased enormously. Since its introduction 1994, revenue collected from service tax has been increasing steadily.

Today, India is a recognised software super power. Indian's exports of services such as software have grown rapidly and these earnings [within the larger income from trade in "invisibles"] have resulted in a healthy balance of payments position.

Even from an education viewpoint, several institutions in India are able to offer quality education in software thus ensuring the presence of a skilled workforce in the future in the software sector.

Demerits

However, increase in service sector's share of the GDP has been marked by a simultaneous fall in the primary sector's contributions and only a smaller rise in contribution from the secondary sector. What worries us is that the growth of services sector is independent growth of the commodity sector. Besides, the share of services in national income is much larger than its corresponding share in employment. This is not desirable as it may lead to inflation or higher import demand for consumer goods. In most countries of the world, the service sector plays a significant role in the expansion of both GDP and employment.

Suggestions and Conclusion

Suggestion

- If the services grow without the commodity sector such growth quite clearly cannot be sustained for too long. Thus, the growth of services should be linked to the growth of output in agriculture and industry. Further it might become necessary to make deliberate effort to improve commodity sector.

- Services sector growth must be driven more by productive services such as trade, tourism, hotel, transport and financial services and not by unproductive services such as community, social and personal services. Private sector should be encouraged to promote productive services.
- The rise in the share of services in GDP itself is not bad. What is important is its direction. For instance, in rural areas, health, educational and transport facilities are very poor. The large employment potential of housing provides a tremendous scope for employment in the present phase of development. If the service sector concentrates on these, it would certainly promote productive employment.
- Public investment must be stepped up to generate demand for capital goods. The Government must step up public investment in railways, power system, health, education, irrigation and other agricultural infrastructure by using additional resources through service tax.
- The share of service sector in national income has increased significantly during reform period. The growth of this sector has to be increased further and must be stabilised in order to raise the overall growth of the economy. The quality of service sector has to be improved in order to attract investments.

Conclusion

The observed changes in aggregate economic activity as indicated by GDP growth showed a significant acceleration in the post-reform years which is entirely driven by the services sector growth. Thus, there is a growing belief that India's economic future lies in the service sector.

Despite certain negative implication of service sector growth, our welfare and the welfare of our economy are now based on the service sector. Service sector is at the very hub of economic activity in any society. It is noted that after Green Revolution and Industrial Revolution, the next popular revolution will be in the services sector. According to the World Development Indicators, 2003, recently released by the World Bank, India's Services Sector has emerged among the top-five fastest growing in the world during 1990-2001.

Thus, it is concluded that the reforms have successful in service sector. The service sector will continue to be India's engine of growth in the coming years. Consequently, higher growth rates in the rest of the decade can indeed be achieved through further deepening of the economic reform process. Second generation reforms have been initiated already and, as their implementation proceeds, further acceleration in economic growth can be expected in the coming years.

REFERENCES

1. Ankit Majumdar, "Challenges and Opportunities in the New Millennium: The Service Sector Beckons", *Ushus Journal of Business Management*, Vol. 1 No.1, July-Dec 2002, pp. 37-40.
2. Chandrasekhar, C.P. & Jayati Ghosh, *"Service Sector Growth: What Does It Mean?"*, www.macroscan.org, Nov. 16, 1999.
3. Corporate Reporter, "Service Sector India's Gngine of Growth", *The Hindu*, Tuesday, Nov. 28, 2000.
4. Damodar N. Gujarati, *Basic Econometrics*, Mc Graw-Hill, New Delhi, 1995, pp. 499-525.
5. Fakir Chand, *"Service Sector to Drive India's Engine of Growth"*, Bangalore.
6. Krishna Mazumdar, "Disproportional Growth of Service Sector in India: 1960-1990", *The Indian Economic Journal*, Vol. 43 No. 2, Oct-Dec. 1995, pp. 102-109.
7. Mahendra Devi, S. & Ravi, C., "Macro-economic Scene: Performance and Policies", *Economic and Political Weekly*, vol. XXXVIII Nos. 12 & 13, March 22-April 4, 2003, pp. 1143-1154.
8. Nagaraj, R., "Indian Economy Since 1980", *Economic and Political Weekly*, Vol. XXXV No. 32, August 5, 2000, pp. 2831-2838.

9. Narasimhan, C.R.L., "The Services in the Reform Era", *The Hindu*, Saturday, June 7, 2003, p.17.
10. Rakesh Mohan, "Decade After 1991: New Challenges Facing the Indian Economy", *RBI Bulletin*, November 2002, pp. 774-788.
11. Rammanohar Reddy, C., "Limits of a Service Economy", *The Hindu*, Saturday, June 21, 2003, p. 10.
12. Rita Bhowmik, "Role of Services Sector in Indian Economy: An Input-Output Approach", *Artha Vijnana*, Vol. XLII No. 2, June 2000, pp. 158-169.
13. Sambandam, V.S., "Changing Pattern of GDP Growth", *The Hindu*, July 5, 2000, p. 16.
14. Satya Sundaram, I., "Trends in Services Sector in India", *Southern Economist*, Vol. 41 No. 6, July 15, 2002, p. 23.
15. Shankar Acharya, "Macro-economic Management in the Nineties." *Economic and Political Weekly*, Vol. XXXVII No. 16, April 20, 2002, pp. 1515-1538.
16. Srivastava, M.P., "Service Sector Revolution at Turning Point", *Employment News*, Vol. XXVI No. 28, 13-19, October 2001, pp. 1-2.
17. Subramanian, P., & Raju, G., "Service Tax: A Bird's Eye View", *Yojana*, Vol. 47 No. 2, February 2003, pp. 25-28.
18. Sukumar Mukhopadhyay, "Globalisation and Indian Services Sector", *Economic and Political Weekly*, Vol. XXXVII, No. 40, October 5, 2002, pp. 4098-4099.
19. ...., "An Analysis of India's Gross Domestic Product (GDP)", *Indiaonstep.com*, April 30, 2003.
20. ...., "The Leading Sector of the Economy", *RBI Annual Report*, September 2000, p. 18.

6

Employment in Organised and Unorganised Sector

Emerging Issues and Future Perspectives

Dr. S. David Amirtharajan

Introduction

India being a nation of developing comes under third world country. She is gradually moving toward all-round development, though she has her own economic problems. Now the whole world looks at India and raises its eyebrow due to its reformation and its impact on growth in various sectors. Reformation is not the new term being used at present. It was developed and tested in many countries among which only few have succeeded their venture and other have failed.

India started this reformation journey from 1991. This shows that the nation has the experience for a decade and more: But the process has been continuing till now; with the stingent policy on employment: since the nation tries to adopt market economy and shifting her agenda of social-welfare state into laissez-faire state, the question of job permanency and individual care raised among all working community. Not it is the right time to think over emerging issues and future perspectives on employment in organised and unorganised sectors.

Reformation in India

In 1985, the then Prime Minister Mr. Rajiv Gandhi sketched out the new trends in economic policy of the Government. Accordingly it was suggested that the improvement in productivity, absorption of modern technology and fuller utilisation of capacity should be the prioritised national agenda. In a nutshell, the focus was made on the private sector. Prof. K.N. Raj pointed out that "there has been however, a general agreement that a very distinctive feature of this policy changes taken as a whole is a greater scope for unfettered expansion they offer to the private sector particularly in the corporate segment of manufacturing industry and the opportunities opened up to multinational enterprises". However, such a great effort did not bring any expected changes; on the other side this led to increase in trade deficit and a serious balance of payment crisis. In order to face this crisis a huge loan to the tune of $7 billion was borrowed from IMF and World Bank.

Again, in 1991, the new Congress government made an attempt to introduce New Economic Policy. On the eve of introducing the same on June 21st, 1991, India had extremely low foreign exchange reserves, i.e. Rs. 2400 crore which was equivalent to the import needs for only three weeks. This situation became still worst when several international agencies lowered the country's credit rating. Further, the national debt exceeded 60 per cent of GNP during this period.

It was also an evidence that the wholesale price index increased to a large extent. In midst of this crisis, the New Economic Policy was introduced with much expectation. As a part of solving these problems, Structural Adjustment Programme was introduced. This aimed at converting deficits of both fiscal and trade into surplus. The reform adopted by Cong(I) under two stages of waves, i.e. 1985 and 1991 was expressed as first generation reforms. In the same pathway was adhered by the then Janata Dal Government under a new format of common minimum programme. Under these regimes, reforms were made at top level.

The second generation reform was introduced by the BJP Government done at deep-root level. However, the agenda of both Government has shown a very large consensus about economic reforms. While calculating the end result it would be necessary to check all-round development at various levels. Among all one is an enlargement of employment potential leading to full employment.

Employment in Organised and Unorganised Sector

The sector which is regularised and controlled through state is called as organised and otherwise it is called unorganised sector. Unorganised sectoral workers and producers include agricultural labourers, small and marginal farmers, forest workers, fisher folk, beedi rollers, garment stitchers, construction workers, rag pickers and the like. Having no fixed employer, these workers are casual contractual, migrant, home-based, own-account workers who attempt to earn a living from whatever meagre assets and skill they possess. Such unorganised way of forming any sector is called as unorganised sector.

The Table 6.1 presents the employment and unemployment in India.

Table 6.1: Employment and Unemployment in General

Details	*1983-84 million person*	*1993-94 million person*	*1999-2000 million person*	*Employment Growth rate % per annum*	
				1983-84 to 1993-94	*1993-94 to 1999-2000*
All India					
Population	718.20	894.01	1003.97	2.00	1.95
Labour force	261.33	339.97	363.33	2.43	1.31
Work force	239.57	315.84	336.75	2.70	1.07
No. of unemployed (2-3)	21.76	20.13	26.58	-0.08	4.74
Unemployment rate (%)	8.33	5.99	7.32	—	—

Source: Planning Commission Report, 2002.

Table 6.1 discloses that the population is moving in an increasing trend whereas the no. of employed is not in the same proportion. However, it is also found that unemployment was declined (from 8.33 to 5.99) during 1993-94 but was again increased to 7.32 in 1999-2000. Further the employment growth fell to 1.0 per cent per annum (between 1993-94 and 1999-2000) from 2.7 per cent per annum in the past (between 1983-84 and 1993-94). This clearly shows that the increasing trend in population and declining trend in employment are in general.

In order to have clear picture the rural and urban-wise classification is done and it is presented in Table 6.2.

Table 6.2: Employment and Unemployment in Rural and Urban

Details	*1983-84 million person*	*1993-94 million person*	*1999-2000 million person*	*Employment Growth rate % per annum*	
				1983-84 to 1993-94	*1993-94 to 1999-2000*
Rural					
Population	546.61	658.83	727.50	1.79	1.67
Labour force	204.18	255.38	270.39	2.15	0.96
Work force	187.92	241.04	250.89	2.40	0.67
No. of unemployed	16.26	14.34	19.50	-1.19	5.26
Unemployment rate (%)	7.96	5.61	7.12		
Urban					
Population	171.59	234.98	276.47	3.04	2.74
Labour force	57.15	80.60	92.95	3.33	2.40
Work force	51.64	74.80	85.84	3.59	2.32
No. of unemployed	5.51	5.80	7.11	0.49	3.45
Unemployment rate (%)	9.64	7.19	7.65		

Source: Planning Commission Report, 2002.

It is inferred from Table 6.2 that there is no significant difference between rural and urban employment. In both, the employment growth rate is not satisfactory. It is very clear that the unemployment problem becomes normal in both rural and urban.

It is very interesting to look into the scenario of employment in organised and unorganised sectors. Table 6.3 depicts this very clearly.

Table 6.3: Employment in Organised and Unorganised Sectors

Sector	*Employment in million*			*Growth rate % per annum*	
	1983	*1994*	*1999-2000*	*1983-1994*	*1994-99 2000*
Employment in organised sector					
Public sector	16.46	19.44	19.41	1.52	0.03
Private sector	7.55	7.93	8.70	0.45	1.87
Employment in unorganised sector	278.74	347.08	368.89	2.23	1.05
Employment in organised sector as % of total employment	7.93	7.30	7.08	—	—
Total labour force as % of population	43.00	42.7	40.4	—	—

Source: Ruddar Dutt, Economic Liberalisation and its implication for employment in India.

Table 6.3 reveals that employment in the organised sector as to total employment in percentage is gradually reducing from 7.93 to 7.08 in 1999-2000. On the other hand, the employment in organised sector is in increasing trend as a whole. But its growth rate is much obvious only in the private sector. This implies that the public sector has shown virtually jobless growth.

Table 6.4: Employment in General

Classification	Status			Growth Rate		GDP Growth Rate		Employment Elasticity	
	1983	*1993-1994*	*1999-2000*	*1983 to 1993-94*	*1993-94 to 1999-2000*	*1983 to 1993-94*	*1993-94 to 1999-2000*	*1983 to 1993-94*	*1993-94 to 1999-2000*
1. Agriculture	151.35 (63.18)	190.72 (60.38)	190.94 (56.70)	2.03	0.02	2.9	3.1	0.70	0.01
2. Mining and Quarrying	1.74 (0.73)	2.54 (0.80)	2.26 (0.67)	3.66	-1.91	6.2	4.7	0.59	-0.41
3. Manufacturing	27.69 (11.56)	35.00 (11.08)	40.79 (12.11)	2.28	2.58	6.0	7.8	0.38	0.33
4. Electricity, gas and water supply	0.83 (0.34)	1.43 (0.45)	1.15 (0.34)	5.29	-3.55	8.4	6.8	0.63	-0.52
5. Construction	7.17 (2.99)	11.02 (3.99)	14.95 (4.44)	4.21	5.21	4.9	6.3	0.86	0.82
6. Trade, hotels & restaurants	18.17 (7.58)	26.88 (8.51)	37.54 (11.15)	3.81	5.72	5.6	9.2	0.68	0.62
7. Transport, storage and communication	6.99 (2.92)	9.38 (3.13)	13.65 (4.05)	3.36	5.53	6.1	8.7	0.55	0.63
8. Finance, insurance, real estate and business services	2.10 (0.88)	3.37 (1.07)	4.62 (1.38)	4.54	5.40	10.1	8.4	0.45	0.64
9. Community, social and personal services	23.52 (9.82)	34.98 (11.08)	30.84 (9.16)	3.88	-2.08	5.7	8.4	0.68	-0.25
All	239.7 (100)	315.84 (100)	336.75 (100)	2.70	1.07	5.2	6.7	0.52	0.16

Note: Figures in brackets are percentages of total employment in the respective columns.
Source: Compiled and computed from the report of employment opportunities, 2002.

In the case of unorganised sector the employment is gradually increasing year by year. In 1983, it is shown as 278.74 million. But there is a hike to 368.89 million in 1999-2000. But the growth rate shows slow growth in 1999-2000 being compared with 1994.

For a clarity on discussion, the organised and unorganised sectors are further classified and presented in Table 6.4.

It is found from Table 6.4, that agriculture is the main employment generation sector as it is counted for about 57 per cent of total employment in 1999-2000. Other side, the employment elasticity is high between 1983 and 1993-94, whereas it has declined to 0.01 between 1993-94 and 1999-2000. It means that during the post-reform period it has been affected to a large extent. There is a slight hike in employment growth in construction, trade, hotels, restaurants, transport, storage, communication, finance, insurance and real estate. Further these divisions are also presented under the heading organised and unorganised sector for 1999-2000 in Table 6.5.

Table 6.5 reveals that 91.66 per cent of the total employment were accounted to unorganised sector. Except mining, quarrying, electricity, gas and water supply, the unorganised sector accounted more in providing employment. Among various employment opportunities in unorganised sector, agriculture, trade, hotels, restaurants and manufacturing are the key sectors for generating employment.

Emerging Issues and Future Perspective

As a whole of discussion on employment, it is emerged to the following issues:

- *(a)* The population of the country is in increasing trend whereas the employment is in declining trend;
- *(b)* The unemployment problem become common issue in rural and urban;

Table 6.5: Employment in organised and unorganised sector in 1999-2000

Classification	*Total*	*Organised Sector*			*Unorganised Sector*	
		Public Sector	*Private Sector*	*Total*	*Col.1-4*	*% of Col.1*
1. Agriculture	190.94	0.52	0.87	1.39	189.55 (61.4)	99.3
2. Mining and Quarrying	2.26	0.93	0.09	1.02	1.24 (0.4)	54.9
3. Manufacturing	40.79	1.57	5.18	6.75	34.04 (11.0)	83.5
4. Electricity, gas and water supply	1.15	0.96	0.04	1.00	0.15 (0.0)	13.0
5. Construction	14.95	1.11	0.07	1.18	13.77 (4.5)	92.1
6. Trade, hotels & restaurants	37.54	0.16	0.32	0.48	37.06 (12.0)	98.7
7. Transport, storage and communication	13.65	3.08	0.07	3.15	10.50 (3.4)	76.9
8. Finance, insurance, real estate and business services	4.62	1.30	0.35	1.65	2.97 (1.0)	64.2
9. Community, social and personal services	30.84	9.79	1.07	11.49	19.35 (6.3)	62.7
All	336.75 (100)	19.42 (5.77)	8.70 (2.58)	28.11 (8.34)	308.64 (100)	91.66

Source: Ruddar Dutt and Sundaram K.P.M., *Indian Economy*, S. Chand & Eompany, New Delhi, 2003, p. 956.

(c) The public sector has accounted virtually jobless growth. In case of private sector, the organised sector marked a gradual taking off in providing employment. There is a virtual growth rate of employment in the unorganised sector;

(d) Agriculture is the main employment generation sector. But the growth of employment is affected a lot during the post-reform period. However, there is a shift of growth and employment to construction, trade, hotels, restaurant, transport, storage, communication, finance, insurance and real estate;

(e) In general, among various employment opportunities existing among unorganised sector, agriculture, trade, hotels, restaurant and manufacturing are the key sectors for employment.

Based on these, it could be possible to sort out the future perspective on employment in both organised and unorganised sectors as stated below:

The percentage of people below poverty line decline from 44.84 per cent in 1983 to 35.11 per cent in 1990-91, and it has increased to 37.23 in 1997. It is the evidence to show that proportion of people below poverty line has increased during the post-reform period. On the other side population of India crossed 1027 million in 2001. It highlights the parallel growth of population and poverty. Further processes of disinvestments and privatisation in major public sector units led to growth in private sector.

Further during the 10 years period of economic reform, food grain production increased from 176.4 million tonnes in 1990-91 to 195.9 million tonnes in 2000-01. This growth was just 1 per cent which was lower than the growth rate of population.

In addition to these it is noted from reform process that the emphasis was given more on manufacturing and service sectors. It reveals that the process of economic reform neglected the agricultural sector. However, it is also viewed that the central public sector enterprises (PSE's) have shown better performance during the reform period. According to the Memorandum of Understanding (MoU) between Government and PSE in 2000-01, the evaluation of 107 PSE's performance reveals that 49 were rated as excellent, 25 very good and 12 as good. But it is very sad to say that the performance of the industrial production during 1993-94 to 2000-01 was not upto the expectation. It is a great set back to the reform process on industrial production.

Correlating these with previous discussion throw light on the future perspective for employment as such that the economic scenario in India paves the way for uphill task to develop the employment opportunity in both organised and unorganised sector. It can be averted if the following measures are taken:

- There is a need to reform agricultural sector. The Government should take measures to establish more number of agriculture-based and related industries;
- There is a need to reform education from primary level to higher education. Such reform should make a way to teach skill-oriented education from the primary level. The Government should take proper steps to strengthen the present education in rural area by adding a strong foundation in English. Because, the present mushroom growth of English medium school in rural area may in future affect the employment in agriculture. The skill-oriented education will help the workforce in agriculture to have their own self employment during season-off season;
- The reformation process in public sector should be stopped and should start to open chances of employment again. The government should encourage investors to invest in agro-based industries.

Summary

India is a nation of having more undisclosed powerful human resources. During the post-reform period there was a set back in employment in organised and unorganised sector. However, the employment growth rate was very low in unorganised sector. But there was jobless growth in public sector. Even after these, agriculture has its own uniqueness to provide employment. If India would have given more importance to agriculture and its allied activities, agro-based industries and education there is a boom period which is not too far. With this human resource and agro-based policy, our nation will become a super nation in near future.

REFERENCES

1. Renana Jhabrala and Subrahmanya R.K. *"The Unorganised Sector—Work Security and Social Protection*, Sage Publication", New Delhi, 2000.
2. Rumki Basu *'Economic Liberalisation and Poverty Alleviation'*, Deep and Deep Publication Pvt. Ltd., New Delhi, 2000.
3. Mahajan V.S. *'Economic Reforms and Liberalisation'*, Deep and Deep Publication Pvt. Ltd., New Delhi, 1999.
4. Ruddar Dutt and Sundaram K.P.M. *'Indian Economics'* S. Chand & Company, New Delhi, 2003.
5. *'India Development Report'*, 2002.
6. *'India 2002'*, Publication Division, Ministry of Information and Broadcasting, Government of India.

7

Economic Reforms and Rural Industries in India

Dr. R. Seerangarajan

Introduction

India is a land of small enterprises. Two-thirds of business enterprises all over the world are small enterprises. They are traditional in their investment, technology, manufacturing process, marketing and quality control. Their range varies from cottage level enterprises to modern SSI units using sophisticated technologies. Their contribution to Indian economy is significant. Small enterprises are characterised by lean organisational structure, capital saving labour intensive methodologies, low research and development input and absence of professional management styles particularly in rural based small enterprises.

During last three decades, small scale sector attracted the attention of several economic schools of thought and small scale sector is considered as an important tool in the process of economic development in developing countries. Hence, small scale policies are pursued for

(a) efficient factor utilisation

(b) employment generation

(c) entrepreneurship development

(*d*) democratisation; and

(*e*) environmental soundness.

Recently, the emergence of flexible production systems and networking among small enterprises provided new ground for innovative SSI policy orientation. Many SSI's are concerned with residual economic activities. However, they take advantage of special market niches, lower costs and their ability to bypass certain laws and regulatory mechanisms. And they largely absorb more unskilled labours who would otherwise unable to find employment. Hence a supportive policy for SSI could best focus on creating favourable conditions on supply side and on demand side. Supply side policies are, provision of training, extending credit facilities at low cost and infrastructure. Demand side policies are increasing effective demand for SSI products, market promotional measures and development of market based assistances.

With the above backdrop, India initiated economic reforms in 1991 which included several policy changes specific to village small industries. Major features of SSI policy are (i) curtailing protective measures offered through SSI's, and (ii) promotion of competitiveness through addressing the basic concerns of the sector, namely, technology, finance, marketing and infrastructure development. These measures were taken to strengthen the competitiveness of SSI units to face the threats internally as well as externally.

As per the Report of the Planning Commission (2000-2001), the comprehensive policy package on SSI and tiny sector are as below:

1. Increasing the investment limit to SSI's at Rs. One crore;
2. Providing credit-linked capital subsidy of 12 per cent against loans for technology upgradation;
3. Raising the investment limit in industry related service and business enterprise from Rs. 5.00 lakhs to Rs. 10.00 lakhs;
4. Grant of Rs. 75,000 to SSI units for obtaining ISO 9000 certification;

5. Capital grants up to 15 per cent for establishing testing laboratories;
6. Raising the limit for composite loans from Rs.10 lakhs to Rs.25 lakhs;
7. Enhancing the family income limit of Rs. 20,000 to Rs. 40,000 for availing financial assistance under PMRY Scheme to establish micro enterprises;
8. Dereservation of readymade garments in order to help the sector to upgrade the technology, enhancement of productivity, quality consciousness, product diversification, increase in exports, innovative marketing strategies and enhancing employment opportunities.

World Trade Organisation (WTO) and Globalisation Issues

WTO was formed in 1995, with modifications in GATT. As GATT was only a treaty and it did not have an implementing authority by negotiations and GATT was ad hoc and provisional. WTO agreements are permanent and it has a sound legal binding. The major principles of WTO are:

(a) Free international trade without quantitative restrictions—In order to encourage international trade, barriers have to be curtailed. The barriers may be higher customs duty and putting quantitative restrictions;

(b) Binding of tariffs—Under WTO, when the countries agree to open their markets for goods and services, they bind their commitments;

(c) Non-discrimination between countries—WTO expects each member country to treat all other countries equally as "most favoured" trading partners;

(d) Non-discrimination within a country—This rule prohibits countries from discriminating between imported goods and equivalent domestically produced goods;

(*e*) Promoting fair competitions—WTO promotes a system of rules to encourage open and fair competition. This encourages competition, promotes efficiency and consumer welfare.

Impact of WTO on SSIs

WTO agreements do not mention about small enterprises. It does not discriminate on the basis of size of industries. In fact, no agreement of WTO has dealt directly with small enterprises. The agreements talk about only the enhanced efficiency thro' better allocation of resources, improving the quality and productivity at a global level. It is anticipated that Govt. of India may plan for complete dereservation of items of SSI units and have to compete not only with large scale units in the country, but with cheap imported goods produced by multi-nationals and other companies from different parts of the world.

Issues arising out of WTO in Respect to SSI's

Reservation Policy

There were about 812 products reserved for SSI's and were not allowed to be manufactured by LSI's. This gave them enough protection and was responsible for their sustained growth. Now 586 items have been put under OGL. They can be imported by anyone. In such case reservation policy will have no meaning and SSI units will have to be phased out and be linked to EXIM perspectives. Only competitive and innovative units alone can survive at global level.

Tariffs and Trade Reforms

WTO insist on prohibition of physical restriction on imports and exports. Thus, from 2005 onwards, more and more goods will be imported in to India without any restrictions. Further WTO agreement force India to bring down tariffs on imported items. This will pave way for the arrival of goods from other countries at a lower cost than the price of products made in India. Thus, many SSI units will be losing their markets to these international players.

Dumping of Goods

Due to liberalised imports and reduction in tariffs, goods are being dumped in the Indian markets at a cheaper price. It will affect Indian producers particularly SSI units. For making a case in anti-dumping, it is necessary to establish the cost of the item and other inputs used in the country of origin etc. Such data collection is costly and SSI's could not defend their case.

Intellectual Property Rights

Many SSI's in India make import substituted products. Under WTO regime such option is completely prohibited. TRIPS agreements will not allow them to copy the design of a product. Thus, appropriate technology tools have to be evolved for SSI units to counter TRIPS.

Government Procurement

Part of Government procurement is reserved for SSI's and price preference are given to them. When WTO is fully implemented in India, all purchases above certain value will have to be made by issuing global tenders.

Multinationals and SSI's

Entry of multinationals in Indian manufacturing has been mainly focusing on simple technology high volume items. These low technology products were produced by SSI units. As a result of entry of multinationals, the existence of SSI's will be a big problem.

Merits of WTO

1. Subcontracting to foreign large scale units may be undertaken by SSI units;
2. WTO may pave way for new business opportunities;
3. Indian SSI's may turn as cheap outsourcing centers for global corporations;
4. Wide scope in service and software development sector;
5. Possibility of improving Indian SSI's to global level;

6. Access to high tech areas for production of quality goods and scope for upgradation.

Subsequent analysis have been made keeping in mind the economic reforms undertaken by the Govt. of India and the impact of WTO in the prospects of small scale industrial sector and khadi and village industries.

Performance of Small Scale Industries and Khadi and Village Industries after Economic Reforms

After the liberalisation process in 1991, village and small industries performance have to be evaluated in terms of production, sales and employment to identify factors responsible for such performance.

Table 7.1: Performance of Small Scale Industry in India after Economic reforms

Sl. No.	*Year*	*No. of units in lakhs*	*Value of production in Rs. Crores*	*Employment in lakhs*	*Exports Rs. in Crores*
1	2	3	4	5	6
1.	1991-92	20.82	1,78,699	129.80	13,853
2.	1992-93	22.50	2,09,510	134.06	17,784
3.	1993-94	23.90	2,41,648	139.36	25,306
4.	1994-95	25.70	2,98,886	146.56	29,068
5.	1995-96	26.60	3,62,656	152.61	36,470
6.	1996-97	28.00	4,11,858	160.00	39,248
7.	1997-98	29.40	4,62,641	167.20	44,442
8.	1998-99	30.80	5,20,650	171.58	48,979
9.	1999-00	32.10	5,72,887	178.50	54,200
10.	2000-01	33.70	6,45,496	185.64	59,978

Source: Report of Ministry of Industries, Govt. of India, 2000-01.

As per Table 7.1 the number of SSI units has shown increasing trend. During the year of introduction of liberalised policy in 1991-92, number of SSI units registered were at

Table 7.1A: Small Scale Industries – Compound Growth Rates

Sl. No.	*Parameter*	*Compound Growth Rate in %*
1.	No. of units	5.68
2.	Value of production	16.42
3.	Employment generation	4.20
4.	Value of exports	18.10

20.82 lakh units. In the span of ten years after liberalisation there was a significant growth in the number of SSI units posting the maximum of 33.70 lakh units. The trends were assessed thro' linear, cubic models and compound growth rate.

In terms of linear equation,

$y = 19.624 + 1.4582 \times R^2 = 0.995^{**}$

Thus, the growth rate in the number of units was at 1.4582, a positive value indicating the positive nature of the growth. High R^2 value signifies the fitness of the variable in linear model.

In terms of cubic model, the number of units recorded following trend.

$y = 19.3916 + 1.3715x + 0.0763x^2 - 0.0078x^3$

and $R2 = 0.999^{xx}$

After differentiation, the differential equation y' is substituted with $x = 1$ and $x = 10$.

$y'_1 = 1.50$ and $y'_{10} = 1.849$

As the value of $y'_{10} > y'_1$, it is a clear indication that the number of units recorded increasing trend.

The compound growth rate was also 5.68 per cent. Thus, after liberalisation and economic reforms, there was a significant growth in the number of SSI units operating in India.

** significant at 1 per cent level.

Value of Production by SSI Sector

Col. 2 of Table 7.1, shows the value of production by SSI sector in the period of ten years. In 1991-92, the value of production was at Rs. 1,78,699 crore and it has grown to Rs. 6,45,491 crore in 2000-01. In terms of linear equation, the trend was

$y = 102675 + 51990.4x;$

$R^2 = 0.992^{xx}$... with positive rate of growth of 51990.4

In terms of cubic model, the trend was

$y = 167340 + 2882.44x + 9326.22x^2 - 508.69x^3$ and $R^2 = 0.999^{xx}$

$y'_1 = 20009$ and $y'_{10} = 47143$

Thus, value of production by SSI sector has shown increasing trend as $y'_{10} > y'_1$ and liberalised economic policies helped to achieve growth.

The compound growth rate of production value was at 16.42 per cent.

Employment Generation

Employment generation has always been one of the main objectives of the SSI policies aimed at economic development and growth of a nation. The rise in economic growth has led to increased employment opportunities and enhanced employment generation help to improve standard of living of a country. Thus, Small Scale Industries are considered to be the employment generators in a nation.

After liberalisation in 1991-92, SSI's provided employment to 129.80 lakh persons. Steady growth in employment could be observed and in 2000-2001, SSI's provided employment to about 185.64 lakh persons.

In terms of linear equations, the growth recorded

$y = 121.934 + 6.2873$

$R^2 = 0.997_{**}$

** significant at 1 per cent level.

Thus, the rate of growth in employment over a period of 10 years was at (+) 6.28 with positive or increasing trends.

In terms of cubic model, the employment values recorded following equation.

$y = 126.594 + 2.2415x + 0.8804x^2 - 0.084x^3$

$R^2 = 0.999^{**}$ and

$y'_1 = 3.87$ and $y'_{10} = 4.748$

Thus, in cubic model also, the growth of employment was significant over ten years period indicating that liberalisation and reform process helped to enhance employment rate in ten year period. Employment values recorded a compounded growth rate of 4.20 per cent which confirms the positive or increasing trends.

Export Performance

Export earnings add to the wealth of a nation and the process of liberalisation and globalisation aim at improving the exports of a nation. In India, SSI exports is one of the major export earner and over 40 per cent of the country's exports are contributed by SSI sector.

The present exercise also gauged the export performance of SSI sector during the study period.

In terms of linear equation, the value of exports of SSI's recorded the following equation:

$y = 8596 + 5073.03x^{**}$ and

$R^2 = 0.989$

The value of growth in exports was very high recording 'm' value of 5073.03.

The export values were also fitted in a cubic model that recorded the following model.

$y = 9067.24 + 4405.33x + 197.869x^2 - 15.104x^3$

$R^2 = 0.989$

** significant at 1 per cent level.

$y'_1 = 4755.8$ and

$y'_{10} = 4996.7$

Thus, in the span of ten years there was a considerable growth in cubic model also. After the liberalised regime SSI's has shown significant improvement in exports also.

In terms of compounded growth rate, exports recorded about 18.10 per cent highest among all parameters observed.

Performance of Small Scale Industries before Economic Reforms and after Economic Reforms

In order to assess the impact of economic reforms on the growth and performance of Small Scale Industries, a paired 't' test was conducted selecting few five years before economic reforms and another five years after introduction of economic reforms as per Table 7.2.

Table 7.2: Performance of SSI's before Economic Reforms and after Reforms

Sl. No.	*Year*	*No. of units in lakhs.*	*Value of production in Rs. Crores*	*Employment in lakhs*	*Exports Rs. in Crores*
1	2	3	4	5	6
Before Economic Reforms					
1.	1980-81	8.74	28,060	71.00	1,643
2.	1984-85	12.42	50,520	90.00	2,563
3.	1987-88	15.86	87,300	107.00	4,373
4.	1989-90	18,26	1,32,320	120.00	7,624
5.	1990-91	19.30	1,58,300	125.00	9,888
After Economic Reforms					
1.	1991-92	20.82	1,78,699	130.00	13,853
2.	1994-95	25.71	2,98,886	146.56	29,068
3.	1996-97	28.57	4,11,858	160.00	39,248
4.	1998-99	31.21	5,38,357	171.00	48,079
5.	2000-01	33.70	6,45,496	185.64	59,978

The '*t*' test results were presented in Table 7.3. From the '*t*' test analysis, the prediction statement that there is a significant difference between the two periods of observation has been proved in all respects. That is, after economic reforms, SSI sector has shown significant growth in respect of number of units, value of production, employment generation and value of exports. Thus, economic reforms and globalisation have helped SSI units to record all round commendable performance indicating its vibrant role in the Indian economic scenario.

Table 7.3: Paired Sample –'*t*' Test

	Mean	'*t*'	*Level of significance*
1. No. of units	2,08,140.00	8.765	0.01
2. Value of production	2,45,805.70	3.876	0.01
3. Employment	129.45	11.852	0.01
4. Value of exports	21,174.10	3.329	0.01

Performance of Khadi during Post Liberalisation Period

Khadi and Village Industries in India

Khadi and Village Industries in India (KVI) occupied a distinct place in pre-independence political scene of India. Gandhiji also felt that khadi and village industries will make Indians economically strong and self-reliant. Revival of khadi and village industries movement will restore the pride and glory of ancient culture and values. Mahatma Gandhi opined that "by reviving KVIs, we shall remodel the nation in keeping with the ideal of simplicity and domesticity implanted in the bosom of the masses". Thus, KVIs are undertaken with the major objective of solving rural poverty and unemployment thro' meaningful economic activity utilizing the local resources mostly the human resources. Large scale industries could not solve the problem of unemployment and they can provide employment to about 5% of total available workforce. The lasting remedy to unemployment problem of India is promotion of khadi and village industries. Promotions of khadi and village industries activities is charged with khadi

Table 7.4: Performance of Khadi and Village Industries

(All India Figures)

Sl. No.	Year	*Value of Production Rs. in Crores*		*Value of Sales Rs. in Crores*		Employment in lakhs	Earnings Rs. in Crores	Per capita earnings in Rs.
		Khadi	*Village Industries*	*Khadi*	*Village Industries*			
(1)	(2)	(3)	(4)	(5)	(6)	(7)	(8)	(9)
1.	1991-92	353.48	2523.34	387.13	2810.12	52.50	1013.62	1930.70
2.	1992-93	357.27	2876.87	409.24	3232.01	53.28	1140.63	1908.22
3.	1993-94	389.71	3234.34	490.85	3578.33	53.46	1269.35	2374.39
4.	1994-95	522.23	3504.22	567.36	3861.78	56.75	1363.84	2703.30
5.	1995-96	626.40	3889.85	581.10	4232.89	58.17	1551.85	2667.78
6.	1996-97	624.09	3895.21	745.90	4319.37	56.50	1588.63	2811.73
7.	1997-98	635.89	4476.48	647.82	4953.18	58.29	1797.59	3083.77
8.	1998-99	551.94	5613.90	631.79	6137.40	59.23	2147.82	3626.23
9.	1999-00	431.57	6491.69	570.55	7384.55	60.07	2332.02	3882.60
10.	2000-01	416.68	7140.52	527.86	8383.48	62.64	2869.67	4581.21

Source: Annual Reports, KVIC, Mumbai, 2001-02

and village industries commission in India. KVIC is also working with other rural development agencies for promotion of KVIs in villages. Thus, KVIC is a catalystic agent for rural industrialisation in India. Recent statistics indicate that KVI sector has created history by reaching Rs. 1039.34 crore sales turnover during 2002-03.

Table 7.4A: Khadi and Village Industries - Compound Growth Rates

Sl. No.	*Parameter*	*Compound growth Rate in %*
1.	Value of production – khadi	3.16
2.	Value of production – village industries	11.90
3.	Value of sales – khadi	4.35
4.	Value of sales – village industries	12.26
5.	Employment generation	1.83
6.	Earnings	11.43

Value of Production—Khadi

Khadi is a textile material produced by using hand spun yarn in a handloom. Khadi occupies a meager share of less than 0.5 per cent of the total clothing produced in India. Khadi production was 62.03 million sq. mtrs. in 2002-03. And it has provided employment to about 8.58 lakh persons including part-time employment. Khadi spinning tools are very simple and can be operated in any rural household that is not even provided with electric supply. As per Table 7.4, in 1991-92, the value of production of khadi at Rs.353.48 crore. It showed a gradual increase up to 1997-98 reaching the peak of Rs.635.89 crore and drastically showed declining trend reaching Rs.416.68 crore in 2000-01. After 1997-98, khadi could not show sufficient progress due to (i) non-release of rebate in time, (ii) inadequate earning capacity of the khadi spinning and weaving tools, (iii) lack of customer acceptance, (iv) high cost of the goods; and (v) competitive forces from mill-sector and handloom sector.

The value of production in khadi was fit in two trend models as below:

(*i*) linear equation

(*ii*) cubic equation

In terms of linear equation, khadi production recorded

y = 416.302 – 13.562x

R^2 = -0.129

The R^2 value was at 0.129 suggesting high fluctuation of the values.

It has recorded negative slope of –13,[illegible] indicating the declining nature of the activity. In terms of cubic model, khadi production recorded the following equation:

$y = 274.01 + 35.96x + 12.03x^2 - 1.468x^3$;

R^2 = 0.852

After differentiation, the value of

y'_1 = 55.616 and Y'_{10} = -163.8 confirming the declining nature of the activity during the study period of ten years from 1991-92 to 2000-01. Appropriate measures in the following lines may ensure orderly growth of khadi sector:

(*i*) Improving the quality of the khadi products;

(*ii*) Production of more value added products instead of plain items;

(*iii*) Improving the productivity of the charkhas and looms;

(*iv*) Modifying the cost chart to ensure competitive pricing;

(*v*) Re-orientation of existing marketing strategies.

Sales Performance

Sales is considered as the harbinger of revenue to any business unit. Khadi sales are presented in Table 7.4. Khadi sales recorded the same trends exhibited by khadi production values. Khadi sales was at Rs.387.13 crore in 1991-92 and increased gradually to reach a peak sales of Rs. 745.90 crore in 1996-97 and thereafter declined gradually to Rs. 527.86 crore.

The trend in linear model was

$y = 439.019 - 21.247x$

$R^2 = 0.351^{NS}$ $\quad$ ^{NS} – Not significant

In linear model the sales of khadi has shown negative growth rate of (-) 21.247.

The trend in cubic model was

$y = 316.11 + 45.66x + 8.47x^2 = 1.118x^3$

$R^2 = 0.880^{**}$ and

$y'_1 = 52.257$ and $y'_{10} = -119.60$

As $y'_1 < y'_{10}$, the declining nature of khadi sales was confirmed by cubic model also.

From the above analysis, khadi production and sales recorded declining trends during post-economic reform period. Though the value of production and sales have shown increasing nature up to 1997-98, and thereafter the decline was very sharp afterwards affecting the future prospects of khadi. Appropriate measures are to be undertaken for rejuvenating the khadi performance throughout India. Khadi goods are produced for the sake of production and not for making sales to meet customer requirements. Khadi must be competitive enough to meet the challenges of powerloom, handloom and mill cloth both in price levels and quality levels. Adequate efforts are not paid in the areas of marketing research in respect of khadi.

The quality of khadi yarn and fabric are not made to the durability requirements of the customers. Poor strength, pick density variations, cracks, patches, snarls and all sorts of fabric defects could be attributed to the low quality levels.

Spinners and weavers must be properly trained to produce defect-free khadi yarn and fabrics. They should keep the spinning and weaving equipments clean and in order to facilitate quality production. Further, khadi institutions must ensure right choice of the raw material, namely, cotton for spinning, fibre testing, yarn testing and chemical testing laboratories are established in major khadi textile clusters all over India facilitating khadi institutions to use such facilities and to upgrade the quality levels of khadi products.

Village Industries—Production Performance

Village industries occupy prominent place in the KVI programme of KVIC. Now 116 industries were brought under village industries classification of KVIC offering scope for entrepreneurs to take up village industrial activities in rural areas. After this wider classification, village industries recorded substantial growth opening up new avenues for employment, entrepreneurship and production of goods using local resources.

As per Table 7.4, the value of production of village industries in 1991-92 was at Rs. 2523.34 crore and it increased to Rs.7140.52 crore in 2000-01, in current prices.

The linear equation has shown a positive growth rate of 495.02 from,

$$y = 1642.03 + 495.02$$

$$R^2 = 0.924^{**}$$

Thus, village industries have shown commendable growth in the span of ten years than the rate of growth in khadi.

In terms of cubic equations, village industries production recorded the following trend with better 'R^2' value.

$$y = 2210.76 + 403.001x - 47.14x^2 + 5.793x^3$$

$R^2 = 0.986^{**}$ and the value of

$y'_1 = 326.10$ and

$y'_{10} = 1198.10.$

As $y'_{10} > y'_1$, it could be confirmed that the production performance of village industries has shown increasing trends during the period of ten years. The reasons for such commendable performance are as below:

** significant at 1 per cent level.

(a) Wider choice of industries and services under village industries to have diversified production and to meet local demands;

(b) Introduction of margin money scheme;

(c) Spade work done by Regional/State offices of KVIC in popularizing the margin money scheme;

(d) Low capital and technological base motivating even the untrained workers to take up village industries activities;

(e) Major village industries activities are agro-based industries facilitating rural people to start activities;

(f) Active involvement of women in village industries activities;

(g) Abundant raw material base, manpower and marketing nexus for VI products.

Village Industries–Sales Performance

Sales performance of village industries recorded similar trend to that of production performance of village industries. In 1991-92, the value of sales was at Rs.2810 crore and it increased to Rs. 8383.48 crore in 2000-01. Sales of village industries products have been fit in to both linear and cubic models as below.

$$y = 1709.84 + 84 + 578.08x$$

$$R^2 = 0.901^{**}$$

As per the linear model, the growth rate was at 578.08 indicating the potentiality and viability of the village industries activity even after the economic reforms and the impact of globalisation.

The cubic model is,

$$y = 2353.48 + 588.43x - 96.81x^2 + 10.005x^3$$

** significant at 1 per cent level.

$R^2 = 0.992^{**}$ and

$y'_1 = 424.83$ and $y'_{10} = 1653.70$.

Thus, in a period of ten years after economic reforms, the sale of village industries products has expanded to four times in terms of growth. As per the above models, sale of village industries products has shown increasing trends indicating the scope of the activity and economic reforms helped the village industries to post-considerable growth in sales. Major reasons for such stupendous performance are:

1. Decentralised production and sales.
2. Less capital intensity, simple to organize and low technology base;
3. Utilizes local markets effectively thro' tailor-made sales efforts and sales service;
4. Tax concessions and exemptions in sales;
5. Efforts of KVIC in popularizing KVI products thro' sales exhibitions, advertisement and publicity campaigns;
6. Lower prices of village industries products than a branded product of equivalent quality.

Employment Generation Thro' KVI

Major chunk of employment generations of KVI activities is generated by village industries. Khadi has provided employment to about 9.56 lakh persons while village industries have provided employment to 53.26 lakh persons in 2000-01. Among the seven major classification of village industries, agro-based food industry has provided maximum number of employment to about 22.86 lakh persons. Widespread employment generation could be observed in agro-based and food industry group thro' (a) processing of cereals, pulses, masala and condiments, (b) manufacture of gur and khandsari, (c) ghani oil industry, (d) bee-keeping, (e) fruit processing, and (f) medicinal plants collection and processing.

The second major employment provider among village industries is mineral based industry group followed by polymer and chemical based industries. Service industry and textile industries provided low employment with less than 1 lakh persons in the profile of KVIC groupings.

As per Table 7.4, Col.7, the employment generation thro' KVI activities was at 52.50 lakh persons in 1991-92. It has shown steady increase up to 1995-96 and again from 1997-98 onwards it has shown increasing trends reaching the maximum employment generation in 2000-01 at 62.64 lakh persons. Such increase in the employment generation could be mainly attributed to increase in the value of production in village industries and decline in the khadi production was also compensated by growth in village industries.

Employment generation trends were fit in to linear and cubic models.

In terms of linear model, the trend line is

$y = 51.4027 + 1.0339x$

$R^2 = 0.918^{**}$

The model has shown increasing or positive trends with a rate of growth of 1.0339. The rate of growth was not in tune with the rate of growth of village industries which was mainly attributed to the declining employment trends in khadi sector.

In terms of cubic model, employment generation has predicted the following trend equation.

$y = 49.804 + 2.4857x - 0.3203x^2 + 0.0192x^3$

$R^2 = 0.930^{**}$

and the value of

$y'_1 = 1.9042$ and

$y'_{10} = 1.9897$ and $y'_{10} > y'_1$

Thus employment thro' KVI activities has increased during the post-economic reform period which was mainly due to the enlargement of village industries activities thro' several policy and developmental efforts undertaken by KVIC,

** significant at 1 per cent level.

Mumbai. It is worthwhile to mention that employment in khadi activity is stagnating or decreasing and the expectation of generating large scale employment under khadi is not being fulfilled. Adequate measures are to be undertaken to ensure that more workers are attracted to spinning/weaving thro' adequate sustainable wage earnings.

Earnings in KVI

Khadi and village industries are promoted by KVIC to generate employment and to provide reasonable earnings to the spinners and village industrial artisans. Though earnings are directly related to the labour productivity, KVI activities are capital saving, low technology based labour intensive activities. And labour productivity has direct relationship with the technology levels used in the production process. As KVI's employ simple technologies, productivity of the machinery and tools are very low that affect earnings of the artisans of KVI's. The key aspect that support these activities are that, they can be installed and operated in any cottages with or without the use of electrical energy even in a remote village or hilly tribal areas and skill requirement is quite minimum permitting rural women to undertake KVI production work and support their livelihood. From Table 7.4, KVI activities could generate earnings to the tune of about Rs. 3305 crore in 2002-03. Thus, it supports to the people particularly rural women thro' adequate wages.

In case of khadi programme, about 80 per cent of full time and part time employees belong to women spinners. Similarly most of the workers assisting the weavers are also women.

It has to be borne in mind that earnings in KVI activities are directly related to productivity of the tools. By modernisation of KVI equipments and tools, proper maintenance of the tools and appropriate training to the artisans will be helpful in increasing productivity and earnings.

As per Table 7.4, Col. 8, the earnings of KVI workers ranged from Rs. 1013.62 crore to Rs. 2869.67 crore recording peak in 2000-01. Total earnings recorded a linear model of:

$y = 681.71 + 186.48x$

$R^2 = 0.928^{**}$

The rate of growth in earnings was positive at 186.48 in terms of linear model. Due to the efforts taken by KVIC in improving the productivity of the tools thro' research programmes undertaken by its research wings.

In terms of cubic model, the earnings of KVI recorded following model.

$y = 803.17 + 232.84x - 35.12x^2 + 3.22x^3$

$R^2 = 0.994^{**}$

After differentiation and substituting x = 1 and x = 10 we get

$y'_1 = 172.28$ and

$y'_{10} = 498.09.$

As $y'_{10} > y'_1$, earnings have definitely improved in KVI sector during post-reform period.

KVI earnings also recorded compound growth of 11.43 per cent which was significant and phenomenal. Thus, KVI sector will play significant role in the era of liberalisation and globalisation particularly in generating earnings to millions of people across the country.

Per capita earnings was at Rs. 1930.7 in 1991-92. This has been steadily increased to Rs. 4381.21 in 2000-01. It can be seen that the per capita earnings has almost doubled in the liberalised economy. Low per capita earnings were attributed to part time employment in khadi. For example, in 2001-02, part time employment was 7.70 lakh persons out of total employment of 9.56 lakh in khadi. That is, about 80 per cent of khadi employment was contributed thro' part time spinners and weavers leading to low wage earnings. In case of village industries, out of 50.51 lakh employment generation, part time employment was at 24.19 lakh persons with a share

---

** significant at 1 per cent level.

of 47.9 per cent. Part-time earnings in khadi was at Rs. 53.73 crore against a total of Rs. 221.53 crore while the part time earnings in village industries was at Rs. 534.67 crore against a total of Rs. 2110.49 crore in 2000-01. It is, therefore, essential to improve productivity of khadi equipments, modernize the charkhas and efforts are to be made to attract more persons to take up khadi activity as full time vocation by adequately enlarging the market base for khadi products.

Conclusion

Village and small industries sector is part and parcel of Indian manufacturing scenario. The preceding analysis have shown that SSIs had recovered significant growth in terms of production, sales, employment and exports. Thus, SSIs will have a dominant role in the era of globalisation and liberalisation. From 2005 onwards new opportunities will be opened up for SSIs to meet specific customer's demands at different parts of the world. Globalised markets require custom built products to satisfy specific demands of particular group which could be possible through SSIs. Networking and Information Technology tools will have to be used to expand marketing of SSIs. Adequate modernisation, upgradation of quality of the products, trained labour and timely marketing information are the prerequisites for meeting global market demands.

In respect of khadi and village industries trends in khadi production, sales and employment were declining or stagnating, while progress of village industries is quite encouraging. Measures are to be ensured to improve the performance of khadi thro' adequate modernisation of tools, improving productivity of khadi equipments, improving the quality of khadi fabrics and adopting cost-reduction methods.

Thus, in the post-liberalisation era, small scale industries and village industries under KVIC have posted considerable growth and generated substantial employment, earnings and exports. They have to keep their present momentum to gain advantage, even after 2005. Policy measures and support mechanisms are necessary to rejuvenate the sagging trends in khadi as khadi sector is one of the major employment generators even to the people located in remote areas at low capital base.

REFERENCES

1. Padalkar, Whither Khadi: The Brighter Side, *Khadi Gramodyog*, KVIC, Mumbai, Vol. XXXVI, No. 3, Dec. 1989.
2. Prabhakar M.V., Relevance of Khadi and Village Industries, *Khadi Gramodyog*, Vol. XXXVI, No.12, Sep. 1990.
3. Sahadeo Pande, A Critique of Problems of Small and Cottage Industries in India, *Khadi Gramodyog*, Vol. XXXVII, No. 2, Nov. 1990.
4. Pulak Charavarthi, Marketing Research and KVIC, *Khadi Gramodyog*, Vol. XXXVII, No. 3, Dec. 1990.
5. Krishnamurthy T. Khadi Marketing—An Introspection, *Jagrith*, Vol. 35, No. 9, KVIC Mumbai, 1991.
6. Jos Frigins, SSIs and Cleaner Production Strategies, *World Development*, Vol. 27, No. 6, Washington, 1999.
7. Y.C. Sharma, *Cotton Khadi in Indian Economy*, Navajivan Publishing House, Ahmedabad, 14, Dec. 1999.
8. Vasant Desai, *Small Scale Industries and Entrepreneurship*, Himalaya Publishing House, New Delhi, 2000.
9. Sadique M & Kandare P.D., S.T. Efforts in KVIC, Mumbai, *Jagrith* Vol. 45, No. 1, Dec. 2000.
10. Economic Survey 2000-01, Planning Commission, Govt. of India, New Delhi, pp. 144-145, 2001.
11. Ramamurthi P.A., Women Development in Tiny and Small Scale Sector, *Khadi Gramodyog*, Vol. XXXXVIII, No. 3 Dec. 2001.
12. Serangarajan R. Rural Entrepreneurship in Natural and Vegetable Dyes, *Khadi Gramodyog*, Vol. XXXXVIII, No. 3, Dec. 2001.
13. Annual Reports, Ministry of Small Scale Industries, 2001-02, GOI, New Delhi.
14. Meenakshi Sundaram N and Serangarajan R., *Developmental Strategies for Small Enterprises*, Department of RIM, GRI, May 2002.

15. L.S. Prasad, Targeting 10 Million Employment in SSI Sector; Vision 2012, *Laghu Udyog,* April-Sep. 2002, pp. 15-16.

16. A. Rashid Khan, Economic Reforms and Rural Development, *Kurukshetra*, Jan. 2003, p. 31.

17. KVI Sector Sets a Glorious Record; *Jagriti*, Oct. 2003, KVIC, Mumbai, p. 6.

8

Women Workers in Petrol Bunks at Madurai City

Dr. N. Namasivayam
Dr. S. Vijayakumar

A nation's greatness depends on how its women enjoy respect and status in the country. Much has been written on Indian women and a mass of literature is being produced daily in the form of books, articles, newspapers, research papers, comments and criticism. The matters concerning, Indian women their employment, their status in the society are much talked and still much is left to be done in the direction of their upliftment.

- Women make up 50 per cent of world population comprise 33.3 per cent of the official labour force.
- Women perform 67 per cent of the world working hours.
- Women earn 10 per cent of the world's income.
- Women produce 50 per cent of world's food supply.
- Own less than 1 per cent of world's property

(*Source:* The voice of the working women UNO 1982).

In India agriculture accounts for about 65 per cent of total employment, but of the women workers are 82 per cent in this sector. In Sri Lanka, 52 per cent of the women workers are engaged in agriculture mainly in plantations. Manufacturing and community, social and personal activities are other sectors where a significant proportion of women workers are employed in most nations. In professional, technical administrative and managerial categories, the share of women is generally low, about 8 per cent in Nepal, 12 per cent in Bangladesh and 23 per cent in India.

In India about 90 per cent of the total employment is in the unorganised sector, but of the women workers a still higher proportion, about 97 per cent is in the unorganised sector. Women constitute about 12 per cent of the organised sector employment, as against 28 per cent in the total employment.

The present study analyses the socio-economic factors influencing job satisfaction of women workers in petrol bunks at Madurai city. In Madurai city (Tamil Nadu), 18 petrol bunks are functioning. They employ 42 women workers.

Objectives

The following are the main objectives of the study:

1. To analyse socio-economic factors influencing job satisfaction of women workers in petrol bunks;
2. To offer suggestions for enhancing and improving job satisfaction of the women workers.

Methodology

The present study is based on primary data. The primary data had been collected by distributing a well-drafted questionnaire to 42 respondents.

The data collected had been analysed by using chi-square test. Besides, socio-economic factors such as age, community, income, family size and marital status have been considered for analyzing job satisfaction of women workers.

Table 8.1: Job Satisfaction

Women workers	*Satisfied*	*Dissatisfied*	*Total*
42	12 (27%)	30 (73%)	42 (100%)

Source: Field Study

Socio-Economic Factors

Table 8.2 : Age

Age	*Total Respondents*	*Satisfied*	*Dissatisfied*
Below 18	7	2	5
18-22	12	4	8
23-30	18	5	13
Above 30	5	1	4
Total	42	12	30

Source: Primary data

Table 8.3: Community

Community	*Total Respondents*	*Satisfied*	*Dissatisfied*
Forward	2	-	2
Backward	34	10	24
Scheduled	6	2	4
Total	42	12	30

Source: Primary data

Table 8.4: Income

Income	*Total Respondents*	*Satisfied*	*Dissatisfied*
Below 1000	4	-	4
1000-1500	28	8	20
1501-2000	7	2	5
Above 2001	3	2	1
Total	42	12	30

Source: Primary data

Table 8.5: Marital Status

Marital Status	*Total Respondents*	*Satisfied*	*Dissatisfied*
Married	11	2	9
Unmarried	31	10	21
Total	42	12	30

Source: Primary data

Findings

The following are the main findings of the study:

1. Out of 42 women workers in petrol bunks at Madurai city, 12 workers are satisfied with their jobs;
2. Socio-economic factors such as age, income and family size have significant and direct influence over job satisfaction. At the same time, factors such as community and marital status have no significant influence over job satisfaction;
3. It is found that out of 12 women workers who are satisfied with their jobs, 9 workers are part-time employees of the petrol bunks;
4. On an average, 27 per cent of the women workers in petrol bunks alone have job satisfaction. Out of 2 workers, 4 workers at the age group between 18 and 22 are satisfied with their jobs;
5. It is ascertained that 73 per cent of the women workers are not satisfied with their jobs on account of four reasons viz.,

   (a) Low wages

   (b) Excessive hours of work

   (c) Ill-treatment, and

   (d) Lack of incentive schemes.
6. It is also found that most of the women workers are spinsters. It is due to the fact that petrol bunk owners employ young girls between the age group of 16 and 24 years;
7. It is found that no women workers belonging to forward community satisfied with their jobs.

Suggestions

1. The working hours of the women workers should be regulated and streamlined;

2. Minimum wages payable to women workers in petrol bunks should be determined on the lines of male workers of the similar organisations;

3. Steps should be taken by the owners of the petrol bunks in respect of incentive schemes which includes payment of over-time, bonus and providing refreshment;

4. Women workers should be given uniform allowance for maintaining their dress neatly;

5. Finally, steps should be taken by the Government to ensure that no exploitation of labour takes place. This will go a long way in the upliftment of the standard of living of women workers in general.

REFERENCES

1. Miridula Bhaduri, Women in India—Some Issues, APH Publishing Corporation, Govt. of India.
2. *A Profile on Human Resource Development,* New Delhi, 1988.
3. Government of India, Annual Report, Part IV, *Development of Women and Child Development,* IIHRD, 1994-95.

9

New Economic Policy: Some Emerging Concerns

Dr. P. Jeya Baskaran

Introduction

The process of economic reform was initiated when Indian economy was in doldrums in the year 1991. Macro economic policy changes were started with devaluation of 18 per cent in the external value of rupee in July 1991. The IMF/ World Bank prescription required the economy to gradually switch over from mixed economy to the marked-driven economy. In addition, it was decided to globalise the economy, making the movement of capital and human resources easier and quicker. Then came the Word Trade Organisation (WTO) Agreement, which further required the economy to achieve globalisation by dismantling various concessions to the trade, industry and agriculture in a given time frame. Under economic reform the main thrust of the economy were three-fold namely, privatisation, liberalisation and globalisation. The Government initiated four major policy changes in fiscal, trade, industrial and public sector policies and attempted to tackle balance of payment problem and to remove the structural rigidities in the economy. The overall objectives of these measures, apart from reducing the fiscal deficit, include minimising government intervention and increasing domestic competition with the aim to accelerate the integration of Indian economy with the global economy. The post-reform period has already covered more than 12 years. This chapter makes an attempt to critically examine the impact of New Economic Policy on the Indian economy during the post-reform period.

Reforms and Gross Domestic Product

Stable growth and higher growth rate were the primary aims of the reform measures. But the growth rate during the last 12 years shows that it has not been stable. A mid-year appraisal of the economy presented by the Finance Minister in Parliament in December 2002 indicated that during 2002-2003 the actual growth rate would be 5.5 per cent against the target of 6.5 per cent. The RBI in its mid-term review of monetary and credit policy for 2002-2003 has also estimated that the rate of growth in GDP in 2002-2003 will be lower than the projected GDP growth rate of 6-6.5 per cent as estimated in April 2002 statements.

The economy at present is in decelerating phase. As against the targeted growth rate of 6.7 per cent for the first year of Tenth Plan 2002-2003, the actual growth has been much lower at 4.4 per cent. Even during the current fiscal the economy may end up nowhere near the target of 7.3 per cent growth rate of the GDP and the slippage may be more than 2 percentage points. The simple average of the annual growth rate of the gross national product (GDP) was 6.8 per cent between 1992-1993 and 1996-1997; this average came down to 5.3 per cent between 1997-1998 and 2002-2003.

Reforms and Fiscal Deficit

One of the areas of grave concern is the finance of the government, which have not shown the desired improvement during the reforms era. The fiscal deficit remains alarmingly higher. The rising ratio of public debt to gross domestic product (GDP) will push the country steadily closer to a debt trap. Fiscal management of the Central government has deteriorated continuously and more particularly, during the Ninth Plan Period (1997-2002) the fiscal deficit was 5 per cent of the GDP and all the attempts to bring it down to a figure below 4 per cent failed. Interest repayments continue to be high. Non-plan expenditure is galloping year after year. The combined balance of current revenues of the Centre and the State has declined from 1 per cent of the GDP in 1996-1997 to minus (-) 4.8 per cent of the GDP in 1999-2002. The debt service of the Union Government, as per Tenth Plan Document, has risen extraordinarily from 30 per cent of tax revenues in 1980-1985, to about 70 per cent at present. It has also resulted in increase in revenue deficit, which was 17 per cent of the fiscal deficit in 1980-1985, to about 50 per cent now. The situation is even worse in the State where many States are on the verge of fiscal collapse.

Reforms and Investment

The investment in the public sector during the post-reform period has declined. On the other hand investment in the private sector, which was expected to compensate for the decline in public sector investment, has stagnated. The trends in private sector investment have been disappointing, to say the least. After rising from around 13 per cent of GDP in the early 1990s to a shade under 17 per cent of GDP in 1995-1996, private capital expenditure has slumped and remained at under 16 per cent since 1996-1997. The fiscal reforms attempted through the 1990s have had their repercussions in the form of a relative decline in capital expenditure. However, this decline did not take place mainly during the first half of the 1990s, when the fiscal reforms began. The decline has been more marked from the second half of the 1990s. Gross fixed capital formation as a proportion of GDP fell from 9 per cent to around 8 per cent during the period 1990-1991 to 1994-1995. But since then the fall has been dramatic, by 2001-2002 investment in the public sector had come down to as little as 5.9 per cent of the GDP.

In a developing country like India, where there is an unequal distribution of income and wealth, the public interests need to be protected. Public sector alone can safeguard equity and distributive justice. The disinvestments of public sector units had caused more loss than benefit. The Comptroller and Auditor General had pointed out that the loss to Government exchequer from the sale of PSU shares in 1992 was hovering around Rs.3,441.7 crore. The Parliament Standing Committee on industry estimated a loss of Rs.10,000 crores to the national exchequer in the disinvestments PSU shares carried on till 1994-1995.

The stagnation in private investment has been on account of a number of factors. New capital outlays in the small-scale sector have almost stopped because of the gradual removal of reservation, inadequate credit, and competition from the organised sector. The exception is in sectors oriented towards exports. Minimal outlays appear to be taking place in these areas. In the corporate sector, sluggish domestic demand and the fear of competition from imports have led to a drying up of investment in industry.

In the emerging liberalised and globalise environment the domestic agricultural sector is becoming weaker with the decline in the infrastructure investment by the State. It has to be acknowledged that the reform process emphasised the growth of manufacturing and service sectors and neglected agriculture. Big drop in public Investment in agriculture including rural development and irrigation will adversely affect economic growth.

Reforms and Employment

On the employment front, a highly depressing situation prevails when compared with the 1980s. The number of employed workers increased by 23 per cent during 1983 to 1993-1994 but the same declined to 16 per cent during 1999-2000. A special Group on Employment Opportunities constituted by the planning commission reported in May 2002 that the rate of employment growth had declined from an annual average of 2.7 per cent in the period between 1983 and 1993-94 to 1.07 per cent in the period between 1993-1994 and 1999-2000. A decline of nearly 5.0 percentage points in rural employment, and about 4.0 percentage points in urban employment, during the 1990's is too harsh a reality for the Indian economy to brush aside for shake of the growth benefits of first, the economic reforms of 1991, and of the WTO membership in 1995.

During 1990-1998, as many as 7 million Indian workers (nearly 4 million in the rural and about 3 million in the urban areas) lost their jobs; it is equally serious that the entire episode of job losses is confined to non-agricultural activities. Added to this, the proposal of the Central Government to reduce the manpower at the rate of 2 per cent per annum adds fuel to the already existing size of unemployment.

Recent data from the National Sample Survey pointed out that even the number of days or work an agricultural worker used to get earlier, had gone down drastically. It indicates the failure of the policy followed since the 1990s—not cause but consequence. Globalisation was supposed to generate employment, but what is happening is the reverse. People from the organised sector have been compelled to shift to the unorganised sector. Together with the rapid casualisation of labour, there is increasing evidence of growing gender disparities and the persistence of the scourge of child labour. The female work participation rate according to the 2001 census was 25.6 per cent, a moderate increase from the 22.3 per cent recorded in 1991. Much of this employment is in the rural sector, in situations of distress and compulsion rather than of choice.

Similarly, the number of child labourers in the country, according to the NSS 1999-2000 survey, is over 10 million. Child labour, which depresses the wages of adult workers and, what is worse, deprives poor children of their basic rights to education and economic and cultural development.

Reforms and Labour Standard

Everywhere there is a slogan of downsizing of manpower. The Voluntary Retirement Scheme is being implemented everywhere. A policy of hire and fire is being suggested in industrial undertakings and as a result regular jobs are being converted to the contractual jobs and so due to globalisation there has been a decline in the wages of workers. In the name of outsourcing, so many jobs have been handed over to the private sector to reduce the cost of production. In that process the working class is a victim as

MNCs employ more and more contract workers. For example, the majority of workers in Hindustan Lever are contract workers. Regular jobs are being constantly denied to workers by the MNCs.

The Government does not entertain any disputes with the MNCs in the name of encouraging foreign capital. The Government does not encourage disputes particularly in the Export Processing Zones. The government made it clear that the labour laws will not apply to the EPZs. Workers are denied minimum wages, have no job security and they work beyond 8 hours a day. All these have affected the working class adversely. The government has decided to increase the EPZs and to call them as Special Economic Zones with many more concessions so that they can export all their capital and profits.

Industrialists in India are clamouring for a drastic amendment to labour laws. They want to be unshackled from the bothers of having to seek permission from the government before closing down factories and establishments. The whole intention is geared at reducing wage costs. This has resulted in the intensification of exploitation of labour. In the unorganised and small-scale sector, there is gross underpayment of wages. It is almost like bonded labour. Given poverty and the galloping unemployment, people have no option but to offer themselves at the cheapest rates in hostile conditions. There is a large-scale violation of labour laws. Employees State Insurance benefits are denied to workers and defaults on payments of Provident Fund are increasing.

At the threat of being kicked out, women are subjected to all kinds of exploitation. Some of the specific policy decisions that have affected the working class include the reduction in the interest rates on Provident Fund deposits and rampant employment of contract labour. The refusal of the Government to remove the ceilings in the payment of Bonus Act has brought a sizable number of workers out of the purview of the Act.

Reforms and Foreign Investment

India is under pressure to agree to negotiate an agreement in the WTO that will constrain the Government's role in guiding the entry and operation of foreign investment in the country. The objective of the major developed countries, particularly the EU and Japan, is to ensure full freedom of entry and operation of their investors in developing countries like India. The normal objective of a foreign investor is to have a high and assured profit in a short time and he will choose the industrial service sector and geographical location accordingly. India's objective is to have foreign investment for development of its infrastructure, upgradation of technology, production of exportable goods, providing innate strength to is production and services and development of economically weak regions. The foreign investors objective did not coincide with India's objective.

Much of the approved FDI in infrastructure did not fructify, as the rupee cost of electricity supply by foreign firms is much high for Indian consumers. Foreign investment in consumer goods industries has increased domestic competition resulting in greater choice and quality improvement while FDI inflow displaced some domestic firms. There are many instances of foreign firms gradually acquiring controlling interests edging out domestic partners.

One of the most undesirable consequences likely to emerge from the infiltration of the MNCs in the Indian economy would be expansion in production of luxury of goods and services for domestic markets in which they expect a greater profitability. This type of consumer durable oriented industrial growth will facilitate consumerism at the cost of production of essential goods and services meant for the masses. International firms with their superior technology, marketing skills and financial strength would wipe out domestic firms in many of these industries. This has indeed happened in the soft drink market, for instance. FDI, in principle, brings in greater market discipline on the incumbent firms by increasing competition. But, as we have seen, foreign firms often acquired dominant positions by taking over domestic firms. This again is best illustrated by coca-cola's acquisition of the dominant domestic competitor, Thumps Up, and Hindustan Lever's acquisition of its largest domestic rival Lakeme.

Reforms and Natural Resource

In a surreptitious manner, several state governments are entering into contracts with multinationals for privatisation of water. In the last 10-12 years, there have been several developments that aided the privatisation of water. Bottled water became easily available in local markets. It is like privatising national assets. The Indian market for water is estimated to be worth over 2000 million dollars. Major global corporations including the top three global water giants Suez and Vivendi of France and RWE-AG of Germany, have shown interest in the Indian market. They are given contracts of service and management, which makes it possible for them not to be directly accountable to the people. But an expose by a non-governmental organisation showed bottled water defaulting on the requisite quality standards, thus bringing into the open and darker side of privatisation. A study conducted by environmentalists warned that the extraction of groundwater by two large cola companies, that have bottling plants in the drought-prone Palakkad district of Kerala, would lead to a deficient rainfall pattern and deterioration in the quality of groundwater owing to over-exploitation.

Again, the people of Sivaganga district in Tamil Nadu are agitating against a soft drink manufacturer's plan to exploit large quantity water from the region, which is already facing scarcity. As per the agreement of soft drink company has entered into with a sugar mill, it will utilise 75,000 litres of groundwater a day. The plant is expected to affect water supply to Sivaganga, Manamadurai and Tirupuvanam towns and 80 villages.

Reforms and Agriculture Sector

In agriculture, the main imperatives of India in its national perspective are production of adequate food for domestic consumption and sustenance of its rural agricultural economy. The latter is significant as the number of people in India who depend on agriculture for a livelihood are 650 millions and it is almost impossible to find alternative means of livelihood for them in other sectors for a long time to come. Both these objectives are hit at present by the 300 billion dollar annual subsidies provided to their agriculture (generally known as "green box" subsidies) by the rich countries. Such a high support to agriculture grossly violates the spirit of free trade and extended market access to developing, countries. If these subsidies continue and there is no control on them, Indian farmers run the grave risk of facing severely unfair competition from imports. At the same time, the rich countries impose high import duties on specific farm products and they do not offer incentives to the Indian farm exporters. The pious hope of providing greater market access for Indian agricultural products would carry greater conviction if some force is used to make the developed countries to observe their part of the subsidy reduction commitment. So far, free trade has not worked as fair trade.

Gradual reduction of subsidies to farm inputs and produce, compulsion to use the seeds manufactured by MNCs are the danger signals that haunt Indian farmers. The impact of higher fertilizer prices is bound to be severe on small and marginal farmers as they cannot benefit much from the higher output prices consequent on their low marketable surpluses and lack of stock retention capacity. Further low resource level will force them to cut the fertilizer use, which in turn would reduce the already low level of marketable surplus. Another important aspect of high fertilizer prices and the consequent increased cost of cultivation is that it would make our agricultural products less competitive in the international market. This will be contrary to the new export-oriented policies.

Reforms and Industrial Sector

In the new Industrial policy of July 1991 industrial licensing was abolished for all but 18 industries. MRTP was amended to help expansion of large units. Areas reserved for public sector was narrowed down. Locational restrictions were relaxed. Automatic approval of foreign equity and clearance of RBI has been initiated. The industrial growth started accelerating from 1993-94 and reached a peak of 12.8 per cent in 1995-96. However, it felt to 5.6 per cent in 1996-97 and improved marginally to 6.6 per cent in 1997-98. The improvement in 1997-98 was due to better performance of mining and electricity generation. But the growth rate once again plummeted to around 4 per cent in 1998-99. Moreover, the new economic policy has distorted the industrial structure, giving fillip to the consumption of durable consumer goods for the elite.

The industrial growth rate has been quite subdued at around 6 per cent during the last two years. In a manufacturing and the capital goods sector which represent the foundation of the entire industrial economy, the continuing decline in growth rate signals an ominous symptom. The supporters of liberalisation whisk away this trend by citing the higher growth in service sector. But the service sector economy cannot compensate the decline in the real economic sector like manufacturing. Despite the concessions to the industry like lowering the rate of interest, taxes, allowing more depreciation, subsidy in export promotion and so on there appear to be no apparent development of industry.

In the last one and a half decades, the new economic policies have led to a loss of livelihoods. Traditional industries like handloom, weaving, fishing and coir have suffered. Foreign imports have killed off thousands of small and medium industries in India. A number of industries have closed in Mumbai, Aligarh, Kanpur, Indore and several other towns. Unable to compete in the open market as many as 4,00,000 units have closed down, according to an estimate. Production has suffered owing to the closure of a large number of units.

Reforms and Financial Sector

The financial sector underwent a major change. Liberalisation paves the way for the opening of the financial and banking sectors to the multinationals. The entry of the foreign banks and the new private banks that are not subjected to the government obligations and stipulations is bound to adversely affect the domestic banking industry. The main aim of the private sector banks is to minimize the cost and to maximize the profit in a global market where there will be exploitation of labour.

During 1991-92, India witnessed the biggest scam in the world banking history. Reports are pouring in about the occurrence of one scam after another during the past few years. On the face of it, it would seem that a few unscrupulous Indian businessman and stockbrokers were behind these scams. But a deeper insight into the forces behind the scam shows that some of the foreign private banks, which have spread their wings throughout the length and breadth of India, were at the root of these scams. Due to reasons known only to them the foreign private banks have been permitted to indulge in unlawful and unethical banking practices with immunity.

Reforms and Social Sector

Human Development Report 2002 of United Nations Development had ranked India 24th out of 173 countries with Human Development Index of 0.577 lower than that of the newly industrialised countries like Indonesia and Malaysia due to the poor achievements in social sector. The allocations made to the social sector as a whole and particularly to education and health during the post-reform period are inadequate relative to our requirements. The expenditure on social services in the year 2002-03 has been less than the budgeted amount.

Human Development Report, 2003, says that India continues to be the home of the largest number of hungry people. Despite big promises of faster economic growth and eradication of poverty given at the time of introduction of globalisation the people have experienced only negative impact of globalisation. India is witnessing a decline in key human development indicators like health-care, education, housing and income-status. It is also shocking to find in the report that forty million children are still out of schools and may be engaged in manual labour. During the course of just one year, our ranking in the matter of human development has gone down by four points, only shows how inadequately we have addressed the dire needs of our social sectors. This also reveals how India is lagging behind in growth as compared to other countries.

Conclusion

The economic reforms giving importance to privatisation and liberalisation even in the essential and most crucial services like health and education had made them the purview of only those who can afford. Necessities have thus become luxuries to the poor. Because of globalisation, in the Prime Minister's words, there is growth, but it is "jobless growth". This kind of growth is not good for development. All this is happening owing to the effects of globalisation. It is a proven fact that the strategy of growth adopted in the 1990s has not benefited large segments of the population.

REFERENCES

1. *Front Line,* September 12, 2003, pp. 4-18.
2. *The Hindu,* August 14, 2003, p. 12.
3. *The Hindu,* August 22, 2003, p. 10.
4. *The Hindu,* August 25, 2003, p. 25.
5. *The Hindu,* September 2, 2003, p. 18.
6. *The Hindu,* September 10, 2003, p. 10.
7. B. Kumar, "Economic Growth—The Emerging Profile" *Southern Economist,* January 15, 2003, pp. 11-13.
8. Mukta S. Adi, "India Under WTO" *Southern Economist,* June 15, 2003, pp. 11-14.
9. Seema Joshi, "Social Sector: Need for Reprioritisation" *Southern Economist,* September 15, 2003, pp. 19-20.
10. R. Nagaraj, "Foreign Direct Investment in India in the 1990s" *Economic and Political Weekly,* April 26-May 2, 2003, pp. 1701-1712.

11. Siddheswar Prasad and Jagdish Prasad, *New Economic Policy*, Mittal Publications, New Delhi, 1993.
12. Peninsular Economist, *Journal of the Association of Economists of Tamil Nadu*. Vol. IV, No. 2, 1991-1992.
13. K. Padmanabhan, *A Decade of Trade Liberalisation in India*, Indian Institute of Public Administration, Tirupattur Branch, 2001.
14. Peninsular Economist, *Journal of the Association of Economists of Tamil Nadu*. Vol. XIV, No.1, 2001-2002.

10

The Impact of Economic Reforms on Rural Employment Opportunities

K. Sivagami and M. Pushpa
T. Tamilselvi

India is a land of villages where 70 per cent of the population resides. The village communities were little republics having nearly everything they want within themselves. With the development of modern means of transport and industrialisation the villages lost their self-sufficiency and were brought into the vortex of commercial competition and world market.

Employment assumes great significance because human beings are not only means of production but also the end of production. Agricultural sector occupies a pre-dominant role in the national economy both in terms of its contribution to the gross domestic product and employment provided by it. Agriculture happens to be the predominant occupation of people in rural areas. It is seasonal in nature and therefore for the majority of people in the agricultural sector employment is mostly seasonal. Thus, there is considerable amount of unemployment and under-employment in rural India.

Economic Reforms

Since July 1991, a series of economic reforms was formulated by the Government of India. These reforms embraced all major sectors of the economy–agriculture, industry, trade, public sector, financial institution etc.

Liberalisation policy adopted by the government resulted in opening of trade by reduction of import duties, removal of quantitative restrictions, and entering the WTO regime. It also resulted in loosening of licensing systems and privatisation of Government companies. There has been deregulation of labour protection, which leads to rapid growth of contract labour and sub-contracting.

Every section of the Indian economy is now linked with the world outside and taking all efforts to adapt itself to the changing economic environment.

Employment in Post-Economic Reform Period

The days of protected domestic market had gone with the formulation of economic reforms. Quality consciousness and price competitiveness have become prime factors for staying on in the market. To cope up with changing scenario, employment market too has to re-orient itself to new, and more stringent, recruitment standards.

After a decade of economic reforms, this is the most appropriate time to assess the effects of the reforms implements. The assessment of economic reforms will answer questions, such as in which direction the economy is moving, the general standard of living of the people and the most important question is the impact of such reforms in employment, especially rural employment.

A market for educated, trained and skilled job aspirants is steadily expanding, simultaneously with sluggishness or steady decline in the job market for the less educated, semi or unskilled and untrained workers. Employment prospects are thus brighter for the more qualified while a squeezing scenario sets in for the untrained and the uneducated job sectors.

Economic Reforms and Rural Agricultural Employment

Although agriculture continues to occupy a predominant position in the Indian economy, its share in the GDP has declined from 44.8 per cent in 72.73 to 27.6 in 1999-2000 and the share of agriculture in employment declined from 73.9 per cent in 72-73 to 60.2 per cent by 1999-2000. This is evident from the following table.

Share of Agriculture in GDP and Employment

Year	*Per cent Share of Agriculture in GDP at 1993-94 prices*	*Per cent Share of agriculture in (UPSS) Employment*
1972-73	44.8	73.9
1993-94	33.5	63.9
1999-2000	27.6	60.2

Source: National Accounts Statistics and Survey on Employment and Unemployment

The post-liberalisation period 1993-94 to 1999-2000 witnessed a sharp decline in employment growth in agriculture. Deceleration in the growth of employment during the post-liberalisation period 1993-94 to 1999-2000 has not been uniform across sectors of the economy. There is sharp decline in employment growth in agriculture during the 1990s. Thus, growth rate in the secondary and tertiary sectors decelerated from 3.62 per cent and 4.02 per cent p.a. during 1972-73 to 1993-94 to 2.43 and 3.01 per cent p.a. respectively. The growth rate in agricultural employment decelerated from 1.49 per cent p.a. to 0.01 per cent p.a. There are several reasons for the near collapse of employment growth in agriculture during the 1990s. The main reason was a sharp deceleration in the growth rate of agriculture in general and crop production in particular. The growth rate of all crops (agriculture sector being dominant) decelerated from 3.46 per cent p.a. from 1981-91 to 2.38 per cent p.a. during 1991-2000. This sharp decline in the growth of crop output adversely affected employment growth in agriculture during the 1990s. Other contributing factors for the deceleration of agricultural growth in India are:

- A decline in the growth rate of infrastructure investment in agriculture over a prolonged time;

- Declining efficiency of input use;
- Technological stagnation and surplus cereal production and falling prices.

The second reason for the decline of employment in agriculture is increasing capitalisation of agriculture over the year. Cost of cultivation data show that for major crops the man-hours used per hectare has declined whereas the interest charges on fixed capital per hectare have increased over the time. For example in Punjab, in the case of paddy, man-hour per hectare declined from 857.5 during 1981-82 to 450.4 during 1998-99.

In agriculture, usually output growth is associated with high growth in employment, but a new development has taken place, i.e. increasing output is being achieved with relatively little increase in employment. This is evident from the data, which shows that employment elasticity in agriculture fell from 0.49 during 1973-74 to 1993-94 to 0.005 during 1993-94 to 1999-2000.

Agricultural growth acts as an important engine of growth for other sectors of the economy. To accelerate agricultural growth, the following efforts should be taken:

- Large-scale public investment for development of irrigation and other infrastructure in rainfed areas would not only accelerate agricultural growth, but will also increase productive employment;
- Promote diversification of agriculture into high-value crops and agro-processing. Diversification of cropping from cereals to higher-value crops like fruits and vegetables would increase employment and provide opportunities for exports. Vegetables are the most labour intensive crops and hence employment in these crops will be much higher than in cereal crops;
- Animal husbandry is an allied activity undertaken by many cultivating households, and this activity

is widely dispersed. Hence, development of animal husbandry offers opportunities for increasing employment. However, development of animal husbandry, requires substantial investment in feed production, processing, marketing and institutional and technological support;

- Rural manufacturing and agro-processing help in creation of productive employment in rural areas. This sector can be expanded by adopting promotional policies and investment in infrastructure at the village levels;
- The tertiary sector is also becoming very important for creating income and employment, both in rural and urban areas. Many services such as consultancies, computer services, insurance and publishing are becoming more international and tradable in character and are less dependent on local or national demand;
- One of the most important areas for generating employment are the special employment and anti-poverty programmes like the Integrated Rural Development Programme (IRDP), Jawahar Rojgar Yojna (JRY), The Employment Assurance Scheme (EAS) and Training of Rural Youth for employment known as TRYSEM. Many of the schemes were able to generate significant Employment opportunities. For example, during 1996-97, the JRY and EAS programmes in rural areas created 4006 million and 4030 million mandays of additional employment. However, since the amount of spending on these programmes has been reduced due to fiscal problems, employment created by these programmes has reduced during 2001-02.

Liberalisation and Women Workers

Liberalisation has caused an increasing inequality in employment opportunities and income. For women at the upper income, upper skill end, the quality and opportunities for employment have improved. However, for other women workers the quality of employment is poor.

Liberalisation has caused loss of employment in some sectors without creating any new employment. For example, in Gujarat, women gum collectors who collected gum from Baval trees, lost their employment due to import of cheaper gum from Sudan.

Women are also affected by changes due to mechanisation. With the introduction of machines, total number of jobs is reduced drastically, and moreover women are generally replaced by men. Technical changes have eliminated many jobs traditionally performed by women and alternative job opportunities have not been created for women at the same rate. For example, chemical spraying has replaced weeding, a female dominated task.

However, the opening of a new market, or expansion of an existing market have created new employment opportunities for women. In the crafts sector employment has grown at a fast pace. The sector witnessed a dramatic increase in number of crafts persons from 48.25 lakhs persons during 1991-92 to 81.05 lakhs on 1997-98. Trends also indicate that while male participation in crafts has been slowly decreasing over the years, female participation is on the rise, particularly in rural home-based crafts sector.

With globalisation, prospects of export of milk and milk products seem bright. Women play a predominant role in dairy operations, which is mainly carried out within the household.

Another growing area of employment is the manufacture of garments and associated work. There is growth both in domestic and export markets, and hence the opportunities for employment of women workers are on the increase in this sector.

Due to the development of micro finance, women are in a position to speed up the process of capitalisation in her life. Studies have shown that micro finance enhances women's employment and livelihoods in a number of ways.

Conclusion

Rate of growth of employment has witnessed varying degrees of decline in many sectors, both in rural and urban areas and for male and female workers. In some sectors the post-reform employment growth rate has been higher compared to the pre-reform years. However, the improved employment growth rates don't compensate for the declining rates, since the number of such sectors is small and these are not the major absorbers of the rural work force.

For rural workers, transport–storage–communications, construction and agro-based manufacturing offered tremendous employment opportunities. However, agriculture, mining, utilities, trade, finance–insurance–real estate, showed negative growth or slowdown in employment. Thus, a mixed picture on employment growth has emerged in the Indian Economy.

REFERENCES

1. C.B. Mamoria, B.B. Tripathi, *Agricultural Problems of India* Kitab Mahal, Allahabad, 1991.
2. *Economic and Political Weekly,* Feb. 15-21, 2003.
3. *Economic and Political Weekly,* Aug. 16-22, 2003.
4. *Economic and Political Weekly,* May 25-31, 2003.
5. *Kisan World,* Oct. 2003.

11

Impact of New Economic Policy on Service Sector with Reference to Early Childhood Care and Development

A. Shahin Sultana

Introduction

India trailed with its protective policies till 1990. It was only in 1991 that it adopted the new Economic Policy and started making efforts to integrate the Indian Economy with the World Economy. In the 1980s India had a fairly good economic performance. But it was only in 1990-1991 the Indian economy faced a lot of problems with the major Indian Trading Partners collapsing the India's credit in the international markets falling considerably. As a result India had to borrow from the IMF and from Bank of England by mortgaging the gold reserves of the country. India had in hand only one alternative of undertaking Drastic Economic Reforms. With the year 2001 India completed a decade of a policy of Liberalisation and now the Government is introducing a second generation of Economic reforms. There are 3 main components of the service sector:

(a) Trade, Hotels, Transport and Communications;

(b) Financial, Real Estate and Business services;

(c) Community, Social and Personal service;

Table 11.1: Sectoral Real Growth in GDP (AT Factor Cost)

Item	Percentage change over the previous year									
	1993-94	*1994-95*	*1995-96*	*1996-97*	*1997-98*	*1998-99*	*1999-2000 (P)*	*2000-2001 (Q)*	*2001-2002 (A)*	*NFYP**
I. Agriculture and allied	4.1	5.0	-0.9	9.6	-2.4	6.2	1.3	-0.2	5.7	2.1
II. Industry	5.2	10.2	11.6	7.1	4.3	3.7	4.9	6.3	3.3	4.5
1. Mining and Quarrying	1.4	9.3	5.9	0.5	9.8	2.8	2.0	3.3	1.4	3.9
2. Manufacturing	8.5	12.0	14.9	9.7	1.5	2.7	4.2	6.7	3.3	3.7
3. Electricity, gas and water supply	-0.8	9.4	6.8	5.4	7.9	7.0	6.1	6.2	5.2	6.5
4. Construction	0.6	5.5	6.2	2.1	10.2	6.2	8.1	6.8	2.9	6.8
III. Services	7.7	7.1	10.5	7.2	9.8	8.3	9.5	4.8	6.5	7.8
5. Trade, hotels, transport and communications	7.1	10.4	13.3	7.8	7.7	7.7	7.7	5.3	6.3	6.9
6. Financial, real estate and business services	13.4	5.6	8.2	7.0	11.6	7.4	10.6	2.9	7.5	8.0
7. Community, Social and personal Services	3.5	3.2	7.9	6.3	11.7	10.4	11.6	6.0	6.0	9.1
IV. Total GDP	5.9	7.3	7.3	7.8	4.8	6.5	6.1	4.0	5.4	5.4

A: Advance estimate Q: Quick estimate P: Provisional
NFYP: Ninth Five Year Plan (1997-2002) annual average growth
Source: Central statistical organisation, Government of India.

It is clear that the growth of GDP that was 7.3 per cent and 7.8 per cent in 1995-96 and 1996-97 has now considerably decreased to 5.4 per cent. The growth in the period before 1996-97 was concentrated in Industry (9%) and from 1996-97 to 2001-02 it was concentrated mainly in the Service Sector. Community Service grew at a rate of 11 per cent on an average rate. Higher growth in the service sector will ultimately be a positive indicator for the growth of the economy. But in India the contribution of the manufacturing sector to the GDP is very low when compared to the other countries.

Programmes Covered for Children by the Government of India

"Development of Children is the first priority on the country's development agenda not because they are the most vulnerable, but because they are our supreme assets and also the future human resources of the country."

Tenth Five year Plan (2002-2007).

The Schemes for children fall into 4 main categories:

1. Child Development and Nutrition;
2. Child Education;
3. Child Health;
4. Child Protection and Others.

Major Schemes Under Child Development and Nutrition

1. Integrated Child Development Services;
2. World Bank Assisted ICDS Programme;
3. World Bank Assisted ICDS Programme—Training Programmes;
4. National Institute of Public Co-operation and Child Development;
5. National Fund for Child Care Services (General Component);
6. National Children's Board Lumpsum Provision;

7. Universal Children Day Lumpsum Provision;
8. Institution of Awards to Individuals and Institutions;
9. National Commission for Children;
10. Creches/Day Care Centres;
11. National Nutritional Mission;
12. Nutrition Education and Extension;
13. Fortification of Milk;
14. Food and Nutritional Board and its Regional Office;
15. Implementation of National Nutrition Policy.

Major Schemes under Child Education

Sl. No.	*Elementary education*	*Secondary education*
1.	Operation Black Board	National Council of Educational Research and Training (NCERT)
2.	Teachers Training Programme	Vocalisation of Education
3.	Non-Formal Education	Information Communication Technologies in Schools.
4.	Shiksha Karmi Project	Education Technology Programme (Insat Cell)
5.	Mahila Samakhya	Quality Improvement in Schools
6.	District Primary Education Programme	National Open School
7.	Mid-Day Meal	Environmental Orientation Programme
8.	Sarva Shiksha Abhiyan	Population Education project
9.	Teacher Education	Access and Equity
10.	National Programme for Women Education	Integrated Education for Disabled Children
11.	Joint Indo-UN Education Programme	Central Tibetan School Society

Major Schemes under Child Protection

Ministry of Social Justice and Empowerment

1. Central Adoption resource agency.
2. Homes for Infant and Young Children for in Country Adoption.
3. Schemes for Street Children.
4. Prevention and Control of Juvenile Maladjustment.
5. Correctional Services.

Ministry of Labour

1. Child Labour cell-Improvement in working conditions of Children.

Schemes Under Health

1. UNDP Assistance to Children with Disabilities.

Ministry of Social Justice and Empowerment

1. Pre-Matric Scholarship for SC, ST & OBC
2. Post-Matric Scholarship for SC, ST and OBC
3. Girls Hostels
4. Boys Hostels
5. Ashram Schools
6. General Welfare of SC, ST and OBC.

Ministry of Health and Family Welfare

1. Kalawati Saran Children's Hospital, New Delhi.
2. Manufacture of Vaccine – BCG Vaccine Lab Guindy, Chennai.
3. Strengthening of National Immunisation Programme and Polio Eradication.

Others

Ministry of Information and Broadcasting

1. Children Film Society of India.

Table 11.2: Sectoral Share of Child Related Programmes of Government of India

Sectors	*Actual 2000-01*	*B.E. 2001-02*	*R.E. 2001-02*	*B.E. 2002-03*	*R.E. 2002-03*	*B.E. 2003-04*
Health	6164.78 (1.06)	7693.00 (1.08)	3424.50 (0.50)	62178.00 (7.03)	48398.00 (6.34)	72746.00 (7.65)
Child Development and Nutrition	125338.88 (21.49)	151403.00 (21.24)	154537.00 (22.58)	185059.00 (20.93)	173431.00 (22.73)	212861.00 (22.39)
Education	445330.33 (76.36)	545052.00 (76.47)	516713.00 (75.50)	624053.00 (70.58)	526901.00 (69.07)	648977.00 (68.27)
Child Protection and Others	6345.50 (1.09)	8635.00 (1.21)	9728.55 (1.42)	12945.00 (1.46)	14156.00 (1.86)	15965.00 (1.68)
Total	583180.55	712783.00	684403.05	884235.00	762886.00	950549.00

1. Every year the expenditure for every sector is increasing.
2. An increase of about 7 per cent is noticed in the allocation of the budgets for child related schemes.
3. About one-fifth of expenditure on children is devoted to Child Development and Nutrition.
4. Education forms the largest share in Public Expenditure on children in the Union Budget but the relative share is declining.
5. The share in the Health sector has increased from 1 per cent in 2000-01 to nearly 8 per cent in 2003-2004. This increase is mainly on account of increase in provision for the programme on Immunisation against Polio, which now includes a component included in the Reproductive Child Health Programme.
6. The Budgetary allocation really shows the commitment of the Government towards the Children but due to problems like lack of resources, lack of personnel, implementation problems and other problems make it sometimes ineffective.

Globalisation and its Impact on early Childhood Care and Development (ECCD)

Globalisation has become a very dominant feature as many nations are just getting connected with each other through trade and capital flows. Actually Globalisation can be traced back to 1870-1914 as capital, trade and labours were all-free to move from one country to another. But today in "Globalisation" only capital is free but not labour or human resources. Chossudovsky (1997) argues that fragmentation of communities and countries are interlinked with globalisation.

The Human Development Report on South Asia 2001, released by UNDP is perhaps the strongest critic of globalisation. The benefits of globalisation have remained limited to a small minority of educated urban population. As a result, income equalities have increased. There are a number of instances where developing countries are not given equitable treatment though globalisation promotes economic growth and prosperity to all nations, promotes technology, free foreign investment supplements domestic savings and encourages more investment in the community.

WTO follows a policy of green room consultancy, whereby only rich nations come together and take decisions. At the meetings of the WTO, the World Economic Forum and meetings of G7 nations, demonstration and protests are organised against the policy of Globalisation by NGO's from all over the world.

ECCD is a fundamental responsibility of the Government of India but due to the access of Globalisation there has been a great pass over ECCD. The child of the age from 0-6 years is totally ignored whether in the way of the policies, programmes and budgets. It has become a necessity for those working for ECCD to join hands with the co-workers in these areas to fight a battle against Globalisation.

Globalisation has shown its effect on:

1. Waning provisions and unavailability of Creches, Immunisation programmes, Nutritional Programmes and adequate healthcare;

2. Pregnant mothers, Mothers and Children are not covered under the maternity care and benefits;

3. Insufficient and poor quality pre-school education, ignoring school-drop out due to sibling care or child labour.

On November 1989 the United Nations General Assembly adopted the United Nations Convention on the Rights of the Child (UNCRC). Today it is the most widely endorsed international human rights treaty signed by all countries in the world.

The UNCRC sets out the full set of rights, which Governments must guarantee to all children, without any discrimination. These include:

- "The right of the child to the enjoyment of the highest attainable standard of health", including measures to ensure "the provision of adequate nutritious food and clean drinking water" *(Article 24);*
- "The right of the child to education" *(Article 28);*
- "The right of the child to be protected from economic exploitation" *(Article 32).*

Some of the key rights in the UNCRC are threatened by globalisation and the rules governing international trade and disinvestment. But Governments must ensure that even after the expansion of trade and investment the ultimate human rights must not be affected. With the process of globalisation there has been a reduction in the availability and quality of health care services between regions, rural and urban areas.

The amount to be spent on the social services in this year have been less than originally budgeted for.

Revised budget	Budget Allocation (2002-2003)
Rs. 25,520 crore	Rs. 26,823 crore

The budget allocation for plan expenditure on social services in the year is Rs. 28,884 crore, which is 13 per cent higher than the revised estimate for 2002-2003.

The revised expenditure has been less than budgeted in education (elementary and secondary), health, drinking water and sanitation. The gap between budgeted (Rs. 4,304.7 crore) and revised (Rs. 3,762.1 crore) for elementary education is the largest among all the categories. Expenditure on elementary education increased from Rs. 3,764.4 crore in (2002-2003) (revised) to Rs. 4,669.4 crore in 2003-2004 (budget)—an increase of 24 per cent.

Child Development and Nutrition

Nutrition is the scientific term used for the study of food. It is a mixture of nutrients and non-nutrients. In Asia, Bangladesh leads the world with a 67 per cent of children below acceptable levels of nourishment and India comes second with 53 per cent. To keep nations well informed of their progress the National Performance Gap a new indicator has been devised which shows the country's actual level of progress and the expected level for the country's income level.

According to the new estimates of maternal mortality, nearly 50 per cent maternal deaths per year occur in the Asia pacific region, followed by the sub-Saharan Africa with more than a third of these cases. A progress has been achieved in areas like immunisation, healthcare, breastfeeding, safe drinking water and a higher enrollment in primary and secondary schools of the developing and least developed countries of the world.

In India the birth rate exceeds the death rate though both the rates are showing a decreasing trend. In fact, the birth rate is not decreasing as much as the death rate. Hence population continues to go up. Emphasis was given on childhood mortality and morbidity and hence in the year 1992, the IMR in India was 79 when compared to 105 in 1982.

The Primary Health Care consists of providing Promotive, Preventive, Curative and rehabilitative service.

The child's health gets affected mainly because:

- Malnutrition or rather hunger due to poverty;
- Unsafe drinking water and sanitation;

- Poor living conditions;
- Poor working conditions in the case of child labourers;
- Unaccessible health care services.

Primary health care services have increased; health workers have been increased and health care budgets. Maternal mortality has declined and there are a lot of gains in fertility control but still there is a lot more to go.

Child Education

Schooling has no doubt been considerably increased over the last few decades. But still the goal of universal education has not been met. The goal of universal primary education is itself not complete but on the other hand the school drop out rate still persists. Most of the children drop out in the earliest stages.

Out of 100 Children in India

40-50 do not enroll in schools at all	50-60 enters primary schools. Of these, about 30-40, soon drop out.	20-25 enters middle school. Of these, a further 10-15 drop out.	5-10 enters higher secondary school 4-6 of these drops out.	Only 1-2 eventua-lly enter college

There is a belief that the parents send their children to work mainly because they have to pay some fees other than the non-fee expenses.

The comparable enrolment rate up to primary level :

	Girls	*Boys*
1990-1991	40.4	57.0
1991-1992	42.3	59.0
1992-1993	44.9	60.5
1993-1994	46.4	61.8
1994-1995	46.8	62.3

Mostly the girls are sent for Domestic work. The other reason remains that the schools are not that good and it does not give much chances for employment. Another reason for the girl child not attending school is due to sibling care and the school curriculum and teaching. The Sarva Shiksha Abhyan, the concept of "Education for all" is of course on its progress move but how far it will be achieved is yet to be seen.

Child Health

The centuries in the past have witnessed a lot of advancements in the field of health. But still there are a lot of health problems arising. Simple facilities say clean and safe drinking water, healthy nutritious food, and cleanliness are still not available to the people. There is a strong co-relation between the child's health and the mother's education. If the child's health has to be improved then the mothers have to be educated. Right from the stage of conception the mother has to be guided to take care of the child as well as her own health.

WHO estimated that the first decade of the HIV/AIDS there were about 5,00,000 cases in women and children. HIV has to be fought by creating awareness, discovering a vaccine and by immunisation programmes. A lot of problem among the children are also increasing due to the increasing population of children. Wars, Migration and the other problems also create a lot of problems among the Children, e.g. the children in Iraq.

Child Protection and Others

The major problems which the children face are Sexual abuse, Rape, Molestations, Child prostitution, Child trafficking etc. The school-drop out and other children who do not have a good family background have more risks of facing such problems.

Child Labour is another threat the children face. It is mainly due to poverty and cheap labour from the employer's side. The International Labour Office estimates that in the world 52 million children (aged less than 15 years) are working. The impact of globalisation has been vast thus employing children in most of the industries thus denying their right to education. Children are also the main targets of the labour market. They can be hired at much lower wages than adults. Many of India's children are forced into the labour market when they are only three years old. According to the Constitution of India (Article 23), no child below the age of 14 must be employed in a factory or mine or engaged in any other hazardous employment. Article 45 says that the State will provide free and compulsory education to all children up to the age of 14.

Female foeticide and female infanticide cases have to be strictly stopped by the laws that would punish the offenders who use unregistered scan centers, which reduces the male female ratio. Globalisation has brought a tremendous effect on this by totally reducing the male female ratio. If this persists then a lot of other problems would crop up.

Thus the new economic policy has had a worse impact on the young child. Right from the basic survival rights Protection rights, Development and Participation rights everything connected to the child have been affected.

Recommendations

Child Nutrition and Development

- The economic system has to be changed with the people having a major role to play in decision-making.
- Policy level changes have to be implemented.
- Collective action must take place so that all of them ensure that their rights are safeguarded.
- The rural areas where poor health care facilities exist have to be specially considered for.
- More awareness about health and prevention of diseases has to be created.

- The prevalent government programmes must be well published so that more number of people benefit from them.
- Privatisation of medical services must be on check.
- Practitioners of other systems of medicine can also be included in the prevention of disease and promotion of health.
- More facilities like day care centers and creches have to be introduced for both the organised and the unorganised women labourers.
- The maternity assistance schemes have to be revised so that the mothers are benefited by the amount when they are in real need.
- The maternity leave has to be increased upto 3-6 months so that breastfeeding is possible.

Child Education

- There is a considerable reduction in the allocations for the Education sector due to globalisation and this has to be considerably increased.
- All measures must be taken to ensure compulsory elementary education.
- Early Childhood Education must be considered as an important component as it is the basis for the entire life of the child and it must be specially focused on.
- Steps must be taken to ensure that the child is given both nutritional facilities and education so that they do not drop out from school and at the same time do not work to earn for food.
- People's participation and in general the community's involvement must be enhanced for effective functioning of the local schools.

Child Health

- Primary Health Centres play a major role in educating the mothers on nutritious food.
- Infant milk substitutes for the first six months have to be totally removed from the market and stringent measures have to be taken to punish the law-offenders.
- The public has to be given awareness on immunisation programmes and other vaccinations to avoid health complications in children.
- The mothers have to be sensitised on how to prepare low-cost nutritious food, how to maintain clean and hygienic environment and food.
- First-aid measures have to be stressed for the mothers as to avoid complications through Media and the Govt. has a larger role to play in it.
- Breast-feeding for the first six months have to be constantly stressed as a lot of health problems can be avoided.
- All this information could be imparted right from the school curriculum itself.

Child Protection and Others

- Child Labour is a serious problem and laws have to be strictly enforced towards both the employers and the parents who get them employed.
- Female foeticide, infanticide has to be stopped by strict legislations.
- The children have to be sensitised on the issues of sexual abuse so that they are aware of what directions to be followed in such cases.
- Counseling and interactive sessions have to be kept now and then in the school premises so that the child gets to know the problems in real life.

- Child trafficking is on the increase and the school authorities and the parents must ensure the total safety of the child.
- The child must be made to realize what will be the problems she might generally face and build her mental framework to confront such untoward incidents.
- They must be informed of the Child assistance lines available in case of emergencies.

"The options before leaders who are striving to do what's best for children and best for their country seem obvious: assure that every child, without exception, is registered at birth and starts life safe from violence, with adequate nutrition, clean water, proper sanitation, primary health care and cognitive and psychosocial stimulation, or fall their moral and legal obligations as set forth in the convention on the Rights of child".

Carol Bellamy, The state of the world's children, 2001 –UNICEF

REFERENCES

1. Ajit Karnik (2003): 'Ignoring Priorities', *Economic and Political Weekly*, March 22-29, 2003.
2. Children on the State Agenda, Budgeting for the Child, An analysis of the Tamil Nadu State Budget (1998-2003), Early Childhood Care and Development, ICCW.
3. Dev, S. Mahendra and Jos Mooji (2002): 'Social Sector Expenditures in the 1990's: Analysis of Central and State Budgets', *Economic and Political Weekly,* Vol. 37, No. 9.
4. Ghosh Shangthi, (1976) *"The feeding and care of Infants and Young Children"* UNICEF, SCAR, New Delhi.
5. *"National Seminar on Nutrition Education"*, (1975) NCERT Publication.
6. Pulapre Balakrishnan (2003): 'Globalisation, Growth and Justice', *Economic and Policial Weekly,* July 26, 2003.
7. Report of the National Commission of Labour, 2002.

Online Resources

www.eldis.ids.ac.uk/children

www.globalresearch.ca/articles/STA206A.html

www.hrea.org/lists/child-rights/markup/msg00092.html

www.infochangeindia.org/bookandreportsst23.jsp

www.usq.edu.au/unit-2001/80.htm.

12

Rural Employment in India After Economic Reforms

M. Raju

Introduction

Ever since the introduction of economic reforms in 1991, there has been an immense debate on the impact of economic reforms on employment, poverty and well-being of the poor in India, especially in rural areas. Although generation of adequate sustained employment opportunities has become the focus of attention of the development paradigm since inception of planning era. Since then, the employment situation in the rural economy as a part of development dynamism through sustained interaction between growth, employment and poverty has stated to witness different facts and dimensions.

Now that the Indian economy has already lived through a full decade of the new policy regime, it is time to know the precise effects of the reforms implemented so for on various segments of Indian economy; what directions the economy is likely to take; and how would the people's working and general standard of living look like after a decade or so, are the questions that are yet to be answered with empirical firmness. Central to all these questions is the issue of employment. It is time to pose questions such directions in which rural labour market is likely to move in the near future now that new technology, production and employment, trade and other policy regimes have taken roots in the Indian economy.

The present chapter looks into the situation on the front of rural employment. This chapter aims to examine the work-force participation in rural economic activities during the pre- and post-reform period. The study is mainly based on secondary data collected from various reports on employment and unemployment published by the NSSO.

Profile of Workforce in the 1990s

According to the recent NSSO estimates, the total population of India has increased by 895 million in 1993-94 to 994 million in 1999-2000. A sharp rise in the growth rate of population is observed in the urban areas as compared to rural areas over the same period (NSSO, 2000). Similarly, the total labour force has also increased from 374 million to 393 million during the same period. The NSS data (2000) reveal that the percentage growth rate of population and workforce has significantly increased in the urban areas as compared to rural areas. But, the percentage growth rate of labour force is found to be more than the population growth rate in the rural economy, leading to overcrowding in the rural labour market, which has eventually resulted in migration of rural labour force to the urban areas in search of better employment opportunities in the late 1990s.

Rural Work Participation

With speedier implementation of economic reforms, the proportion of workers participating in different economic activities has stated to exhibit a dismal scenario in India, especially in the rural economy. Table 12.1 presents the data on workforce participation according to usual status during 1972- to 1999-2000. It is evident from the data that the all-India level, the labour force registered a marginal decline in the late 1980s, even before the reform period and sharply increased in the early 1990s, and again steeply declined in the late 1990s, the post-reform period. The decline in the labour force participation, which stated even before the reform measures, is found to be not only higher but also accelerated in the rural areas as compared to the urban areas during the

Table 12.1: Workforce Participation During 1972-73 to 1999-2000

(Usual Status)

Year/NSSO Round	*Rural*			*Urban*			
	Male	*Female*	*Persons*	*Male*	*Female*	*Persons*	*Total*
1972-73	53.6	31.4	42.8	49.8	13.2	32.6	40.7
1977-78	54.4	32.6	43.8	50.0	15.3	33.9	41.6
1983	54.3	33.7	44.2	50.9	14.9	34.0	41.8
1987-88	53.9	32.3	43.4	50.6	15.2	33.7	41.2
1993-94	55.3	32.8	44.4	52.0	15.4	34.7	42.0
1999-2000	53.1	29.9	41.7	51.8	13.9	33.7	39.5

Source: NSSO (1981, 1988, 1996 and 2000)

post-reform period. Moreover, it is also quite clear that the percentage share of female participation, although it is small, has witnessed a significant reduction in the rural areas as compared to urban areas. This implies that the employment opportunities for rural females are getting limited as compared to urban females in recent years. The poor workforce participation can be attributed to the following reasons:

(a) A decline in the age specific workforce participation;

(b) A rise in the student population ratios at different age levels;

(c) Lack of employment opportunities which reflect in terms of a decline in employment growth rate, increased informalisation, casualisation and feminisation of rural employment during post-reform period.

Rise in Unemployment

The most daunting challenge of the present development paradigm is to provide employment not only to the new entrants into the labour market but also reduce the backlog of unemployment in the past.

It may be observed that the unemployment rates by current daily status (CDS) have also gone up. The data on unemployment rates based on CDS during 1972-73 to 1999-2000 are provided in Table 12.2.

The data reveal that the problem of unemployment in the rural economy is more acute than in urban economy as the workforce in rural areas can't remain unemployed for long term. Although the employment opportunities for women, especially for the unskilled, seem to be deteriorating in recent years, the differential rate of unemployment between men and women has come down over recent years. This reveals that there is gradual increase in female proportion in the development process.

Table 12.2: Unemployment Rates During 1972-73 to 1999-2000

(Current Daily Status)

Year/NSSO Round	*Rural*			*Urban*			
	Male	*Female*	*Persons*	*Male*	*Female*	*Persons*	*Total*
1972-73	6.83	11.22	8.21	8.02	13.67	8.99	8.35
1977-78	7.12	9.18	7.70	9.40	14.55	1.34	8.18
1983	7.52	8.98	7.94	9.23	10.99	9.52	8.28
1987-88	4.58	6.91	5.25	8.79	12.00	9.36	6.09
1993-94	5.64	5.55	5.61	6.72	10.52	7.43	6.03
1999-2000	7.20	6.80		7.20	9.80		

Source: NSSO (1981, 1988, 1996 and 2000)

Table 12.3: Percentage Distribution of Workers Between Agriculture and Non-agriculture During 1972-73 to 1999-2000

Year/NSSO Round	*Rural*			*Urban*		
	Agricult.	*Non-agri.*	*Total*	*Agricult.*	*Non-agri.*	*Total*
1972-73	85.6	14.4	100	14.8	85.2	100
1977-78	83.4	16.6	100	15.2	84.8	100
1983	81.5	18.5	100	14.8	85.2	100
1987-88	78.3	21.7	100	13.6	86.4	100
1993-94	78.4	21.6	100	12.3	87.7	100
1999-2000	76.1	23.9	100	8.8	91.2	100

Source: NSSO (1981, 1988, 1996 and 2000)

The unemployment rates for women both in rural and urban areas continued to register a decline trend during the pre- and post-reform periods except for rural females in the year 1999-2000. This means that employment opportunities are getting limited and bleak for rural women as compared to urban women in the post-liberalised era. Similarly, during the post-reform period, while unemployment rates among males declined both in the rural urban areas, it started rising during the post-reform period.

Rural Non-Agricultural Employment

In the view of the increasing population pressure on agricultural, diminishing land frontiers, decline employment elasticity in agriculture and urban organised manufacturing sector, higher incidence of unemployment and poverty and excess supply of labour force, etc., rural non-agricultural activities are expected to play an important role in combing the problem of rural employment during the post-reforms period.

It is since the 1970s that the rural economy has been diversifying away from agriculture to non-agriculture absorbing the bulk of the rural labour force who are mostly unable to find adequate employment in the agricultural sector. Table 12.3 presents the data on percentage distribution of workforce between agricultural and non-agricultural in the rural and urban areas during the period between 1972-73 and 1999-2000. The data show that while agriculture continues to be a major occupation for the rural people, for urban people non-agricultural employment is not only the main occupation but also has been increasing in the post-reform period.

Conclusion

There is an apprehension that the economic reforms have had an adverse impact on the employment and poverty particularly in rural India. Although it is premature to assess the impact of economic reforms, the data on employment and unemployment published by NSSO for 1999-2000, the percentage growth rate of labour force has increased much faster than the population and eventually has lead to migration of rural workforce to urban areas in search better livelihood opportunities. While there is a marginal decline in the growth rate of workforce in India, a dramatic decline is observed in the case of female participation, particularly in the rural areas. The decline in workforce participation can be attributed to a decline in the age specific workforce participation, a rise in the student population ratios at different age levels, lack of employment opportunities. The growth rate of employment, which was on the rise for all categories of workforce (except rural female) in the early reform period, has steeply declined and a negative growth rate of employment for rural female is observed. Similarly, the unemployment rates, which started to register a declining trend on the eve of economic reforms, have begun to go up during the post-liberalisation era. In the view of changing employment scenario in the rural economy, a multi-faceted and multi-prolonged strategic package needs to be worked out to face the challenge in the market driven economy.

REFERENCE

1. Arindam Bandyopadhyay and A.K. Giri (2001), "Pattern of Employment in India and Major States" *Indian Agricultural Journal,* Vol. 56 No. 3.
2. Biradar R.R. and Bagalkoti S.T. (2001), "Changing Facets of Employment in Rural India: Emerging Issues and Challenges" *Indian Agricultural Journal,* Vol. 56 No. 3.
3. National Sample Survey Organisation (NSSO) (1981), "Report on Second Quinquennial Survey on Employment and Unemployment (All India)', NSS 32nd round, *Sarvekshana* Vol. 5 Nos. 1 and 2.
4. NSSO (1988), "Report on Third Quinquennial Survey on Employment and Unemployment (All India)", *Sarvekshana* Vol. 11, No. 4.
5. NSSO (1990), "Results of Fourth Quinquennial Survey on Employment and Unemployment (All India)", 43rd round, *Sarvekshana* special number.
6. NSSO (2000), "Report on Employment and Unemployment in India, 1999-2000 Key Results", NSS 55th round, Report no. 455(55/10).

13

Economic Reforms and Labour Force Participation in Rural Sector

Dr. M. Soundarapandian
Dr. S. Jagadeespandi

Since the beginning of the Five year plans there has been persisting worrisome trends in the rural labour market. They are (1) Inadequate growth of productive employment in the rural areas. (2) Casualisation of masses of rural workers without a safety net. (3) Feminisation of agricultural labour with low wages and (4) Persistence of child labour. The Present chapter attempts to examine the impact of economic reforms bring about a change in the labour force participation in rural areas. The key issues are:

(i) Whether the reforms have adversely affected the employment opportunities in rural sector;

(ii) Whether reforms have accentuated casualisation and if so which sections have been suffered most; and

(iii) Whether the casual workers, the most vulnerable section among the rural labour class have been benefited in the reforms period in terms of real wage rise.

The chapter examine the issues in detail:

These issues have been studied by comparing the relevant parameters before and during reform period. The database for these analyses derived from NSSO reports, Economic Surveys, and other Government Reports.

Trends in Employment

During the last two decades there have been some perceptible trends in the structure of rural employment. The table 13.1 shows the trends in the quality of employment in rural areas.

Table 13.1: Growth of Employment in Agriculture and Non-Agriculture Sector in Rural India

(Fig. in percentage)

Period	*Agricultural*	*Non-Agriculture*	*All rural*
1977-78-1983	1.43	3.83	1.97
1983 to 87-88	0.12	5.79	1.14
1987-88 to 93-94	2.32	1.41	2.10
1993-94 to 99-2000	0.20	2.34	0.16

Source: National sample survey organisation 55th round (2000).

The Table 13.1 shows that the share in growth of Agriculture labour force declined from 2.32 per cent in 1987-1993 to 0.20 per cent in 1993-1994 to 1999-2000. While the Non-Agricultural sector shifted to rise from 1.43 per cent to 2.34 per cent in the same period. It indicates the Non-Agricultural rural households in the rural areas are gradually withdrawing from cultivation to concentrate on the main non-agricultural occupation in the agriculturally developed states. The shift of the workforce from agricultural to non-agricultural activities is shown to be an outcome of growth rather than a "distress" phenomenon. The expansion of the rural non-farm sector has been influenced by growing commercialisation in the rural economy. It means that the employment potential on the non-farm sector appears to be directly related to the commercialisation of Agriculture.

Table 13.2: Age specific Labour Force Participation Rates by Sex in India

Year	*Male*					*Total*	*Female*					*Total*
	5-14	*15-29*	*30-44*	*45-59*	*60 above*		*5-14*	*15-29*	*30-44*	*45-59*	*60 above*	
1977-78	13.1	86.1	90.0	95.9	64.6	63.7	9.1	39.7	49.2	41.1	16.1	30.5
1987-88	7.4	79.7	98.7	95.7	64.9	61.4	6.3	36.9	47.6	42.2	16.3	29.2
1993-94	5.9	77.7	98.8	96.4	60.3	63.0	5.5	32.2	42.7	43.1	17.3	27.2
1999-00	4.3	75.9	98.4	95.4	62.4	53.3	3.8	31.6	44.5	40.7	17.4	23.5

Source: NSSO 55th round data (2000)

Labour Force Participation

Regarding the labour force participation in rural India, it has gone up from about 208 millions in 1983 to 263 million in 1993-1994 and to 291 millions in 1999-2000. The Table 13.2 is presented in Age-wise labour force participation rates by sex.

From the Table 13.2 there is a declining trend in labour force participation rates and among so female workers. The male labour participation declined from 61.4 in 1987-88 to 53.3 in 1999-2000; while the female rate declined from 29.2 to 23.2. The annual average growth rates of labour force were 2.6 and 1.8 per cent respectively during these two periods. A steep fall in percentage of female workers due to the efforts of the state and other development agencies a discouraging child labour could be one of the plausible reasons for this. To explore the reasons for substantial decline in labour force participation of female workers, the LFPF in the Age group 5-14 declined from 9.1 rate in 1977-78 to 3.8 in 1999-2000. Similarly a case can be seen also in male workers. The rate declined to 13.1 to 4.3 in the above two periods. Further the participation rate during 1993-94 and 1999-2000 found that female rates dropped negatively in the states of Haryana, West Bengal, Punjab, Assam, Uttar Pradesh and Bihar. Above all, the work population ratios have been showing a declining trend revealing a rise in the economic dependency ratio's. The fall in the worker population ratios in 90s needs further probing. Unless compensated by a rise in the duration of employment and wage rates, these trends will have adverse affect on the livelihoods of rural people.

On the occupational distribution of workforce the composition of work (self, employment regular and casual) has been changing. While self-employment is on the decline, casual employment is on the rise. The share of the self employed in the rural workforce declined from 62 per cent in 1977-78 to 56 per cent in 1999-2000. While the proportion of casual labour increased from 30 to 37 per cent during the corresponding period. Regular employment declined marginally from 7.8 to 6.7 per cent during the same period. The Table 13.3 and 13.4 is present the distribution of workers and occupational divisions of employed.

Table 13.3: Distribution of Workers in Rural Areas *(percentages)*

Employed status	*1977-78*	*1987-88*	*1993-94*	*1999-2000*
Self-employed	64.3	59.4	58.0	55.6
Regular	9.3	7.7	6.4	6.7
Casual	25.4	32.9	35.6	37.7

Source: NSSO 55th round data (2000).

Table 13.4: Occupational Distribution and Status of usually employed in Rural Areas *(percentage)*

Sector	*1983*		*1993-94*		*1999-2000*	
	Male	*Female*	*Male*	*Female*	*Male*	*Female*
Primary	77.8 (107.9)	87.8 (55.7)	74.1 (123.3)	86.2 (80.2)	71.4 (132.9)	85.4 (85.7)
Secondary	10.0 (14.1)	7.4 (4.8)	14.7 (24.46)	7.6 (7.0)	12.6 (23.4)	8.9 (8.94)
Territory	12.2 (17.3)	4.8 (3.1)	11.2 (18.63)	6.2 (5.8)	16 (29.8)	5.7 (5.7)

Source: NSSO 55th round data (2000)

(Figure in parenthesis are the persons employed under each sector in millions.)

It is inferred from the occupational distribution of workforce, there is high degree of dependence in primary sector. Although the millions of people increased from 1993-94 to 1999-2000 the percentage rate have mild decreased from 77.8 to 71.4 per cent in males, while 87.8 per cent to 85.4 per cent for females during the corresponding period. The availability of males and females in secondary sector increased from 14.1 to 23.4 and 4.8 to 8.94 respectively from 1983 to 1999-2000. Similarly a case in territory sector is also seen. It can be gleaned that primary sector has been losing its share but at a slow pace. In the reform period, a rise in the share employed females in secondary sector was more conspicuous while territory sector could improve its share as far as male workers are concerned. Thus, it reveals that rural labour market have been gradually diversifying.

Regarding the casualisation in the workforce of rural workers, the rate of male workers have gone up than the female workers more steeply among the self employed in non-agriculture. The Table 13.5 explained the incidence of casualisation in rural workers.

Table 13.5: Incidence of Casualisation among rural workers *(percentages)*

Type of employment	*1983*		*1993-94*		*1999-2000*	
	Male	*Female*	*Male*	*Female*	*Male*	*Female*
SE Non-Agri	2.41	3.14	7.37	16.9	5.99	14.3
SE-Agri	0.86	5.46	2.99	4.67	2.9	4.20
Agri Labour	64.9	49.8	88.1	83.1	91.9	85.3
Other labour	71.8	66.4	70.5	56.4	72.4	57.6
All	28.3	34.7	33.8	38.7	37.68	44.36

Source: Rao and Rajalakshmi (NSSO), SE – Self employment

From the table there is high level of casualisation seen in agricultural and other labourers. The percentage rate rose from 88.1 to 91.9 for males and 83.1 to 85.3 for females during the period of 1993-94 to 1999-00. Thus the incidence of casualisation was not only high but also rising among labour class. On the whole, the incidence of casualisation has been higher among females than males and among labour class compared to self employed.

As far as the wage rate is concerned the real wage rate gone up moderately in 1993-94 but remarkably in 1999-2000. The Table 13.6 present the wage rate in rural labour market.

From the table 13.6, in spite of the sluggish growth of rural employment during 80s real wages increased. This could be due to both an expansion of employment in non-agricultural activities such as construction and services. Real wage registered an improvement during the post-reform

Table 13.6: Duration of Employment and wage rate—Rural India (days/year)

Item	1983		1993-94		1999-2000	
	Male	*Female*	*Male*	*Female*	*Male*	*Female*
Employment 15-59 years	320	212	331.7	241	327	246
Wages (Rs/day) of casual workers (at 1983 prices)						
Public works	-	-	10.9	8.19	15.8	12.7
Agriculture	7.21	4.89	9.56	6.68	14.9	9.23
Non-Agri	10.3	5.10	13.3	7.74	19.2	12.03
All activities	-	-	10.3	6.81	12.7	-

Source: Rao and Rajalakshmi (NSSO).

period despite a deceleration in agricultural productivity and a slow down in rural non-farm employment. While the gender disparities in labour markets are evident from the declining ratios of female wages to male wages in agriculture. But in non-agriculture sector the ratio of benefit has been rising for females.

Conclusion

With the introduction of new economic reforms the rural labour market has undergone qualitative changes. The labour force participation ratios have declined, and its annual growth was less than the population growth in the reform period. The deceleration in growth on female labour force and employment in the post-reform period. Casualisation has been on rise and more conspicuously among female workers and labour class. In fine, the effects of reforms are adverse to rural labour markets and more so to female workers.

REFERENCE

1. D. Narashima Reddy, (2002), "Changing Agrarian Relation and Rural Labour; Certain Emerging Issues" *Indian Journal of Labour Economics*, Vol. 45, No. 1.

2. Rao and Rajalakshmi (2002) "Structure of Employment and Casualisation in Rural India" *Journal of Rural Development.*

3. Kumar B. L. (1996), "Changes in the Composition of Rural Labour Force: Some Evidence from a Village Resurvey" *Indian Journal of Labour Economics*, Vol. 39, No. 4 October – December.

4. Vaidyanathan, A (1995), "Employment Situation in India; Some Emerging Perspectives" *Economic and Political Weekly*, Vol. 29 (50) December.

5. Naidu R.M. (1993), "Unemployment and Employment in India; An Overview" *The Indian Journal of Labour Economics,* Vol. 36, No. 1.

14

Economic Reforms and Employment

Dr. M. Nagesh Kumari
C. Renuka

Reforms in India

Since July 1991, the Indian economy has witnessed a series of reforms, encompassing all major sectors of the economy (agriculture, industry, trade, foreign investment and technology, public sector, financial institutions, and so on); it has marked a steady break from the past policy regime. The government followed an export-linked strategy in the place of import substituting strategy. Being a member of World Trade Organisation from 1st January 1995, India got further integrated into the global economic system and became an adherent of the multilateral trade system. Finally, beginning April 1, 2000, all types of quantitative restrictions on imports stood nearly completely removed since April 1, 2001; exports and imports are now free of all restrictions. Foreign investment is now invited by all regions of India, in a wide range of areas, most significantly for removing the so-called infrastructural bottlenecks. Every sector of Indian economy is now attuning itself to the changing economic environment. The state itself is struggling to demarcate the balance between its development and welfare functions. Production and marketing management now needs new visions, initiatives and networking, both at home and abroad. Concerns for environment, labour standards and product acceptability among others have acquired added significance.

Quality consciousness and price competitiveness become prime considerations for staying on in the market. Coping with new production, product quality, marketing, and networking norms, the quality of work force acquires supreme significance. In this back drop, this chapter discusses the employment scenario in India in post-reform period.

Orientation in Labour Market

The employment market has to substantially reorient itself to new, and more stringent, recruitment standards; even for those aspiring to self-employ themselves, up-to-date knowledge of the trade and market networking are as inescapable prerequisites as are higher educational, training and skill accomplishments. Never before did the Indian economy in general, or its rural counterpart in particular, face such labour-market challenges as during the 1990s or would face in the coming years.

Dualism in Labour Market

Employment prospects are brighter for the more qualified while squeezing scenario set in for the untrained and the uneducated job-seekers; differences in employment prospects get magnified between self-employment and wage-paid jobs, and still more significantly, between urban and rural areas. Rural job aspirants, especially females, suffer far more severe setback, primarily because of the own educational and skill deficiencies.

Demand and Supply of Labour

The total employment of an economy is an issue determined both by the demand as well as the supply factors. In fact, the prime concern in a labour market evolves around the demand and supply of labour and the factors determining the operation of these two forces. The ability of the economy expand output, in response to the needs of the economy, will decide the employment generating capacity of the various crucial sectors of the economy. In a similar fashion response by the labour force, in terms of their ability to adopt themselves to the productive and technological transitions in the economy, coupled with their competitive strength, are the critical factors, which determine the supply of labourers.

In India, out of the economically active population of 550 million at present, only 28 million people have had the benefit of employment in organised sector. 249.29 million are either employed or under-employed in the unorganised sector, while the services of the balance 272.71 million remain unutilised.

Under organised sector the percentage share of public sector in total employment is showing a declining trend in recent years (Table 14.1). It can be observed from the table that the private sector continued predominently to the increase in the organised sector employment in the reform period except in the year 1993. The deregulation has helped to generate new employment in the services sector as well as in the unorganised sector. Studies on informal sector shows that employment has been growing in unorganised sector. Another significant factor is that informal sector employment in smaller towns with a population of the order of one lakh has been growing at 12 per cent per annum as per studies conducted by the Institute of Applied Manpower Research. These smaller towns accounts for about 40 per cent of the urban population and are also the points of first migration for rural-urban migrants. Synergy between the formal and informal sector in economic growth and development is the primary imperative of this millennium.

Formal sector employment is undergoing structural change. It is leading to the creation of high skill intensity jobs. Human Resource Development efforts to promote skill requirements, therefore, assume significance. This calls for closer interaction and collaboration between the corporate sector and the education and training infrastructure to bring about required transformation in skill development.

India's organised labour strength of 28 million is only 7-8 per cent of the total workforce and over 90 per cent belonging to the unorganised sector, with no wage determination or social protection. While real wages and productivity of labour increased in the 1990s in the organised sector—where public sector employment makes up 70 per cent of the total—India's labour productivity is the lowest among the 47 countries listed in the World Competitiveness Report.

Elasticity of Employment

Elasticity of employment to growth measures the percentage increase in jobs created for every percentage growth of Gross Domestic Product (GDP). The higher the elasticity the more labour intensive one can expect the GDP growth to be. The elasticity of employment creation of growth has been declining between the early eighties and mid-nineties.

Table 14.1: Percentage Share of Organised Public and Private Sectors in Total Employment

Years	*Public*	*Private*	*Total*
1990	71.23	28.77	100
1991	71.29	28.71	100
1992	78.46	21.54	100
1993	78.51	21.49	100
1994	70.30	20.70	100
1995	70.72	29.28	100
1996	69.53	30.47	100
1997	69.25	30.75	100
Average	73.54	26.46	

Table 14.2: Sector-wise Growth Rate of GDP, Employment and Elasticity

Year	*Public Sector*	*Private Sector*	*Total*	*GDP*	*Employment Elasticity*
1981-82	2.98	2.06	2.68	5.8	0.46
1982-83	3.20	0.07	2.20	2.6	0.85
1983-84	2.50	2.72	0.86	7.9	0.11
1984-85	2.38	(-) 0.50	1.50	3.8	0.39
1985-86	2.40	(-) 0.89	1.95	4.1	0.48
1986-87	1.92	0.14	1.32	4.0	0.33

(Contd...)

Table Contd...

Year	*Public Sector*	*Private Sector*	*Total*	*GDP*	*Employment Elasticity*
1987-88	1.64	(-) 0.38	1.28	4.1	0.31
1988-89	0.69	0.83	0.73	10.2	0.07
1989-90	1.71	1.73	1.71	6.9	0.25
1990-91	1.58	1.25	1.48	5.2	0.28
1991-92	0.80	2.61	1.20	0.5	2.40
1992-93	0.60	0.06	0.45	5.2	0.09
1993-94	0.62	1.01	0.73	6.0	0.12
1994-95	0.11	1.63	0.71	6.9	0.10
1995-96*	(-) 0.20	5.62	1.51	7.6	0.20
1996-97*	0.66	2.04	1.08	7.8	0.14

*Figures relate to the end of December every year.

Source: Economic Survey (Various years).

REFERENCE

1. K.C. Pant, *India's Development Scenario—Next Decade and Beyond,* Academic Foundation, New Delhi, 2003.
2. S. Murthy, *Economic Reforms Today—Pros and Cons,* RBSA Publishers, Jaipur, 2002.
3. *Southern Economist*, 1 and 15 December, 2002.

Human Resource Development in the Context of Economic Reforms Relating to Information Technology

Dr. G. Themozhi, P. Sorubarani
Dr. J. Chandrakantha

India is a country of enormous potential. With the right set of economic policies, India can be a major player in the global economy. Economic growth and development of India can alter the fate of a large section of the poorest people in the world. While India has recently made considerable progress in its economic performance since the balance of payments crisis of 1991, economic reforms in India remain an unfinished task. If the country is to achieve higher growth then its economic institutions and policies need to undergo major changes.

Human Resource Development offers a full range of programs and services to help enrich the capabilities of individuals and work teams while improving organisational systems and processes.

One major trend with implications for Human Resource Development is Globalisation. It is fostered by technological changes.

Globalisation impacts on Human Resource Development in various ways. Thus, compared to the past enterprises will head to update much more regularly the spells mix of their employees to respond to the opportunities or threats created by Globalisation and rapid technological change. Indeed intense global competitions reconfiguring the mount place.

Enterprises are increasingly having to compete by differentiating themselves from their competitions by the quality of the human systems and processes behind their products and services.

Changing Organisational Structure/Work Pattern

Changing Organisational Structure and Work Patterns are another trend. Technological changes especially information technology and telecommunication and competition in the vast competitive Global mount place have changed work organisations and working patterns.

Information Technology and the advances in and falling cost of telecommunication mean that it is no longer critical to site offices or companies near the customers. The workforce has become more mobile one, impact on work patterns that is emerging is relationship organisations or virtual corporations.

A virtual corporation is an organisation which uses information technology to link various independent companies, suppliers, customers and even competitors in a temporary organisation to share skills and costs and access to one another's markets. The virtual organisation has a very small core with many resources supported from the outside but without a physical set up.

Virtual offices are emerging as companies are leveraging cyberspace and electronic technology to cut costs like rentals and to boost productivity. In such virtual offices workers stay out of the office but retain contact through high technology gadgets which could be handheld devices that can receive and send e-mail and faxes. Telecommuting is one form of the virtual office where workers work from the home or just about anywhere outside the office.

The development of virtual organisations has HRD implications. Virtual corporations need workers who are highly skirted, reliable and educated, able to understand the new forms of information, adaptable and can work efficiently with others. Employees need not just technical skills but also the skill of learning how to learn to cope with continuous and radical change of virtual businesses. New forms of training which are flexible on demand and interactive will have to be devised for employees of virtual enterprises. These work pattern changes are already taking place in the industrialised world. They are also increasingly affecting enterprises in the developing countries. Human Development Policies and programmes will have to change in response to these changes.

Taskforce on Human Resource Development in Information Technology—Business Process Outsourcing

Business Process Outsourcing is the delegation of one or more business processes to an external service provider who in turn owns, manages and administers the selected processes based on defined and measurable performance metrics.

An important aspect of business process outsourcing is its ability to free corporate executives from some of their day-to-day process management responsibilities. Once a process is successfully outsourced, the ratio can be reversed. Executives get more control over their most valuable resource time. Time to explore new revenue streams, time to accelerate other projects and time to focus on their customers.

Companies that outsource business processes are often able to reengineer those processes and capture new efficiencies. Then they can reallocate resources to other important projects and leverage their investment in technology. For example, processes that are handled in a shared production environment for multiple companies save everyone money.

India's Hopes on BPO—IT Enabled Service

There is not one Hope but Hundreds. India is now pinning its hopes on the IT enabled services business.

If one million Indians can serve the world.

- Answering Phones and E-mails in contact centers
- Developing Software
- Analysing X-rays
- Providing medical advice
- Processing Insurance claims at even an average of US$ 10 (Rs. 460) per hour, it would add US$ 20 billion a year. Nothing wrong with this picture, especially considering that we have no shortage of Indians to serve the world. In fact, the latest mantra among the Indian Software companies in BPO.

BPO has been hyped as one of next big things in IT. Forrester Research believes that the BPO market will grow to $146 billion in 2008. Noting that it surveyed 82 senior business and IT executives and held in-depth interviews with 12 early BPO adopters, the Forrester said many organisations experimenting with BPO reported inflexible contracts, difficulty managing vendors, and a lack of performance metrics.

It's Time to Face the Threat...

BPO and call centre billing rates have gone into free fall, with no signs of recovery. Even the larger, branded companies are now quoting at billing rates of less than $10 per hour and even $5 per hour within the next year or two. Of course, such pricing is likely to spell disaster for many IT-Enabled Services (ITES) companies, which were planned and built on a revenue model of $15 per hour. So what to do? To prepare for the above said one needs to spend some time re-visiting the validity of one's existing business model. Typically this would result in four broad opportunities.

- Straight forward reduction of unnecessary or inflated expenditures that creep into every large organisation.

- An opportunity for process re-engineering to optimize resource utilisation and thereby cut costs.
- Opportunity may involve a capital expenditure in order to drastically change variable costs.
- There may be ways to work closer with one's customers—reduce transaction costs, and in some cases help re-engineer their processes in order to reduce overall costs.

Conclusion

The importance of HRD cannot be overemphasised. The Chinese philosopher, Guanzi (551-479 BC) said that

"When planning for one year,

there's nothing better than planting grain,

When planning for ten years,

there's nothing better than planting trees,

When planning for a lifetime,

there's nothing better than planting men".

In his own words he explained that grain is something that is planted once and produces only a single harvest. Trees are planted once but may produce ten harvests. Men are things that are planted once but may produce a hundred harvests. HRD contributes to economic development. It does not by itself make such growth possible.

India is a country rich in natural and human resources. It has an impressive entrepreneurial base, growing capital markets and an agricultural sector with food self-sufficiency. It has a diversified industrial structure and excellent centers of advanced education. The central objective of economic policy in India should be human development, poverty alleviation, improvement of the infrastructure. These are feasible objectives which can be achieved with economic growth and greater democratisation of political power. To direct economic policies in favour of the majority, the people of India must organize politically.

REFERENCES

1. Proceedings of the International Seminar on Industrial Structural Change and Human Resource Development in the Asia and Pacific Region (7-8 Dec. 1994-Tokyo) Tokyo.

2. Asian Productivity Organisation (1993) *Asian Dynamism Through Human Resource Development*, Tokyo.

3. John Ribeiro, March 22, 2002 1:01 pm PT—*"BPO Bound for Bombay"*.

4. "The Next New Thing" *Tech Talk*—Feb. 15, 2002.

5. *Business Today*—Nov. 25, 2001.

6. *Business Line—e-World*—March 14, 2002.

7. *Business India*, Jan. 21-Feb 3, 2002.

8. *Business Line—e-World*—September 17.

16

Impact of Reforms on Social Indicators in India—A Statistical Appraisal

Dr. C. Sivapragasam
Sri. M. Jeganathan

Introduction

India is one of the world's largest and most heterogeneous countries. It suffered famines and secular stagnation before Independence. It has successfully eliminated famines and severe epidemics in the last few decades. Five-Year Plans and programmes were introduced since 1951 for raising the human resources and improving the living conditions of the people in the country. Uplifting the poor and integrating them into the main stream is a recurrent theme of India's Five-Year Plans. Universal access to education is enshrined in the constitution. India has made tremendous progress in reducing poverty and in its social development indicators, the world's worst at the time of Independence in 1947. Since Independence, India's growth rate has risen, poverty has declined, social indicators have improved – literacy and school enrolments have risen, morbidity and mortality have declined and the gender gap has narrowed. Its continued developmental efforts and economic reforms are the major factors for these achievements. The objective of this chapter is to highlight India's achievements on selected social indicators in the context of reforms.

Economic Development

India's GDP growth rate was 5.4 during 1990-91 while it was 6.0 during 1998-99. The average growth in GDP was 5.7 per cent per annum during the period 1981-99. During 1998-99, India's per capita income was Rs.14682 while it was Rs.237.5 in 1950-51 (at current prices). The growth rate of national income increased from 3.6 per cent per annum during 1951-56 to 6.6 per cent during 1992-97. During the same period the growth rate in per capita income was 1.8 per cent and 4.6 per cent (Ministry of Finance, 2000). The per capita income was Rs.5365 during 1990-91 which has increased to Rs.17182 during 2000-01. As a consequence of growth in the national and per capita income, the population below poverty line has declined significantly to 26.1 per cent during 1999-2000 from 54.9 per cent in 1973-74. By 1993-94 the incidence of poverty was 35 per cent. Economic reforms have also made a significant impact on the households of different income groups. For example, 58.8 per cent of low income HHs during 1989-90 has been reduced to 48.9 per cent during 1995-96. The percentage change was 9.3 (negative).

Agricultural Development

India's performance in agriculture was poor during 1951. Reforms in the early 90s led to higher growth in agriculture. Agricultural production increased nearly 4 times from 1950-51 to 1998-99 mainly due to the success of the Green Revolution since 1970s and reforms in 1991. The yield has increased by 65 per cent. Further agriculture contributes nearly one-fourth of the GDP (RBI, 1999). It provides employment for about two-thirds of all workers in the country (CSO, 1999). The agricultural productivity index of 134 during 1990-91 has increased to 149 during 1999-00, an index of agricultural development in the reform period.

Industrial Development

India had a very weak industrial base before independence. Since 1948 India adopted the concept of mixed economy for overall industrial development. As a result, the industrial production index increased to 155 in 1999-2000 which was only 8 during 1950-51. Further, India has been made to compete with the developed countries of the world. The production of finished steel goods has increased from 1 million tonne in 1950-51 to 24 million tonnes in 1998-99. The generation of electricity has increased from 5 billion kwh to 448 billion kwh. From 1950-54 to 1998-99 exports have increased from US $ 1.3 billion to US $ 33.7 billions. The export which was 75.4 per cent of imports during 1990-91 has risen to 86.6 per cent in 2000-01 as a consequence of globalisation.

Social Development

India has made tremendous progress in social sectors also. The Tenth Five Year Plan has accorded a top priority to social sector development. It emphasizes growth with social justice and equity. The key sectors such as education and health have been performing well, especially after 1991. For example, during 1991 the life expectancy was 58.2 years, literacy rate 52.2 per cent, birth rate 29.5, Death rate 9.8 and IMR 80 per 1000 while the corresponding figures were 63.0 years, 65.4 per cent, 26.1, 8.7 and 70 respectively during 2001. These are crucial for accelerating development and change in the demographic scenario of the country.

Education and Demographic Achievements

With regard to education, a significant progress has been achieved by increasing the literacy rate from 18 per cent in 1951 to 52 per cent in 1991. From 1991 to 1997, the overall literacy rate increased from 52 per cent to 64 per cent, rising from 64 per cent to 73 per cent for males and 39 per cent to 50 per cent for females, according to NSS. The literacy rate improved further to 65.4 per cent with 75.9 per cent for males and 54.2 per cent for females (census, 2001).

The demographic and other development achievements in different sectors of the economy are given below:

- The gross enrolment in the age group 6-11 years increased from 43 per cent in 1951 to 90 per cent in 1997-98 and for the age group 11-14 years, the figures were 13 per cent and 59 per cent respectively.

- The average number of persons per dwelling was 6.0 in 1971, which declined to 5.4 persons during 1998-99, showing an improvement in the housing condition.
- The per capita annual consumption of electricity for domestic purpose increased from 7 kwh in 1970-71 to 57.1 kwh during 1995-96, showing an improvement in the index of economic development.
- The population covered by T.V. was only 5 per cent and radio 55 per cent during 1961, which increased to 87 per cent and 97 per cent during 1997.
- The population growth rate declined from 2.1 per cent in 1990-91 to 1.7 per cent in 2000-01.
- The crude birth rate declined from 32.5 in 1991 to 27.2 in 2001.
- The crude death rate declined from 11.4 in 1991 to 8.9 in 2001.
- The infant mortality rate declined from 146 in 1951 to 80 in 1991 and to 71 in 2001.
- The total fertility rate declined from 6 in 1951 to 3.4 in 1992-93 and to 2.9 during 1998-99.
- The couple protection rate increased from 10 per cent in 1971 to 44.1 per cent in 1991 and to 46.2 per cent in 1999 due to revision of policies and programmes of FP.
- Life expectancy (at birth) increased from 37 years in 1951 to 62 years in 1998 and to 65.4 years in 2001, largely due to improvement in health and medical facilities in the country.
- The telephones and post offices were available at 47 and 10 per 100 thousand population during 1950-51 while the figures were 55 and 16 during

1996-97 showing and improvement in the communication facilities.

Further, significant changes have been noticed in the villages in rural India in respect of social development indicators. The findings of the National Family Health Survey conducted during 1992-93 (NFHS-1) and 1998-99 (NFHS-2) by the International Institute for Population Sciences, Bombay revealed the following improvements among the households in rural India.

- The illiteracy was 63.1 per cent during NFHS-1 which has declined to 58.2 per cent during NFHS-2.
- 51 per cent of the households who had electricity during 1992 has increased to 69 per cent during 1998.
- 33 per cent of the households with piped drinking water has increased to 39 per cent.
- 70 per cent of the households without toilet facilities during 1992 has declined to 64 per cent during 1998.
- About 75 per cent males and 51 per cent females aged 6 and above are literates, an increase of 6 to 8 per cent from the literacy at the time of NFHS-1.
- 79 per cent children age 6-14 years were attending school, which is up from 68 per cent in NFHS-1.
- The infant mortality rate has declined from 79 per 1000 during NFHS-1 to 60 during NFHS-2.
- The child mortality rate has declined from 32 during NFHS-1 to 29 during NFHS-2.
- Knowledge of contraception was almost universal in India. 99 per cent of currently married women know at least one modern FP method; 98 per cent

of women are more familiar to female sterilisation, followed by male sterilisation (89 per cent) and IUD (71 per cent). Knowledge of modern spacing methods have increased from 10 to 13 per cent since NFHS-1, due to revised FP policies and effective Family Planning programmes after 1991.

- 48 per cent of the women were using some method of contraception, up from 41 per cent at the time of NFHS-1.
- 34 per cent of women were sterilised whereas it was 27 per cent at the time of NFHS-1.
- 47 per cent of children (under the age of 3 years) who are underweight was slightly down from 52 per cent at the time of NFHS-1.

The above statistics, particularly show a significant improvement in the social indicators of development in rural India in 90s. Consequently its impact on the human development resources and Human Development Index in India.

Human Development Index in India

The Human Development Report (HDR) defines 'development', as a process of widening people's choices. The HDR proposes a Human Development Index (HDI) based on: access to income and assets needed for a decent standard of living, knowledge acquisition and enjoyment of a long and healthy life. Accordingly, India has been categorised by HDR, 2001 as a medium human development country. The HDI of the country has risen gradually from 0.406 in 1975 to 0.510 in 1990 and stood at 0.57 in 1991. In 1996, India's HDI was 0.436 and its rank was 135th among 174 nations of the world (UNDP, 1996). Latest HDR places India at 128th rank in HDI in the world (UNDP, 2000). The report emphasizes the need for giving top priority to sectors like education, health and poverty eradication. These areas are also crucial for accelerating development in the country.

The HDI of a particular country provides an insight into the level of socio-economic development and quality of the people. However, as an aggregate measure, HDI conceals the inter-regional or inter-state variations. To formulate strategies for human development, it is therefore necessary to analyze human development Index in different states in India.

The National Human Development Report-(2001) has brought out human development index for 15 major states in India for the periods 1981, 1991 and 2001.

Analysis revealed that HDI varies between 0.638 for Kerala and 0.367 for Bihar in 2001. By and large the states maintained their relative position between 1981 and 2001 with a few exceptions. For example, Tamil Nadu improved its ranking by 4 positions from 7 to 3, Assam deteriorated from 10 to 14; and Bihar, and Madhya Pradesh continued to the tail-enders in the HDI race. The all India HDI was 0.472 in 2001 while it was 0.302 in 1981 and 0.381 in 1991. Kerala continued to retain rank position 1 while Bihar rank position 15 among the major states in India.

Further analysis was carried out to quantify disparity in HDI values among the states. The average HDI score was 0.3212 with S.D. 0.0725, the disparity measure showed 23 per cent variation in HDI values among the states in India during 1981.

States in India continued to show improvement in human development from 1981 to 1991. The average of HDI values increased to 0.4027 in 1991 from 0.3212 in 1981. During 1991 the overall variation in HDI values was 19 per cent among the states, which is less by 4 per cent during 1981.

The average HDI further increased to 0.4631 during 2001 with S.D. 0.0755. The variation in HDI among the states was found to be 16.3 per cent indicating a further reduction in HDI disparity among the states from 1981. Such a reduction in disparity value in HDI among the states was mainly due to the economic reforms and other development measures introduced in the country particularly after 1991.

Human Development Index in Rural India

Analysis of human development Index for rural areas in the selected states were carried out starting from 1961 to 1987-88 for which data were readily available. The rural HDI has significantly improved to 0.4387 in 1987-88 while it was just 0.1967 in 1961, 0.2387 in 1971 and 0.3573 in 1981. The variation in HDI values among the states (rural areas) has also shown decline from 33.2 per cent in 1961 to 23.4 per cent in 1987-88 while it was 28.8 per cent in 1971 and 30.3 per cent in 1981. In fact, during 1981, the performance of the states in India with regard to HDI was highly heterogeneous or more variable among various states in India for varied reasons. In the last decade it must have shown further decline in disparity in HDI values which requires further analysis.

Conclusion

Reforms and development measures introduced in the country have made a significant impact on the performance of social indicators and human development in India over the past decades. Further the disparity in HDI values has declined among the states over the decades with improvement in living conditions and infrastructure developments as a consequence of developmental efforts since Independence and particularly due to reform measures initiated in 1991 in the country.

REFERENCES

1. National Family Health Survey, IIPS, 1992-93.
2. National Family Health Survey, IIPS, 1998-99.
3. Economic Survey 1996-97, Ministry of Finance, Govt. of India, New Delhi Found in "Fifty Years of R.D. in India: Retrospect and Prospect, NIRD, Hydarabad, 1998.
4. Census of India, Series I, Paper I, 2001.
5. South India, Human Development Report, NCAER, New Delhi, 2001.
6. *India: Reducing Poverty, Accelerating Development,* A World Bank Country Study, Oxford, 2001.

7. Planning Commission (2002), National Human Development Report (2001).

8. Ruddar Draft and K.P.M. Sundharam, *Indian Economy*, Chand and Company Ltd., New Delhi, 2002.

Impact of Economic Reforms on Dalits in India

Dr. N. Markkendayan
M. Ponniah

Introduction

The Economic Reforms launched in July 1991 in India were in nature of a crisis management response to the economic and political crisis that erupted in early 1991. The economic crisis comprised a steep fall in the foreign exchange reserve, galloping inflation, large public and current account deficits and mounting of domestic and foreign debt. In politics, the fall of two governments in a sort span of four months, from November 1990 to March 1991; deferment of presentation of the union budget, fairly long political interregnum till the elections, the assassination of a former prime minister Rajiv Gandhi in their midst and the emergence of a minority government with a leader sans charisma, reflected an unprecedented crisis. These events led to a sharp erosion of confidence in India among lenders, down-gradation of India's credit rating and consequently cut off of international credit lines from private or commercial sources. Indian Reforms thus, were essentially of a 'crisis driven' variety. They did not represent strategic choice with a vision of long-term development of Indian people.

Dalits in India

Dalits, as the ex-untouchables prefer to be called, are

a very distinct social group. While belonging to a broad class of have-nots they suffer an additional disability of social oppression. Economically, most of them are still the poorest of poor. The balance minuscule minority has managed to escape poverty limits and to locate itself on to a continuum ranging up to a reasonable level of prosperity. The main factor that has catalysed this transition is the reservation policy, which has provided them a basic opportunity enter the modern sectors of economy. In social terms however, all dalits, irrespective of their economic standing, still suffer oppression. This social oppression varies from the crudest variety of untouchability, still being practised in rural areas, to the sophisticated forms of discrimination encountered even in modern sectors of urban areas. Although the statistics indicate that dalits have made a significant progress on almost all parameters during the five post-independence decades, the relative distance between them and non-dalits seems to have remained the same or increased. More than 75 per cent of the dalit workers are still connected with land; 25 per cent being the marginal and small farmers and balance over 50 per cent are the landless labourers. In urban areas, they work mainly in unorganised sector. Out of the total dalit population of 138 million, the number of dalits in services falling in the domain of reservations does not exceed 1.1 million; a mere 0.8 per cent.

Objectives of the Study

An attempt has been made to study the Impact of Economic Reforms on Dalits in India. The specific objectives of the study are:

1. To study the food security in India.
2. To study the inflation rate in India;
3. To study the employment position in India;
4. To study the poverty in India;
5. To study the reservation and financial assistance in educational, institutions in India.
6. To study the reservation in services in India.

Methodology

This study is based on secondary data only. The data relating to the various aspects of Impact of Economic Reforms on Dalits in India were collected from various journals and magazines.

Analysis and Interpretation

Food Security

Food security mainly relates with the production, distribution and pricing of foodgrains and thus brings agriculture, Public Distribution System (PDS) and the subsidy structure in to focus. The reform measures that predominantly affect them are reduction of fiscal deficit, reduction of subsidies, devaluation of rupee, export orientation and reduction of agricultural credit. Considering the pattern of the budgetary outlays of the government, the fiscal contraction inevitably resulted in a disproportionate cut in capital expenditure. Agriculture sector also bore the share of this cut. The average annual increase in public sector outlay on agriculture and irrigation during 1985-90 fell from Rs. 1.3 billion to an average of Rs. 0.68 billion during 1990-92. This cut is bound to have a depressing effect on the agricultural production.

The subsidy on fertilizer had played a crucial role in quadrupling foodgrain production from 46 million tonnes for a population of 363 million in 1951 to 170 million tonnes in 1991 for a population of 832 million. But, after the launch of the Reforms, the subsidy was reduced. It slide from 0.82 per cent of GDP in 1990-91 to 0.75 per cent of GDP in 1995-96. The prices of the phosphatic and potassium based fertilizers were decontrolled and that of nitrogen based fertilizers were reduced by 10 per cent. The prices of phosphatic and potassium based fertilizers soared to international level resulting into sharp fall in their consumption.

This inherent threat to food security is further magnified by the devaluation of rupee by about 25 per cent effected in July 1991. It resulted in making our foodgrains cheaper in the international market. As a result, even the ordinary (non-aromatic) rice [besides the usually exported superfine aromatic (basmati) rice] was exported in huge volumes. The policy impetus to export of rice and wheat is reflected in the actual exports overshooting the targets. For example, in 1995-96 (October- September) actual rice export had reached 5.51 million tones as against the target of 2.5 million tonnes. Increasing exports and free market sales of foodgrains have contributed to a drastic reduction in the stocks of foodgrains with the public procurement agencies.

The reforms in banking led to a severe squeeze on agriculture lending. The share of agriculture in net bank credit consistently declined and fell from 17.4 per cent to 12.4 per cent between March 1990 to March 1995. As a measure of ensuring food security to the large mass of Indian population, public distribution system was instituted in India in the wake of the calamity of the Great Bengal Famine of 1942-43 and the World War-II. The system comprises over 4,24,000 fair price shops spread all over the country in rough proportion of the population. The food distributed through PDS is subsidised by the Government to the extent of the difference between the issue price of foodgrain. It devours a significant part of the government subsidy. With the FCI-costs ever increasing, the impact of any reduction in subsidy has to hit the poor directly.

For ensuring supply of foodgrains to the PDS system in face of export attraction due to the devaluation of rupee, for maintaining their level of production in spite of sharp rise in input prices and for political consideration of assuaging the rich farmers' lobby, the government had to increase the procurement prices of rice and wheat. The procurement prices of rice and wheat were raised by 67.56 per cent and 62.8 per cent respectively between 1989-90 and 1993-94. This rise was passed on to the consumers by increasing the issue prices of these commodities by 85.81 per cent and 75.14 per cent respectively between June, 1990 and February, 1994, apparently for reducing the food subsidy. The impact of this rise was reflected in a significant fall in the off-take of foodgrains. After the Reforms, off-take of wheat and rice as a percentage of the allocation has shown considerable decline. Since, the difference between the consumer-end PDS retail prices and market prices became marginal, the not-so-poor left the PDS and owing to unaffordable prices the poor cut their consumption.

The cumulative effect of the above could be clearly seen in a trend of falling per capita net availability of cereals per day for the Indian population. During two years of the Reforms, there was 8.43 per cent fall in per capita availability of cereals and 12.02 per cent fall in that of pulses. Considering the acute inequality of Indian population, the impact of this declining trend on the poorer and disadvantaged sections would be far more severe than indicated by averages. Pulses being the only source of vegetable protein for poor people, a sharp decline in their availability certainly indicates malnutrition. The incidence of malnutrition further would be disproportionately injurious to women and children because of the male preference in Indian tradition.

Inflation

Inflation hits the poor people the hardest. Being employed mainly in the unorganised sector, they do not have even the partial protection their counterparts in the organised sector have, by way of dearness allowance. Most of their earning is spent of the basic needs like food, clothing and shelter, and hence any price rise directly dampens their level of consumption. Devaluation of currency directly contributes to the inflation by raising the cost of imports that enter into domestic production or consumption. Large part of our import comprises petroleum crude and its products; chemicals, machinery, iron and steel, etc. which enter as raw or intermediate materials in our production process. Most of these products are of common use in the economy. Any escalation in their cost therefore directly results in contributing to the rise of general price level.

Employment

The rate of growth of employment in the organised sector dropped from more than 1.7 per cent per annum in the late 1980s to 1.2 per cent in 1991-92 and to 0.6 per cent in 1992-93. Creation of jobs in the public sector fell from 11.0 million in the preceding four years to the 6.2 million in the succeeding four years of the Reforms. For the Private Sector, the corresponding figures rose form 2.08 million to 2.49 million. In the Central Government establishment there were 4.03 million jobs on 1st March 1991 which went up next year to 4.14 million. But for the next two years they came down to 3.97 million and 3.84 million respectively.

Poverty

Poverty is a sum total of all the deprivations. In India governmental definition of poverty is based on the sole criterion of minimum food requirement for survival. Thus, the poverty line is decided by the income sufficient to buy food equivalent of 2400 calories in rural and 2100 calories in urban areas. The data base for poverty estimates is provided by the quinquenial surveys of NSS. NSS also collects the consumer expenditure data by decile group on an annual basis. The Reforms have reversed the two decades long declining trend of poverty. The rural poverty went up from the pre-reform low of 33.7 per cent to 41.7 per cent in 1992 and slightly declined to 40.2 per cent in 1993-94. The urban poverty also showed the same trend shooting up from the pre-Reform low of 36 per cent to 37.8 per cent and then coming down to 36.2 per cent.

The social disadvantage suffered by dalits in India was taken note of in the Constitution of India which was drafted under the chairmanship of Dr. Ambedkar—a person who had spearheaded the most momentous anti-caste movement of the depressed classes. It provided dalits with many safeguards, viz., (1) social, educational, cultural and religious safeguards, (2) economic safeguards, (3) political safeguards and (4) safeguards for employment. The free market ethos of the Reforms, conceptually can nether confirm to the democratic spirit of the Indian Constitution of 'one vote, one value', nor can it coexist with the system of positive discrimination embodied in these safeguards.

Reservation and Financial assistance in Education Institutions

Reservation in the educational institutions and the financial assistance in the form of scholarships and free ships constitute perhaps the most important factor in the development scheme for dalits. For, it is primarily responsible to make the basic input of education available to them. Without education, all the constitutional safeguards including the reservation in services would be in fructuous. Under this scheme the dalit students whose parental income is below a specified level, get free ship, reservation in admissions to all the colleges getting grants-in-aid from the government, and scholarships. Without this assistance, even today, it would be difficult for dalits to send their children to school.

The Reforms have already resulted in freezing the grants to many institutions and in stagnating, if not lowering, the expenditure on education. The free market ethos has entered the educational sphere in a big way. Commercialisation of education is no more a mere rhetoric; it is now the established fact. Commercial institutions offering specialised education signifying the essential input from utilitarian view point have come up in a big way from cities to small towns. Their product-prices are not only based on the demand-supply consideration in their market segment but also are manipulated by their promotional strategies. In a true spirit of globalisation, many foreign universities, are invading the educational spheres through hitherto unfamiliar strategic alliances with non-descript commercial agencies, of course at a hefty dollar equivalent prices. Many elite institutions like IIMs, IITs, suddenly facing fund crunch had to raise their fee structure and other prices manyfold. They were already beyond the reach of dalits. When they eventually turn self-financing, their prices would be benchmarked against their international counterparts, which any way would be affordable to the same top market segment that constitutes the focus of all the Reform-talk. As the job markets become acutely competitive, owing to a sharp decline in job opportunities, the polarisation between the elite and commoner would also sharpen. Various kinds of price barriers would be erected to thwart the entry of downtrodden.

Even the sphere of primary education the coverage of which has been so miserably inadequate as to leave out multitude of children in villages as illiterate, could not remain unaffected, notwithstanding it is already existing divide between the vernacular and English schools. Corporatisation has entered this arena, transforming the education into an enterprise for profits. The quality of input these expensive schools will provide, benchmark the products in the contracting job markets. Even today, because of preponderance of the English language in business circles, the divide between village and towns is almost complete in the field of education. It is so difficult for a village student, educated in vernacular medium to compete with his convent educated (now an understatement !) counterpart in cities and towns.

Reservations in Services

Whatever may be the other costs, the government policy of reservations in employment sphere has undoubtedly played an important role for dalits. The policy broadly envisages representation of dalits in proportion to their population in all the public services which includes the government, public sector, autonomous bodies and institutions receiving grant-in-aid from the government. A cursory glance at the figures of this representation is enough to get a pathetic state of implementation.

Howsoever, unsatisfactory the results of the implementation may be, the importance of reservations from the dalit viewpoint cannot be overemphasised. As could be evidenced by the organised private sector, where it would be difficult to find a dalit employee (save of course in scavenging and lowliest jobs), without reservations dalits would have been totally doomed. The importance of reservations thus could only be assessed in relation to situations where they do not exist. Whatever be their defects and deficiencies, they have given certain economic means of livelihood and some social prestige to the sons and daughters of over 1.5 million landless labourers. Whether they get real power or not, over 50,000 dalits could enter the sphere of bureaucratic authority with the help of reservations. Besides these tangible benefits promised by the policy, it has instilled a hope in dalit community. This hope predominantly manifests in the form of spread of education among them. Their emotional bond with the nation and its Constitution despite heaps of injustice and ignominy they bear every moment of their life may also be significantly attributable to the Reservation Policy.

The winds of privatisation under the Economic Reforms have already shaken the very foundation of the Reservations. The Reforms clearly envisage the minimalist government. Wherever the Reforms patterned on the Structural Adjustment Programme of the World Bank were carried out, denationalisation of the public sector and privatisation have come in a big way. Being the late starter, India has not reached the scales achieved by others, say, the Latin American countries. However, the start has not been any unimpressive. Almost all sectors of economy stand opened up for private investment. The disinvestments in existing public sector companies has already been allowed upto 49 per cent by the policy. The public stake being more than 50 per cent, the public sector as such is not yet dismantled in policy. It continues to be the State, as before, and hence attracts application of the reservation policy. However, the Reform package has already endangered, if not abolished, the reservations through back doors.

The policy of limited disinvestments of PSUs not being in conformity with the spirit of the Reforms, is bound to be relaxed in favour of privatisation any time. But still, all the PSUs may not get privatised at once. The better ones would be gobbled up by the bigger sharks. The worst ones may be closed down or distress-sold. And the middle ones may for quite some time, continue to be the relic of their past. Whatever the scenario, the residual structures of the 'reformed' PSUs are never going to be the same, as far as dalits are concerned. The ethos of provatisation and the excuse of competition, superimposed on the traditional caste prejudice, will never allow reservations to happen, any more.

The caste atrocities are an integral feature of dalit life. The government machinery keeps on collecting their statistics year after year and issues it in a report of its Commissioner for SCs and STs (now the National Commission for SCs and STs). There are at least three Articles (15, 17 and 23) in the Constitution of India which seeks to mitigate the evil. To give effect to these Constitutional provisions the following acts also have been in operation:

1. The untouchability (Offences) Act, 1955, later amended and re-titled as the Protection of Civil Rights Act, 1955;

2. The Scheduled Castes and Scheduled Tribes (Prevention of Atrocities Act) 1989 and The Bonded Labour System (Abolition) Act, 1976.

Despite this, the statistics of the registered atrocities read like a balance sheet of a blue chip company with consistent rise every successive year. It is pertinent to remember that owing to the dependency relationship of dalits with the perpetrators of atrocities, not every occurrence of the atrocity gets registered. Rather, it can be safely assumed that behind each registered atrocity over ten atrocity cases go unreported. As per the latest statistics, every day nearly 50 cases of atrocities are registered all over the country. Over three dalit women are raped and six are disabled on each day round the year. The National Commission analysed the causes of each of the atrocities in a sample of 45 cases. The analysis shows that out of 45 cases 13 are clearly attributable to the economic reasons. The balance can also be explained out by some kind of weakness of dalits. Coupled with the weakness of dalits, their growing assertiveness and refusal to submit to the casteist dictates of the village lords, rebellion ethos assimilated through the Ambedkarian struggle and process of general awareness, also cause atrocities to increase.

The atrocities occur where the dependency relationships are more pronounced and bear economic implications. Villages, where dalits as landless labourers depend upon landlords or rich farmers for their livelihood and where the traditional caste equations have potential to yield economic surplus to the latter, provide ideal setting for atrocities. What impact would the new regime have on the socio-economic setting of Indian villages? In face of it, the unbridled capitalism inherent in the Reforms is not compatible with any feudal structure. But this thumb rule does not seem to be entirely validated by the developmental experience in India. The capitalism in India did not have to sprout through the bedrock of contradictions of feudalism as in Europe. It was planted in the fertile soil of Indian feudalism. It has grown here on its nutrients. Thus, it would be too mechanical to have theoremic expectation about the demise of feudalism and thence the end of the caste through the growth of capitalism. The caste institution moreover, has defied the classical mould of feudalism by possessing many unique features. The most important being its resilience and adaptability. What we experience in the mysterious growth of casteist politics today in India is precisely this ability of caste of adapt to changing times. The annihilation of caste is only possible through economic empowerment of dalit masses and waging an uncompromising and concerted struggle against its non-economic manifestations.

Can the new regime afford these economic empowerment of dalits? Can it, for instance, grant them land? Does it have the wherewithal or motivation to catalyse their struggles against the caste system? The answer to all these questions will be in negative. Instead of talking of land reforms, the new regime will promote depeasantisation of Indian agriculture and consolidation of their holdings to start corporate farming. Barring perhaps the example of East Asian countries, the Bretton Wood institutions sponsored reforms have always aggravated the economic inequality everywhere. The experience of other countries where similar Reforms were brought in, bears testimony to the fact that with increasing inequality the social tensions also increased as a result of the Reforms.

The capital influx in the rural areas will have natural ally in the rich farmers who have hegemonic hold over their areas. These sections, will be the main beneficiaries of the improved terms of trade and capitalist development in the rural areas. All the dalits would be thrown into the job market along with many non-dalit marginal to middle farmers. The vast army of unemployed thus created by this developmental dynamics will need appropriate instruments for being controlled. The history bears ample testimony to the fact that whenever the people tended to come together with a common identity, the ruling classes have deftly used the time-tested weapon of castes to divide them. Unlike elsewhere, the Reforms thus are likely to enliven and rejuvenate the archaic value system.

Conclusion

The economic reforms in the mould of macro-economic stabilisation and structural adjustment programme of IMF and World Bank have essentially a pro-rich bias. Wherever they were implemented, they have worsened the situation of the masses of poor people in absolute as well as relative terms. Some contrary data to this general observation (say, of the east Asian countries) are rather attributed to the departures from the standard blueprint given by the Bretton Wood institutions. The dalits in India, being the poorest of the poor have been hit the hardest. Their social disabilities, largely reinforced by and sustained on the economic deprivations, are bound to get accentuated with these policies. The Indian reforms were essentially 'crisis driven' and not 'strategy driven' when they were adopted. There have since been changes in the formation and key persona. The new government for instance has imparted them a form of 'strategy' through their Common Minimum Programme. However, there has not yet been any evidence of this strategy being any different from the course followed by the previous government. The complete discourse of Reforms appears to be either grossly off the mark of Indian freality or to assume out its momentous features.

The broad Indian reality is that India has too many poor. As per the Human Development Report, 1996, there are 229 million income poor but more than twice as many, 554 million are capability poor. In terms of capability poverty, its 61.5 per cent population is poor. Its rank according to descending poverty among the 174 countries of the world, is 135. Even today India is predominantly an agrarian economy, with over 70 per cent of its population living in villages. No statistics moreover can adequately capture the heinous socio-cultural inequality that is an abiding part of Indian reality. It has acute inequalities not only in economic terms but in the socio-cultural terms.

The free market oriented reforms ought to take this grave Indian reality into consideration. Unless there is a wide-spread purchasing power in the economy the market can never be free and sustainable. The reform strategy thus should embody sustainable economic empowerment of rural masses; investments to enhance their capability and effective measures for accelerated development of the disadvantaged sections like dalits. The per-requisite to reforms therefore could be the radical land reforms, massive investments in rural areas into agriculture-related infrastructural projects, universalisation of primary education, primary health care system and reinforcement of positive discrimination in favour of dalits. The devil of casteism could be tamed only by freeing general masses of people from the anxieties and uncertainties about basic survival. The general condition of deprivation has rendered them vulnerable to be the preys to the frequent machinations of the vested interests that make them see the enemy within their own class. The relative equality thus can be the bedrock for launching the socio-cultural offensive in the form of mass-education programmes. But this all may still not be enough. The policy of positive discrimination in favor of dalits will have to be reinforced much more vigorously in all the sectors of economy, than ever before. They need to be reframed and simplified for effective implementation. Unlike the current provisions, this may be stopped once their representation comes on par with the general population. The specific reform package can be formulated in terms of the conditions existing then.

18

Entrepreneurship Development Under Liberalisation

Dr. V. Mohanasundaram

Introduction

The relationship between innovative ideas turning into improved production technologies on the one hand and increased production (with or without lowering cost) of quality items on the other has been well established. This makes an economy/institution/an individual firm to achieve higher rate of growth. Ideas galore when challenges thrown, difficulties faced, risks revealed and competition clouds an individual/ institution or a nation. In this context, there is no second opinion that the Liberalisation, in otherwords, opening up of the Indian economy has brought challenges of a dimension hitherto not thought of. To face these challenges a powerful coin with two glaring sides—Innovation and Entrepreneurship–is the head of the hour.

Theoretical Background

The discussion in the present chapter can be opened by introducing certain theoretical perspectives regarding Innovation and Entrepreneurship.

In the Development Economics literature a vast scope has been given to the concepts Innovation and Entrepreneurship. As early as in 1800, J. B. Say, the famous Classical Economist opined that the Entrepreneur shifts economic resources out of an area of lower and into an area of higher productivity and greater yield. Then came Joseph Schumpeter to establish and advocate the impact of entrepreneurship on the economy through innovations. After widely quoting and appreciating the Schumpeterian version, Peter Drucker has made the following comment to establish a different view point: "Every Economist knows that the entrepreneurship is a 'meta-economic' event, something that profoundly influences and indeed shapes the economy without itself being part of it. And so too, for economists, is technology.... Indeed, the events that why entrepreneurship becomes effective are probably not in themselves economic events. The causes are likely to lie in changes in values perception, and attitude, changes perhaps in demographies, in institutions, perhaps changes in education as well... entrepreneurs see changes as the norm and as healthy. Usually, they do not bring about the change themselves. But—and this defines Entrepreneur and entrepreneurship—the entrepreneur always searches for change, respond to it and exploited as an opportunity.

The same has been postulated in an other way by Schumpeter: the dynamic disequilibrium brought on by the innovating and entrepreneur rather than equilibrium and optimisation, is the "norm" of a healthy economy and central reality for economic theory and economic practice.

Entrepreneurship Characteristics

The characterisation of an entrepreneur also invites complex and varying ideas depending upon the perception of the person who describes it. For Max Weber (1930) an innovator is one who is having unusual will and energy, clarity of vision and ability to act. On the basis of an empirical study on Women Entrepreneurs Poonam Sinha has the following to say: entrepreneurs should have abilities to coordinate, organize, supervise to whole process apart from bearing the risk at each and every stage.

How to Create Entrepreneurs?

A Manual prepared on Entrepreneurship Development, by a Manila Group says : We can create entrepreneurs and self-employed through the educational process. We must produce free thinking individuals, willing to take risks, capable of identifying and developing business opportunities, especially within their skill or discipline, who are comfortable in making or adopting to change.

Liberalisation and Entrepreneurship

At the global level, as pointed out by Hinterhuber and others, globalisation of markets, new information technologies, reduced logistic costs and the governments retreat from the economy have led to an unprecedented level of competition. This type of competition even exposed the vulnerability of the giant and mighty MNCs. This can be observed from the words of Theodore Levitt (1983). "A powerful force drives the world toward a converging commonality, and that force is technology. It has proletarianised communication, transport and travel. It has made isolated places and impoverished peoples eager for modernity's allurements. Almost everyone everywhere wants all the things they have heard about, seen, or experiences via technologies. The result is a new commercial reality...corporations geared to this new reality benefits into reduced world prices, they can decimate competitors that still live in the disabling grip of old assumptions about how the world works—The globalisation of markets is at hand. With that, the multinational commercial world nears its end, and so does the multinational corporation.

As a way out from turmoil in some of the largest and most visible MNCs, Bartlett and Ghosal suggest that the Top-Down approach hitherto followed in the MNCs should be given up and the entrepreneurial function must now be focused not at the top of the hierarchy but at the bottom.... Companies will be required to build an organisation in which a well-linked entrepreneurial process will drive the company's opportunity-seeking, externally focused ability to create and exploit avenues for profitable growth wherever they may arise.

What in the store for the nation/to the Indian corporate and business houses?

In the words of Desai, "the abolition of Industrial licencing has unleashed competition; industrial firms today have no protection against competition except to grow and become more efficient—which is innovation". Former Finance Minister P. Chidambaram declares that the Government must allow the industry and the entrepreneurs to discouver the country's "hidden" competitive advantages and dismantle all trade barriers and controls impeding international trade and economic growth. The Management guru Prahlad has urged Indian Industry to evolve a new paradigm of competitiveness based on entrepreneurship, innovation, leveraging existing resources, creating new markets and global orientation. Instead of focusing on problem areas and blaming them for India's lack of competitiveness, the companies must look inward to innovate and compete at the global level. According to him, a competitive India Inc. based of entrepreneurship and innovation was needed to meet the national priorities of achieving ten per cent annual growth.

The above type of comments and suggestions made only to touch the consciousness of the big industrialists and corporate bigwigs. Then, what about the fate of the millions of small-scale entrepreneurs under the liberalisation framework?

Though many have return a skeptical note on this account—that the SSIs are being increasingly marginalised after liberalisation—Balasubrahmanya found a different scenario on the basis of a survey conducted in Karnataka covering 2006 small firms and tiny sector units during 1999-2001, it was found that the competitive environment made a sizeable number of SSIs and tiny units to spend more on R & D and Technological Innovations. External forces in the form of competition, technology change and consumer requirements have driven majority of these units towards R & D, rather independently, with objectives of equality improvement, cost reduction and meeting consumer needs. In the process, they not only achieved improvements in quality and productivity but also positioned themselves to face a higher degree of competitiveness.

The lesson implied here is: SSIs need not require protection in the form of reservation and import restrictions.

A study by Morris and others at IIMA covering 1200 SSIs found that the reserved firms are technologically less dynamic and functioning at sub-optimal level. This study covered different product groups and stated that the argument for reservation on the grounds of employment elasticity was weak.

The lesson is: competition makes forces efficient resource allocation and utilisation leading to reduction in costs and increase in productivity.

Infrastructure, Innovation and Entrepreneurship

Can Innovations take place in a Vaccum? Can entrepreneurship flourish independent of an economic environment that is conducive for such growth? Is there any sort of (equal) level playing field that exists in the economy where the ugliest forms of dualism (technological, social and cultural) is the order of the day? In other words, how can one expect a 'level' common to all in such a segmented and fragmented economy?

Finally, is liberalisation per se will bring forth the required rate of innovations and entrepreneurship development?

The answer to all the above questions is a big 'No'. This is because, the sailing is not smooth for an individual to become an innovator and/or to become an entrepreneur as basic infrastructure, conducive economic environment and reasonable as well as responsible government are lacking today in the economy. The overall evaluation of developments and constraints in infrastructure in India reveals that there exists a large number of perversities such as

(i) Distortionary prices

(ii) Systematic exclusion of the poor

(iii) Very inefficient operations and

(iv) Large allocative failures

that run through nearly all the sectors. This clearly brings out the need for a "Political entrepreneurship" that would mobilize and activate the real growth potents (Intellectual capital, incentive compatibility, sensitive institutions and information technology) to be the vanguards of change as visualised by Morris. He further stated that reform of infrastructure creates opportunities for 'leap frogging' and for innovations in technology and design when the space for multiple providers, including private players, is created.

Implied from the above line of thinking is that the precondition for the development of entrepreneurship is the creation of opportunities by the state at the first instance.

Competitiveness and Confidence

The two closely related phenomena in the realm of Innovation and Entrepreneurship Development are competitiveness (of a product/brand/industry) and the confidence level (of innovators and entrepreneurs). An analysis and understanding of the level of competitiveness (of a brand/product) helps to distinguish between 'core-competencies' form that of incompetencies. Similarly an enhanced confidence level makes new investment forthcoming via innovators and entrepreneurs.

In this context let us see what is the position / condition of India at the global level and also in the national level by taking into account only two important indicators, namely competitiveness and confidence.

Competitiveness

The Global Competitiveness Report, 2000 jointly prepared by the World Economic Forum, Geneva and Harvard University placed India only in the 37th position out of 58 countries that it studied on the basis of current competitiveness Index *(see Chart I)*. Of course, it showed an improvement: from the 44th position in 1998 to 42nd position in 1999 to 37th position in 2000. Similarly, India is placed in 50th position in 1998 when the ranking was accorded for company operations and strategy; after a slight improvement in 1999 (48th) it has got a significant place in 2000 (40th position). And in terms of quality to the National Business Environment Ranking, India got only 42nd rank in 1998 which also came down in the following year (43), only to standup in the year 2000 when it got the rank of 37.

The above poor rank points are due to the low values India got in the Economic Creativity Index (ECI) as well as Innovative Index. The following is the details of the points that India got in the respective indices:

Chart–1
Explanation of the Economic Creativity Index

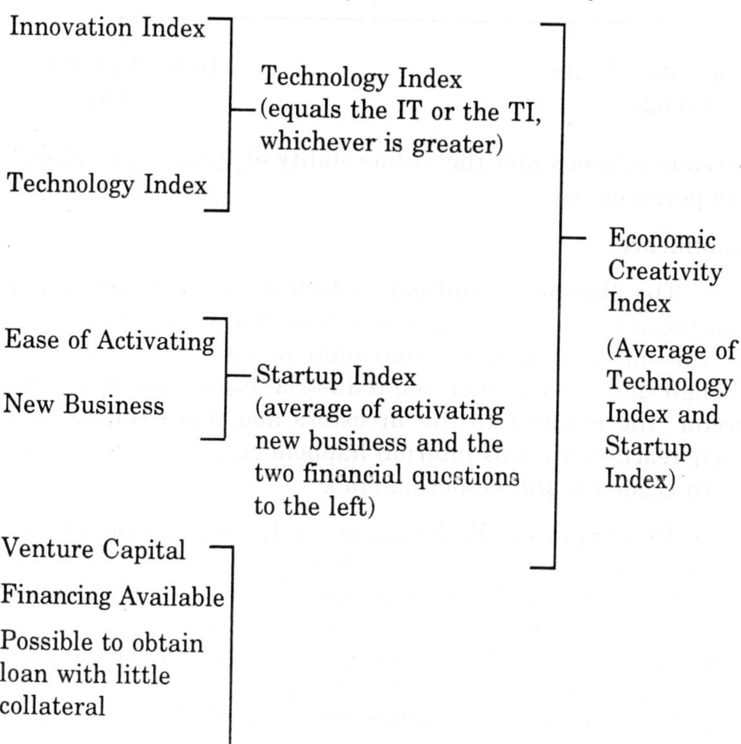

The points are very very low and show India in a very poor image. The innovative index was highest in the case of America (2.02) and technology index was also higher in the case of USA (2.02) followed by Singapore (1.95). This speaks

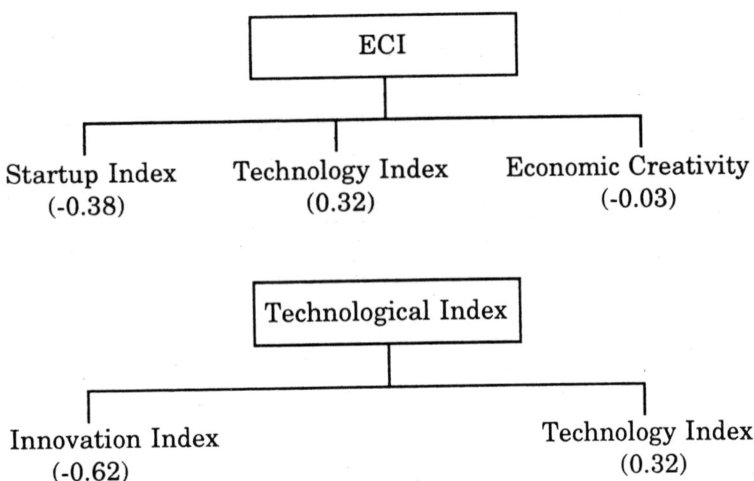

spreads volumes and the vulnerability of India to the global competitiveness.

Confidence

The Business Confidence Indexes are prepared and constructed every year (quarterly basis/half yearly basis) both at the national and international levels. These indicate, though they are based on the industrial houses and corporate sector, the mindset to the investors and industrialists and their reaction towards internal happenings and external risks (both economic and non-economic).

In India the Federation of Indian Chambers of Commerce and Industry (FICCI) conducts Business Confidence Survey (BCS) on quarterly basis; National Council of Applied Economic Research (NCAER) constructs Business Confidence Index (BCI), again on quarterly basis, by making use of the result of the Business Expectation Survey (BES); and the Confederation of Indian Industries (CII) also conducts the Business Outlook Survey (BOS) biannually and its BCI forms a part of it. It prepares the BCI and its survey results are weighted aggregate of current situation index and expectation index.

The following are the highlights of the latest BCS of FICCI (fourth quarter of the fiscal 2002-03):

- Almost 56 per cent expect the economy to perform moderately to substantially better in the next six months as compared to 68 per cent in the last survey;
- Weak demand, threat of imports, availability of credit, cost of credit and inadequate infrastructure were also pointed out as factors adversely affecting business performance;
- The overall Business Confidence Index is down by 8.4 per cent to 63.3 per cent;

NCAER survey (April 2003)

- More than 50 per cent of the respondents said they had new investments proposed in 2002-03. About 42 per cent of the plans are for improving quality of products and improving efficiency and about 28 per cent plan to move into new lines of business and remaining 33 per cent plan to add to the existing capacity;
- The overall BCI was up by 10.8 per cent.

NCAER survey (July 2003)

- The increase in the BCI was 14 percentage points;
- There is an overall improvement in business expectations;
- The improvement in all the four indicators (overall economic condition, financial position, investment climate and capacity utilisation) suggest a broad based recovery in business confidence;
- Government Services were not perceived to be adequate by a majority of the respondents;
- The improvement in the last five years was more conspicuous in the southern region than in the others.

The CII BCI (Oct 2002-Mar 2003)

- Indicated bullish business prospects for the next six months;
- After surveying 186 member companies the BCI showed 61.6 points, which is a good positive indication with respect to business confidence;
- Only a small percentage of firms are expected to witness decline in profits.

The above results indicate volatility in business confidence due to internal factors like government's budget policies, postponement of change over of VAT, drought factor, dip in agricultural GDP by 7.9 per cent and tense situation on the Indo-Pakistan border and the external risks like Iraq war and SARS syndrome. All these can only be managed by adopting well thought out stabilisation policies and strategies.

Concluding Observations

There is a resemblance of improvement in the innovative and entrepreneurial activities during the post-liberalisation period. The surge in new industrial ventures, patents and foreign investment inflows reveal that the rate of innovation is on the increase. For innovation enables a country to attract foreign capital as well as to put it to good use.

Two points to be kept in mind in the liberalisation agenda are:

(a) The investments in advanced technology (plant and equipment) will not increase if there is a uncertainty prevails about the future. That is, even an open economy will not stimulate investment unless future prospects are clear and bright.

(b) A lot of homework should be done by the State. It should act as an efficient entrepreneur to ensure not only a higher rate of growth but also quality of the growth: it is essential if the creative forces inherent in Indian intellect are to be unleashed. It is a fact that most innovations start

Chart–II
Entrepreneurship Development and Promotion

Factors affecting/Influencing Entrepreneurship Development	Possible Sources of Help and Motivation
Skills	Education and Training
Finance	Institutional Sources
Project Planning & Guidance	Specialised Agency
Infrastructure Support	State/Quasi—government/Private sector
Technology	Import/Foreign Collaboration
Marketing	Specialisation—Agencies—Boards—Processing Standardisation—Grading—Packaging—Marketing Intelligence
Expansion	Space and Scale (economies)—Removal of Information bottlenecks—Promotional Schemes
R & D Investment & Innovation	Incentives—Building-up of Business Confidence
Competition	Networking of Institutions like Finance, Marketing, Insurance Education, Training and Trading

with some stimulus driving the company to respond to a perceived opportunity or threat. Similarly our country got a stimulus to innovate in the form of liberalisation. However, the controversy is about the perception: whether it is (Liberalisation) a threat or an opportunity. The answer is : which strategy is better is not a matter of opinion but of necessity.

REFERENCES

1. Ashok V. Desai, "Innovation and the Indian Economy", *Margin* 35 (2) January-March 2003, pp. 1-8.
2. Balasubrahamanya, M. H. and others *R & D and Technical Innovations in SSIs,* Bangalore, Allied, 2002,
3. Christopher A. Bartlett and Sumantra Ghosal, *Transnational Management: Text, Cases, and Readings in Cross-Border Management,* New York, Irwin Mc Graw-Hill, 2000.
4. Colombo Plan Staff College for Technical Education, Manila (Prepared) and Adopted by Centre for Research and Industrial Performance, Bhopal *Entrepreneurship Development,* New Delhi, Tata McGraw-Hill, 1999.
5. Hans H. Hinterhiber, Stephen A. Friedrich, Eric Krawthammar and Kurt Matzler, "Leadership for Worldwide Competition: A European Perspective" *Productivity* 39 (2) July-Sept 1998, pp. 259-271.
6. Manimekala, N and Thangamuthu, C "Education and Entrepreneurship", *Productivity* 35 (4) Jan-March 1995, pp. 697-701.
7. Mohanasundaram, V. "Reservation Policy and SSIs in the Post-Liberalisation Period: From Benevolence to Insolence?", Paper Presented in the State level Seminar on *"Impact of Economic Reforms on SSIs in India"*, Dept. of Economics, PSGR Krishnammal College for Women, Coimbatore, 22nd February 2002.
8. Naik B. M., "Technological Innovation in Higher Education Institutes for Global Competitiveness" *University News* 41 (39), Sept 29-Oct 5, 2003, pp 6-10.
9. Peter F. Drucker, *Innovation and Entrepreneurship: Practice and Principles,* New Delhi, EWP, 1991.
10. Poonam Sinha, "Women Entrepreneurship in the North-East India: Motivation, Social Support and Constraints" *Indian Journal of Industrial Relations,* 38 (4) April 2003, pp. 425-441.
11. *The Global Competitiveness Report,* 2000, Geneva, World Economic Forum and Harvard University, OUP, 2000.

19

Impact of Micro Credit Scheme—An Economic Reform

Dr. M. Swaminathan

Micro finance is being practised as a tool to attack poverty the world over. The experience of all over the world have yielded notable success stories in Indonesia, Thailand and Bangladesh. In India during the last couple of decades substantial work has been done in developing and experimenting. The different concepts and approaches to reach financial services to the poor. For the last few years we hear a lot about micro credit/micro financing through self-help groups and NGOs. In recent years, often at the behest of non-governmental organisation, public welfare agencies have begun to allow experiments and demonstration projects, waiving asset and income limitations for some low-income entrepreneurs and allowing them to participate in micro credit programmes. The declaration of micro summit held in Washington, D.C. in 1997 defined micro credit schemes as programmes "extending small loans to poor people for self employment that generate income allowing them to care for tnemselves and their families." The declaration also states that in most cases micro credit projects offer a combination of services and resources to their clients in addition to credit for self employment, these often include saving facilities, training, net working and peer support.

Diversification of lending particularly in the urban and semi-urban areas towards small business has been recent trend. For cooperatives this is the opportune time for planning a notable venture for the upliftment of weaker sections especially women engaged in small business. In this context, the Tamil Nadu Government has come up with a noble scheme on 1st October 1999. Providing micro credit for small business through cooperatives. The helpless poor and downtrodden people will get special consideration and possible assistance through the scheme. The scheme well promote enthusiastic participation in small business and create the habit of savings among the people.

The vital features of micro credit schemes are:

- Very small loans ranging from Rs. 500 to Rs. 5,000;
- No collateral security;
- Borrowers are poor people;
- Loan for income generation through market based self-employment;
- Quick disbursement of small, short-term loans;
- Clear recovery procedure and strategic;
- The incentive of access to larger loans immediately following successful repayment of first loans;
- A culture, structure, capacity and operating system that can support sustained delivery to a significant and growing number of poor clients.

Need of the Study

The employment of women is an index of their economic status in the society especially with reference to social equality women's employment has a direct bearing on the improvement of the quality of life of the family. Thirty-five per cent of small households are headed by women and thus depend exclusively on female income. In order to bring women in to mainstream of economic activities in the society, the Government of Tamil Nadu has launched a new programme called micro credit within the auspices of cooperative sector. The ultimate effort is to make women economically independent and self-reliant. The Thanjavur Central Cooperative Bank has launched the scheme on 19th January 2002. There are 1929 beneficiaries and disbursement of loan amount was Rs. 28.69 lakhs as on 31st March 2003. Hence the present study is undertaken to-know the impact of micro credit scheme on women beneficiaries in Thanjavur town.

Objectives of the Study

The study has following objectives:

1. To analyse the socio-economic background of the selected respondents;
2. To assess the impact of micro credit system; and
3. To arrive at major findings, suggestions and conclusions.

Methodology

Both primary and secondary data were used for this study. Secondary data were collected from the Central Cooperative Bank, Thanjavur. An interview schedule was prepared for collecting information from the women borrowers who obtained loans from the bank selected for the study. For the purpose of this study of the micro credit scheme five activities financed by the bank with the coverage of 50 borrowers are selected in simple random sampling method. The selected activities are given below (1) Flower vendors (2) Idly vendors (3) Vegetable vendors (4) Eatables and (5) Tailoring. Simple statistical average was used to analyse the data.

Analysis

It is a commonly accepted code that human beings are generally motivated by the socio-economic conditions, particularly Indians who are mostly conservative and orthodox in outlook. It is, therefore, relevant to mention here that the effectiveness of any scheme well be influenced by one's socio-economic background. The various socio-economic factors considered for the study are analysed, presented and discussed in the following paragraphs.

Table 19.1: Age-wise Distribution of Respondents

Sl. No.	*Age*	*No. of Respondents*	*Percentage*
1.	Below 20	5	10
2.	21-30	19	38
3.	31-40	11	32
4.	Above 40	10	20
	Total	50	100

Source: Primary Data.

From the above table it is clearly found that a bulk of respondents are in the age groups of 21-30 (38%) and respondents belonging to less than 20 years and above 40 years represent relatively a lower proportion with a reasonable number of respondents between age group of 31-40 years being 32 per cent. From this, it would be inferred that the adult women are actively participation in micro credit scheme as they have more responsibility in supporting and stabilising their family income.

Table 19.2: Community-wise Distribution of Respondents

Sl. No.	*Community*	*No. of Respondents*	*Percentage*
1.	Forward	5	10
2.	Backward	9	18
3.	Most Backward	10	20
4.	Scheduled Caste	26	52
	Total	50	100

Source: Primary Data.

Table 19.2 reveals 52 per cent of the respondents belonged to scheduled caste, 20 per cent belonged to most backward community, 18 per cent to backward community and the rest belonged to forward community. It is observed that the scheduled caste respondents are highly benefited by this scheme than others. The Government of Tamil Nadu is committed to improve the economic status of scheduled caste people.

Table 19.3: Educational Status of the Respondents

Sl. No.	*Educational Status*	*No. of Respondents*	*Percentage*
1.	Illiterate	19	38
2.	Primary	10	20
3.	High School	16	32
4.	Higher Secondary	5	10
	Total	50	100

Source: Primary Data.

Education is an important element for doing any business activity. From the above table it is observed that 38 per cent of the respondents do not have any education at all. This is a discouraging situation because they cannot improve their business with their illiterate background.

Further it is observed that the occupational status of the respondents. Most of the respondents are self-employed, the scheme is very much beneficial to the self-employed women entrepreneurs.

Table 19.4: Loan availed by the Respondents

Sl. No.	*Loan amount*	*No. of Respondents*	*Percentage*
1.	500	26	52
2.	1000	15	30
3.	2000	9	18
4.	5000	—	—
	Total	50	100

Source: Primary Data.

The Table 19.4 reveals that the amount of loan availed by the respondents through micro credit scheme. 50 per cent of respondents availed credit upto Rs. 500 and 30 per cent of the women entrepreneurs availed credit upto Rs. 1,000. The above table clearly shows that more than 50 per cent of respondents availed small amount of Rs. 500 only. It could be inferred from the table that the cooperative banks disburse small amount to needy poor people and inturn it will improve the economic status of the poor.

Further it is observed that more than 50 per cent of respondents were availing loan facility three times in a year. The credit requirement of entrepreneurs though very small and quite frequent.

Table 19.5: Repayment Period of the Loan in Instalments

Sl. No.	*Repayment Period*	*No. of Respondents*	*Percentage*
1.	Daily	—	—
2.	Weekly	40	80
3.	Monthly	10	20
	Total	50	100

Source: Primary Data.

The success of the micro credit is based on repayment made by the beneficiaries. Table 19.5 clearly shows that more than two-third of borrowers repay their loan instalment amount weekly. Only 20 per cent of respondents repay their instalment amount monthly. Weekly repayment is more convenient for the women entrepreneurs. This shows that micro credit has generated additional employment and income. In addition it generated small assets with which the beneficiaries are repaying the instalments promptly.

Table 19.6 clearly state that more than 50 per cent respondents had earned Rs. 51-75 per day. Which is more reasonable return on their investment in small business.

Table 19.6: Daily Income Earned by the Women Entrepreneurs

Sl. No.	*Income (Rs.)*	*No. of Respondents*	*Percentage*
1.	Below Rs. 50	8	16
2.	Rs. 51 to Rs. 75	26	52
3.	Rs. 76 to Rs. 100	13	26
4.	Above Rs. 100	3	6
	Total	50	100

Source: Primary Data.

Income generation is one of the important determinants to measure the impact of micro credit scheme. It could be found from the survey, the average annual income of the women entrepreneurs availed loan under micro credit scheme was higher than before availed the loan.

The survey inquired about the asset created through micro credit scheme. More than 70 per cent of respondents clearly stated that the asset creation in the form of purchasing sewing machine, watch, business equipment vehicle and increasing savings are more than before availing loan.

The survey also inquired about the economic impact of micro credit scheme the women borrowers came under this scheme clearly stated that after availing the loan they got the following benefits:

(a) Additional man-hours employment opportunities;

(b) Additional loan-increase in volume of loan;

(c) Increasing production and sales;

(d) Promote entrepreneurship;

(e) Rise in the standard of living.

However, the above tangible benefits of the micro credit scheme enjoyed by the respondents (Women entrepreneurs) they are facing the following problems:

(a) Marketing problem

(b) Non-cooperation by the family members

(c) Competition from better quality production.

Findings of the Survey

More than 70 per cent respondents are in the age group of 20-40. This is a good shine of active participation in the scheme as they have more responsibility in supporting and stabilising their family income.

The higher proportion of women entrepreneurs under this scheme belonged to scheduled caste. It can therefore be inferred that people belonging to scheduled caste below poverty line, who are illiterate, which makes them to get micro credit and highly beneficial in this scheme.

Majority of women borrowers depend on self-employment and thus suggest that the women are capable of engaging non-farm sector activities. Regarding the amount of loan availed by the respondents. More than 50 per cent of respondents availed credit upto Rs. 500 and they felt that the weekly repayment is very easy and convenient. The frequency of availing loan are also three times or more than three times in a year.

Due to this scheme, the beneficiaries earned additional income, got self-employment and created assets and thereby improving their economic conditions. The banks are also enjoyed some tangible benefit with low amount of loan disbursement having large number of borrowers and about 100 per cent recovery and discharge its accountability to improve the standard of living of the poor and downtrodden people who are all associated with the scheme.

Suggestions

The micro credit scheme is offering loan to the weaker sections of the community particularly self-employed women. They are relieved from clutches of money-lenders and avail the loan at low rate of interest. However, the system had certain defects. The following suggestions are offered to improve the quality of the scheme:

1. At present the borrowers are getting low amount of loan. The amount is insufficient to run the business. As such there is a 100 per cent recovery and hence the loan amount may be raised to Rs. 10,000 and thereby concrete business development by the small entrepreneurs could be made only by means of enhanced loan amount;
2. The scheme recently (19th January 2002) introduced in Thanjavur district and majority of rural and urban people do not aware of the existence of scheme. Hence the bank must come forward to propagate the scheme to each and every one especially poor people;
3. Some women entrepreneurs experienced low profit margin, marketing problems, difficulties in obtaining loan and competition. These could be overcome by proper training and regular consultancy;
4. Encourage the prompt repayers by way of giving more loan and giving proper guidance and propagate the scheme through them.

To conclude that maximum limit of the loan should be increased from Rs. 5,000 to Rs. 10,000. To make this scheme more popular, more awareness should be created and give proper training and motivation to self employed women.

REFERENCES

1. Gupta, Das, A., "SHGs and Micro Credit Rural Banking for Women", *Social Welfare,* March 1999, Vol. 45, No. 12, p. 21.
2. Joshi, N.N. and Vyas, P.C. (eds.), "Self-Help Groups vis-à-vis Cooperatives". *Metaphysics of Co-operative Movement,* pp. 159-167.
3. Madhura, M. Chartrapathy, "Women Technocrat Entrepreneurs", *The Economic Times*, 6th August 1990, p. 5.
4. Misra, R.V., "Co-operative and Weaker Sections", *Co-operator*, March 2000, p. 420.
5. Mohan, S., "Micro Credit and Employment, Role of NGO's", *Yojana*, February 2000.

6. Shanta Kohili Chandra, *Development of Women Entrepreneurship in India,* New Delhi: Mittal Publications, 1991.

7. Sharma, R.H., "Micro Financing Self Help Groups and Non-Government Organisations by Commercial Banks", *The Journal of the Indian Institute of Bankers,* July-September 1999, pp. 19-23.

8. Zahir Hussain, A.K., "An Innovation in Micro Credit; A Scheme for Women in Tamil Nadu", *The Co-operator,* New Delhi, 1999, pp. 507-508.

20

Entrepreneurship Development Under Liberalisation

Dr. A. Venkatachalam
Dr. M. Inbalakshmi

Introduction

The Government of India has included a New Enterprise Policy in its current framework of industrial policy reforms. For the first time, a policy was framed exclusively for protecting and strengthening small, tiny and village industries on 6th August 1991. These policy measures have given thrust to simplification of regulations and procedures, economic viability of the SSI units, improving their competitive strength, export promotion, credit flow and development of integrated infrastructure for the sector. The main objects of the policy of liberalisation are to promote small scale industrial units and to generate employment.

Methodology

This study aims at analyzing the growth of small scale industrial units during the period of liberalisation. In doing so, the effect of liberalisation is also studied. The present study is primarily based on secondary data. Secondary data were collected mainly from the books reports and journals.

Trend of co-efficient has been calculated for finding out the growth trend of small scale industrial units in terms of number of units, value of production, number of persons employed and the value of export.

It is an appropriate one to give the meaning of liberalisation and the different spheres of introduction of liberalisation.

Liberalisation

Liberalisation means freedom from closed and regulated economy. The situation, wherein the government has minimum interference in the activities of private sector enterprise and allowing private sector to take up activities, which were previously restricted to public sector is termed as liberalisation. It is commonly understood to mean reducing the role of the State in regulating and controlling private economic resources of the society.

Spheres of Liberalisation

Liberalisation has been introduced in different spheres. The first solid attempt to give a grit to the new policy in the wake of the liberalisation of the economy was the constitution of a committee to review the arrangements for meeting the working capital requirements of small scale industries and for the rehabilitation of sick small scale industrial units. This committee was announced in December 1991 and came out with a policy paper for sick units and submitted its recommendations for the entire gamut of credit problems faced by small scale industries.

Procedures have been streamlined and deregulation and delicencing have been introduced to provide and expand role to the private sector vastly. The open policy towards foreign investment and technology is expected to enhance the efficiency and competitiveness of Indian industry and to enable it to integrate effectively with global economy. A climate has been created to enthuse Indian and overseas entrepreneurs to invest in India.

The new Industrial policy of 1991 contemplated several changes in the old policy relating to small scale sector with an intention of making small enterprises economically viable and financially strong. The new policy proposed several measures for ensuring supply of adequate raw materials to SSI units.

Another feature of the policy related to equity participation upto 24 per cent by other units in smaller units. In as much as participation will come largely from large units, it will gave a great boost to the flow of funds to the SSI.

The policy also introduced a new legal form of organisation for this sector namely, restricted/limited partnership. Under this form, the liability of at least one partner has to be unlimited, whereas other partners can have limited liability, that is limited to the extent of their equity investment in the units. This would motivate his friends and relatives to invest in this industry, who earlier used to shy away from small units because of the unlimited liability in the partnership firm. At the same time, the active partners who may have ulnlimited liability would be left generally free to make their own decisions without consulting other sleeping partners.

A curious phenomenon is that following liberalisation the states have also started competing with each other in soliciting investment, offering attractive packages. This in the new policy importance is given to the accelerated growth of tiny, small and village industries.

It is observed that the private sector has been freed from many regulation such as licensing, permission to import raw materials, regulation of price and distribution, and restriction on investment by large business houses. In fact, many formalities have been simplified to facilitate entrepreneurs to promote industries in India.

Growth of SSI Under Liberalisation

An attempt is made to analysis the growth of SSI in India after the combined thrust of government policy of liberalisation, comprehensive programmes of development and network of institutions providing infrastructural facilities. It has been studied in terms of trend and growth rate of number of units, value of production, employment and exports facilities.

It has been studied in terms of trend and growth rate of number of units, value of production, employment and exports.

Growth in Number of Units

The number of SSI units registered in India during the period of one decade of liberalisaiton from 1991 to 2000 is collected and computed results of trend and growth rate of the same is presented in the Table 20.1.

Table 20.1: Trend and Growth Rate of the SSI Units

Particulars	*A*	*Trend co-efficient B*	*Compound Growth Rate*
Number of Units Registered	2.857	0.0161* (33.146)	6.33

* Significant at 5% level.

Figures in bracket are 't' values.

It is inferred from the table that the trend co-efficient of the number of SSI units in India is found to be statisfically significant at the 5 per cent level. It indicates that there is a significant growth of number of SSI units during the period of one decade of liberalisation. The compound growth rate for the same is found to be 6.33 per cent per annum.

Growth in Production

The value of goods produced by the SSI in India during the period of ten years liberalisaiton is collected and the computed results of trend and growth rate of the same is presented in the Table 20.2.

Table 20.2: Trend and Growth Rate of Production of SSI Units

Particulars	*A*	*Trend co-efficient B*	*Compound Growth Rate*
Production	11.632	0.158* (53.684)	17.16

* Significant at 5% level.

Figures in bracket are 't' value.

It is observed from the table that the trend co-efficient of the value of production of SSI is found to be statistically significant at the 5 per cent level. It indicates that there is a significant growth in production during the period of one decade of liberalisation. The compound growth rate for the same is found to be 17.14 per cent per annum.

Growth in Employment

The employment opportunity generated by SSI during the period of ten years from 1991 to 2000 is collected and the computed results of trend and growth rate of the same is presented in the Table 20.3.

Table 20.3: Trend and Growth Rate of the Number of Persons Employed by SSI

Particulars	*A*	*Trend co-efficient B*	*Compound Growth Rate*
Number of persons employed	4.742	0.041* (56.641)	4.18

*Significant at 5% level
Figures in bracket are '*t*' values

It is noted from the table that the trend co-efficient of the number of persons employed is statistically significant at the 5 per cent level. It shows that there is significant growth in the generation of employment opportunities during the period of liberalisation. However, the growth rate is not sufficient to meet the increasing job requirements in the country. The compound growth rate of the employment is 4.18 per cent per annum.

Growth in Export

The value of goods exported by SSI during the period of liberalisation of ten years is collected and computed results of trend and growth rate of value of exports of SSI is presented in the Table 20.4.

It is understood from the table that the trend co-efficient of value of exports is statistically significant at the

Table 20.4: Trend and Growth Rate of Value of Exports of SSI

Particulars	*A*	*Trend co-efficient B*	*Compound Growth Rate*
Value of Exports	8.82	0.211* (13.226)	23.50

*Significant at 5% level.

Figures in bracket are '*t*' values.

5 per cent level. The compound growth rate is 23.50 per cent per annum. It is worthy to note that one-third of total exports of the country is the contribution from SSI. So, in a longer period of time there is a significant growth in the exports from SSI in India.

Effect of Liberalisation

There has been marginal increase in India's share in the international and domestic trade of goods and services, though our progress is very low as compared to other countries. The foreign direct investment to India has increased from Rs. 174 crore in 1991 to Rs. 9338 crore in 2000. Our foreign exchange reserve has increased from Rs. 4822 crore in 1991 to Rs. 1,52,924 crore in 2000. The price rise in the year 1990 was 12 per cent and it has slowly declined to around 5 per cent in the year 2000. it can be observed that the liberalisation policy of India has led to many economic changes in the country during the past one decade.

One of the objectives of the new policy is to eradicate unemployment problems by way of generating employment opportunities. Though new employment opportunities are generated, it is not sufficient to meet the increasing job requirements in the country. It is said that the new policy has failed to generate additional employment opportunities, especially in rural areas, where 70 per cent of the population live. It can be solved by way of creating an awareness of entrepreneurship in the minds of people in rural areas.

Conclusion

The present study has made an earnest attempt to probe into the growth of Small Scale Industries in India after introducing the policy of liberalisaiton. The study reveals that there is a significant development in the field of enterpreneurship under liberalisation.

REFERENCES

1. SIDBI Report on SSI Sector, 1999.
2. Guide to SSIs, STICON-2000 issued by TANSTIA.
3. Vasant Desai, *Dynamics of Entrepreneurial Development and Management,* Himalaya Publishing House.
4. NCERT Publications, New Delhi.
5. Government of India, *Economic Survey,* Ministry of Finance, Economic Division, New Delhi.

21

Globalisation and Human Development

Dr. K. Alamar
Dr. N. Murali

Historical Perspective

Globalisation is not a new phenomenon. It can be better understood in a historical perspective. Globalisation is traced back to the 16th century phenomenon of using trade and military power to open up large number of countries of Asia, Africa and Latin America. By a mix of military and political coercion, coupled with various instruments of persuasion, these countries were ruthlessly reduced to colonies that would supply cheap raw materials, natural resources and labour for the capital accumulation in the European countries. In 1914 Britain had sixty dependent colonies plus India. She paid the penalty for her over-extension. History confirms the weakening of both Britain and Germany by the end of the First World War giving the U.S. the chance to acquire power and exercise it. If the 19th century belonged to the UK with the inter-war period of the 20th century showing its decline, then the end of the Second World War showed the beginning of Americanisation of the second half of the 20th century with Britain in a subordinate position though still assuming an important role. History gives the lesson that the hegemon has to consolidate her position and protect it for maintaining her position as number one. Rather than trying to 'go alone' the 20th century hegemon thus plans to 'go global' by forming an inner group viz., G7. Post-cold-war period apparently has given the hegemon a 'breathing space', though internal latent challenges remain. So comes the game plan of 'Extensive Globalisation' for extension of production boundary not only for the hegemon but also for the group. The game plan of the hegemon is rationalised through empowerment of G-7. Transnational Corporations (TNCs) with headquarters in countries in G-7. are the army for execution of this 'Extensive Globalisation'. The hegemon thus plans her consolidation in global power structure (Sauvant, 1981).

Each member country of the IMF has a quota determined by the country's GNP, foreign trade and currency reserves. Voting rights of each country and its borrowing facilities are determined by this quota. For Developed Market Economics (DME) including the U.S., this voting share declined over time; for Developed Market Economies as a whole it fell from 78.5 per cent in 1950 to 66.5 per cent in 1980 while for U.S. alone it fell from 34.7 per cent to 21.5 per cent. G. 7 has to maintain their voting power in IMF.

Intra G. 7 trade has reached its limit for sale of the output that produce, this requiring markets beyond their national boundaries. In other words, trade within G.7 is inadequate to sustain the uninterrupted growth of G.7. Thus there is a compulsion for G.7 to grow. Market expansion is a necessary pre-requisite.

The demand for globalisation did not come from any developing countries. Following the World Bank's recommendation it came unexpectedly from USA. President Ronald Reagan first proposed the 'free market" approach to the third world economic development at the Cancun Summit Conference in 1981. Again in 1983 he stated that "the United States believed that international direct private investment played a vital and expanding role in the US and world economies" and that an open international investment system responding to market forces provided the best and most efficient mechanism to promote global economic development.

The ideology of free trade dates back to Adam Smith and David Ricardo. Globalisation is but a modern version of theory of comparative cost advantage which was propagated by the classical economists to provide theoretical foundation of unrestricted flow of goods from the developed countries to the less developed countries at the time of colonies. It was argued that the international specialisation benefits the countries which enter into trade relations. Adam Smith in his 'Wealth of Nations' published in 1776 strongly advocated free trade. But from 1783 America opposed Adam Smith's advice and expected protective barriers against the inflow of manufactures from Britain and Europe and built up their own industry in a process of import substitution. Because they did so the USA is today the World's leading capitalist country: had they listened to Adam Smith's version of 'free trade' it would have been at most an Argentina. As the leading capitalist and imperalist country in the world the USA follows today in turn policies to encourage its growth at the expense of the Third World's freedom to industrialize (Utsa Patnaik, 1999). The same arguments have been put fourth by the advocate of globalisation now. They advocate and export-led pattern of growth to replace the import substitution trade policies. They also argue for capital and technology flow.

Economic Impact

It is argued that globalisation shall enable free flow of goods, capital and technology and thus it becomes a motivating force for the nations to develop themselves on such a faster pace and creates more gainful environment in the world scenario for each economy. This logic is that low growth economy gets capital and technology from the developed countries to build their economy for higher growth rate and the developed countries get market for their products so that they become free from secular stagnation.

But historical evidences reveal that all these trade, capital and technology flows helped the developed nations which thrived at the cost of developing nations. Globalisation in being promoted for the economic interest of developed nations, with little regard for the interests of others. It is not conceived as an act of charity towards the developing countries nor it is designed to promote their interests. Half of the developing countries signed the WTO accord without fully understanding their implications. They neither have legal expertise nor the means to stand up to the expertise of the developed nations. Generally the developed countries brought collective pressure, sometimes silently, sometimes with threat on the developing countries to open their frontiers. A situation has thus come about where no country has any choice except to join the globalisation race. In this race, the developed countries always succeed and the most developed is an absolute winner all the time. In other words the entire world has been converted practically into one big market and the market is determining the fate of many countries today.

The developed countries and the multinational corporations have vast amount of capital. They invest in developing countries aiming at highest possible return. They have no commitment to eradicate poverty or to increase the Gross Domestic Product of any poor country. The countries having economic and political power control and use the market for their welfare. In other words, globalisation is more about power than about trade and markets.

The MNCs are protagonists of globalisation. These corporations are controlled by a microscopic minority of the rich in the North. With unending quest for profit they ruthlessly spread the net of market in all corners of the world. With the active support of WTO, World Bank, IMF and with blessing of G.7 countries they become new instruments of domination. Now the global corporations control more than 70 per cent of the World trade. The top 100 MNCs accounting 70 per cent of the total foreign direct investment controls 25 per cent of the world productive assets (*The Economist,* 1994). It is true that the production is decentralised all over the world but the finance control and power remain concentrated in the hands of managerial elites.

Economic Growth and Human Development

Attaining and sustaining the high level of human development for all the people is the prime concern of the nation. Adam Smith, J.S. Mill, Kant, Marx, etc. considered human beings as the real end of all activities. Hirshchman,

A.O. (1958) opined that growth is only a means and not the end, the end is human development. But the so-called Globalisation process put excessive accent on growth and miss the people for whom such growth is meant (Alamar, 1997).

The concept of human development is well brought out in UNDP's Human Development Report. Human development is the development that not only generates economic growth, but distributes the benefits equally; that regenerates environment rather than destroying it; that empowers people rather than marginalizing them, that which gives priority to the poor, enlarges their choices and opportunities and provides for participation in decisions that affect life and it is that which is pro-people, pro-nature, pro-jobs and pro-women (UNDP, 1996).

The proponents of globalisation spread the myth that it ensures the well being of everyone through the trickle down effect. But the facts and figures tell different story. A close look at HDR-2000 would reveal that increase in per capita incomes is not the end of economic development. With low Human Development Index (HDI) the complete human development does not take place. For instance, Canada with per capita income of US $23,582 per annum ranks at first place in the HDI value, while Kuwait with a higher per capita income at $25,314 ranks as low as 36 with lesser life expectancy and lesser literacy rate. Similarly, countries like Poland, Estonia, Chile, Uruguay and Slovakia with less than $10,000 per captia GDP, figure among 46 countries with high human development but a country like Saudi Arabia having per capita GDP at above $10,000, figures at 75th place owing to its relatively poorer socio-economic indicators and is still called a developing country. The HDR-2001 ranked India at 115th position among 162 countries and India's human development ratio is increasing but its ability to convert its rising per capita income into a better average standard of living weakened during the later half of the 1990s. In other words, what India has been witnessing is a deterioration and not an improvement in its ability to rise the human development of its citizens. This in a way reflects the fact that even as the economy has grown by more than 6 per cent per year in the second half of the 1990s, the state provisioning of health and education services has deteriorated. The net effect has been growing 'inefficiency' in the conversion of India's rising per capita income into better education and health. What is also important is what use a country can put this income to translate into better lives of their people.

Jobless Growth

Globalisation creates financial volatility and economic, cultural, job, health, environment and family insecurities. All these insecurities effect the poor and the disadvantaged groups more than the rich (UNDP, HDR-1999).

The new empire of globalisation run by the Multinational Corporations and their mega technology and computers will make most members of the middle classes jobless within two decades. Even in the so-called developed countries the present form of globalisation creates jobless growth that eventually make up fragmentation within the society. In Europe and Canada the unemployment rate has risen to 11 per cent. As per the United Nations estimates round 700 million people in the developing world are unemployed. As per International Labour organisation, the global unemployment reached 1 billion in 1994. Over 20 per cent of the jobs are part time or temporary in the United States of America. In the 20 per cent contingent workforce, vast majority are women and coloured people.

In the entire world millions of well-paid workers are now on the warpath to fight against closure and retrenchment. The heroic workers of South Korea and Argentina have set an example to fight against the master of modern capitalism. At home everyday hundreds of thousands of our workers are sent out of factories on one pretext or other. When this is not possible a new name is given 'retrenchment'—'voluntary Retirement Scheme or Golden Handshake'. An estimated 2 lakh workers have been retrenched during 1991-94 through Voluntary Retirement Scheme—75,000 in the public sector and 1,25,000 in the private sector. A number of factories have been closed down in order to beautify the Indian towns. In Delhi alone around one lakh workers are rendered jobless (Bhattacharya, 1997).

Inequalities in Income and Consumption

The rich are on the fast track of prosperity and the poor are condemned to squalor and misery. The inequality between countries is on the rise. The share of the poorest fifth of the world's population in global income has dropped from 2.3 per cent to 1.4 per cent over the past ten years while the proportion taken by the richest fifth has risen from 70 per cent to 85 per cent. The assets of top three billionaires are worth more than the combined GNP of 48 least developed countries nearly one-fourth of the population in the developing world, i.e., an estimated 1.2 billion people live under poverty line. Among them 44 per cent live in South Asia. We know that trade can create wealth. Yet 80 countries containing a third of the World's Population are being increasingly marginalised, and over the past 20 years developing country's share of global trade fall from 0.8 to 0.4 per cent. There are more Internet connections in Manhattan than in all of Africa. The bottom line is that 3 billion live on less than $ 1 a day.

Human Development Report, 1998 is focused on consumption and brings out the glaring disparities in the levels of consumption between industrialised countries and developing countries. Globally the richest 20 per cent are seen to account for 86 per cent of total private consumption expenditure while the poorest 20 per cent consumed a miniscule 1.3 per cent. The HDR 1998 certainly makes use of shock therapy to jolt the conscience of the rich world when it compares the amount spent by them on conspicuous luxurious or even criminal consumption when a fraction of this expenditure would alleviate the suffering of all humanity in certain spheres where they are deprived of such as health care and education. The annual expenditure in Europe and the U.S. on perfume is $ 12 billion whereas reproductive health for all women would cost $ 12 billion. The estimated annual cost to achieve universal access to basic social services in all developing countries is $ 40 billion. However, due to the reverse global priorities, the expenditure on icecream in Europe is $ 105 billion, on narcotic drugs $ 400 billion, and the global military spending is $ 780 billion. In contrast, basic health and nutrition would cost only $ 13 billion for all (Human Development Report, 1998). In his speech on the eve of the Golden jubilee of Republic in 2000, the Indian president, Mr. K.R. Narayanan reflected the grim consumption pattern of the people: one section of the society guzzles with aerated beverages, while the other has to make do with palmfuls of muddied water.

Cultural Impact

Globalisation is indeed a new dramatic religion. It uses the media to create a sense of lack: Here we are driven to earn more in order to acquire more, yet can never reach a point of contentment. Since the process of globalisation is under the control of corporations the media is used to direct us blindly towards the monoculture of ever increasing technology of the McDonald for fast food and junk and of the "Cola and Jeans" syndrome (Sulak Sivarakha, 1998).

A small minority of middle class with tertiary level education and technical skill get gainful employment and join the ranks and file of global middle class to consume more and more. But the same process also pushes down a vast majority of the middle class with less education and skills to a vulnerable condition. The frustration and anger of the vulnerable class find expression in violence, corruption, criminalisation, religious fanaticism and reactionary skills. The present kind of globalisation creates the real forces that perpetuate deprivation, unemployment and fragmentation. Economic problems are being blamed not on the economic system or those who control it but on racial, ethnic, religious and material scape goats. Various form of extremists nationalism, racism, religious fanaticisms are aggravated by the impact of globalisation.

Environmental Degradation

The process of globalisation has adverse implications on environment. It has encouraged and increased in the extraction and export of raw materials in many countries thus, contributing to resource depletion and degradation. The ecological effects of globalisation are strikingly catastrophic. There is a lot of evidence now available to prove that export-led increase in the catch of fish and in rice production have both had an adverse effect on environment. Foreign exchange earnings from exports encouraged many entrepreneurs and private companies to use large mechanised trawlers to harvest fish at a rate faster than that at which fish can be regenerated. This over-fishing has not only accelerated the loss of species and genetic resources but also has caused the loss of livelihoods of those poor artisanal fisherfolk who exclusively depend on fishing. In addition, the trawlers have destroyed the natural habitat of the fish, i.e. corals and reefs and fumes from the engines of the trawlers and motor boats have polluted the sea water. Under the fiscal pressure, the developing countries sell off more and more of their public reserves—forests, mining, natural resources, maritime resources thus, affecting the inter-generational equity which is essential for sustainable development. Only exports of those primary commodities and manufactured good which do not deplete natural resources and degrade environment and which benefit the poor would help improve and maintain the quality of environment and attain sustainable development (Katar Singh and Pundir, 2001).

Unfair Trade Practices

The term globalisation has four components: free flow of goods, free flow of capital, free flow of technology and free movement of labour. The advocates of globalisation especially from developed countries limit their definition of globalisation only to three parameters; namely unrestricted flow of trade, capital and technology. They insist on the developing countries to accept their own definition (Ruddar Dutt, 1997).

The developed countries especially United States raises the issue of labour standards to cut down the exports of carpets, textiles from India, in the name of child labour. Linking of labour standards with trade is a form of disguised protectionism. The developed countries invent "social class" to prevent the exports of developing countries. The richer countries also use non-tariff barriers of various sorts to regulate exports from the poor countries. At the same time, by heavily subsidizing agricultural exports, the rich countries succeed in depressing global prices of such commodities. The US has subsidised export of maize. It has been calculated that this will adversely affect the livelihoods of half a million small producers of maize in phillipines (Kurien, 1997).

The U.S. has a legal doctrine called 'caveat emptor' meaning 'let the buyer beware'. That is, even those products that are totally banned within the U.S. because of the harm they cause can be exported to other countries without any restriction. A lot of goods–hundreds of medicines, pesticides such as DTT and other materials like asbestos–which are totally banned in the U.S. and other western countries because of the harm they cause to people's health and lives are aggressively marketed by the multinationals in India and other Third World Countries as safe products, blatantly violating the human right to safety and security.

Throughout 1990s the public policy of Indian Government was entirely concerned with how to accelerate economic growth, reduce fiscal deficit and subsidy, integrate India with world economy and make India super power in information technology. However, the ultimate test of the reforms should be judged in terms of the success of human development. It is about time, the government should pay more focus on human dimensions instead of income-centered economic growth. The Secretary General of the United Nations, Mr. Kofi Annan expressed his concern that globalisation should become "a positive force for all the world's people instead of leaving billions of them behind in squalor. This requires massive investment on basic services like education, health, sanitation and provision of safe drinking water. The government should take deliberate efforts to make the process of growth and and human development mutually reinforcing so that one sustains the other. A link between growth and human development can be created by a major expansion of social spending, providing equal access to social service, equitable access to productive assets through land reforms and a wide dispersal in the ownership of industrial capital and by the removal of barriers to the entry of the people in economic and political spheres.

REFERENCES

1. Alamar, K, "Growth Versus Human Development" *Arul Anandar Journal of Economics,* 4(1). 1997:35.
2. Bhattacharya, N, "First Manifestation of Globalisation", *Mainstream,* March 15, 1997: 15.
3. Human Development Report, 1998.
4. Katar Singh and R.S. Pundir, "Some Environmental Impacts of Liberalised International Trade in Agricultural Commodities". *The Asian Economic Review,* 43(2) Aug-2001: 199.
5. Kurien, C.T., "Globalisation and the Poor", *Frontline,* 5 September, 1997.
6. Ruddar Datt, "Who are the Real Beneficiaries?", *Mainstream,* 12 July 1997:15
7. Sauvant, Karl, P. in Sauvant, Karl, P. (ed.). *Changing Priorities on the International Agenda,* "The New International Economic Order", Oxford, Pergamend Press 1981.
8. Survey of Multinationals, *The Economist,* March 27, 1994.
9. Sulak Sivaraksa, "Applying Gandhi for Alternative Consumption", *Gandhi Marg,* 19 (4) Jan-Mar, 1998:396.
10. Utsa Patnaik, "The Cost of Free Trade: The WTO Regime and the Indian Economy" *Social Scientist,* 2 (11-12) Now-Dec., 1999:5.

Post-Reform India

Emerging Trends (With Special Reference to Human Resource Development)

Dr. R. Shashi Kumar

Introduction

The Indian economy broke off from long years of colonial rule in 1947 after independence, characterised by an extremely low GDP growth rate, a near zero industrial base and predominance of extractive industries. The Government of India, therefore, at the very outset ushered in a highly regulated and controlled economy, backed by the argument that the infant industry in India needs protection from external competition. The Government's approach gained further credence due to the protectionist policies pursued by other countries. The unpleasant memories of the colonial era the fears of the hostile global economy also influence India's thinking at that point of time.

Though the initial phase of economic growth was slow, India soon reaped the benefits of a diversified industrial base. With the agricultural sector making significant progress and attaining self-sufficiency, the growth rate of the economy reached around 5 to 5.5 per cent during the late 1970s and the early 1980s.

Problems surfaced thereafter. The protectionist policies had outlived their utility. The regulated regime, in the absence of completion, incentives and innovations, brought in inefficiency in the production system countrywide and the economy's dependence on foreign savings in the form of foreign aid and commercial borrowings began to increase. All this culminated in a serious foreign exchange crisis in 1991.

Meanwhile, the fast growth of emerging countries of the East Asian and Pacific Region made an impact on the Indian intelligentsia and policy-makers. They began to appreciate the virtues of liberalisation and competition. The 1991 reforms were ushered in against this very background. These constituted an ambitious and comprehensive programmed conditioned and influenced largely by the IMF. The reforms embody three major objectives: (i) to absorb the shocks of the foreign exchange crisis by restoring the macro-economic balance and by helping in the stabilisation of the economy; (ii) to bring in structural changes through policy measures in order to reach the high growth path, and (iii) to combine growth with equity, to give reforms a human face. The 'human angle' essentially constituted an Indian approach and had nothing to do with the IMF package.

Dimensions of Economic Reforms

In its attempts at globalisation, India has to undergo a profound process of economic transformation involving trade-offs in maintaining a social consensus in support of economic reforms to become integrated into an increasingly interdependent and highly competitive global market. Thus, a review of the sequencing of the basic reforms measures is urgently called for, particularly in respect of the critical issues which must received the first priority in economic agenda. It is quite satisfying that the government has been taking several measures to dilute or do away with these critical problems and hopefully the country would usher in the coming years with resilience and confidence. The following are the important dimensions of the Indian economic reforms.

Agricultural Policy

A draft Agricultural Policy Resolution was placed in Parliament in December 1992. the draft resolution seeks to dovetail the agricultural development and research programmers to the challenges in Indian agriculture and addresses itself to the problems of under-employment, unemployment and malnutrition by generating activities through diversification of agriculture and promotion of agro-based industry. Augmenting facilities for processing, marketing and storage, development of rain-fed and irrigated horticulture, augmentation of biomass reduction and increased utilisation of irrigation potential and promotion of water conservation are some of the major objectives of the Draft. It also aims at reviving and strengthening the cooperatives and local communities and increasing the involvement of non-Governmental organisations in agricultural development. The draft was passed as a policy in the conference of Chief Minister on 5th March 1993.

Industrial Policy

In the root of the industrial policy, 1991 was the liberalisation policy of the government. The New Industrial Policy aims at: to maintain the gains from industrial already made, contraction of public sector, privatisation of public sector, industrial licensing decontrol, abolition of registration, new ventures for foreign capital, adoption of foreign technology in a massive level, concessions from MRTP Act, etc. The objectives are similar to those of earlier Industrial Policy Resolutions, but the differences lies in the strategy to achieve these objectives. The strategy now shifts from controls to liberalisation and from nationalisation to privatisation.

Fiscal Policy

The complexion of India's fiscal policy has undergone some change after the Economic Reforms. Reliance on Deficit Financing, reliance on indirect taxation, long-term fiscal policy, eradicating of black money, inflationary potential, use of administered prices, rationalisation of product classification codes, introduction of MODVAT, common accounting year for income tax are some of important measures of fiscal policy.

New Trade Policy

During July-August 1991, the Government announced far reaching changes in trade policy, these policy changes aimed at strengthening export intensives, eliminating a substantial volume of import licencing and optional import compression. Essential imports of sensitive items were fully protected, but other imports of raw material and components were linked to export performance (EPZ and EOU) through enlargement and restructuring of the replenishment licencing system.

All the above lead one to conclude that the final reform objective: "to elevate India to higher growth path matching India's fast growing emerging neighbors". By moving away from subsidy and charity-oriented measures, the emphasis is now on steps that would enhance the efficiency and opportunities in a free market set-up, leading to better allocation of resources and more equitable distribution of wealth and income.

An Assessment of Economic Reforms

India launched an ambitious reforms programmed in 1991, following an acute foreign exchange crisis. This programme aimed to take the economy to a high growth path, breaking from its past, with sound macro-economic balance in the external and domestic sectors on a sustainable base. But the experiences after Economic Reforms show that this goal has not yet been fulfilled.

General Trends of the Economy (With Human Face)

The record of India's performance judge in terms of the growth rate of GDP is quite evidently commendable. India's mixed economy in the post-reform period has so far witnessed about 7 per cent growth in GDP. Thus, the growth performance is seemingly encouraging. However, accelerated growth has been accompanied by growing incidence of poverty, unemployment, inequality and deprivation. It may, therefore, be observed that the condition with respect to human development in India is appalling. In 1991, the literacy rate in India was only 52.1 per cent with 324 million in the age group of seven years and above being classified as illiterates. India has the largest pool of children in the world who do not attend school. Significantly, in 1991 out of 100 million children in less developed countries that were not in school. The bulk, i.e. 72.9 million was in India. The dropout ratio at the primary level in 1989-90 at 46 per cent for boys and 50 per cent for girls makes a mockery of high gross enrolment ratios reported. Thus, human development strategies are important not for enhancing the quality of human resources but also as a means towards a more egalitarian distribution of income.

During the post-reform period agricultural growth could not pick up primarily because the main agenda of reform excluded agriculture and the public sector. After a brief period of acceleration, the industrial growth rate started declining due to a number of factors—an uncoordinated and improper sequencing of official policies on exports, foreign investment and financial reforms, and lack of proper integration between fiscal and monetary policies of the Government, an inadequate focus on India's preparedness to meet the global challenges, and the domestic political instability.

Thus, the growth in the post-reform period has been largely achieved by a comparatively higher growth of the services sector rather than the goods sector. In the goods sector, there were years when agricultural growth provided the main growth momentum. But at the same time, there were years when agricultural growth was very low. In general, the performance of agriculture during the reform period, in the context of its long-term secular growth, although satisfying, has not reflected any breakthrough. It was, in fact, lower than the agricultural growth of the late 1980s and its contribution to total GDP measured in terms of elasticity to GDP has proved to be much lower in the post-reform period, compared to the pre-reform period.

There is concern among the economists with regard to the frequent changes made in the estimates by the CSO, with long retrospective effect. More important is the fact that inmost emerging countries, the engine of growth is industry and industrial exports. India cannot be an exception. In future our emphasis should be on an industry led growth. Agriculture cannot be an engine of growth in the near future, since it is still largely dependent on the vagaries of nature. It has many long-awaited reform areas constrained primarily by socio-political considerations. At the same time, Indian industry is now under heavy infrastructure constrains. Subject to these constraints, growth in industrial production above 7 to 8 per cent will not be sustainable. For example, the elasticity of GDP to the growth of the power sector has been seen to be less than one. Given the low growth of the power sector into the near future, only a GDP growth of around 5.6 to 6 per cent will be sustainable.

While ritual obeisance has been considered as a peripheral welfare activity rather than as the central pivot on which success of planning rests. The allocations to social sectors have been low and even the same have been witnessing a declining trend. Ironically, even as the emphasis on human development in the Plan documents has been increasing, the proportionate allocations made to these sectors have been the decline. Despite much proclamation, there has been no significant increase in the allocation for social sectors. Besides, the plan allocation targets have not been met in actual practice. In the India case, not only were the public funds available for human development low, they were also allocated in a distortionary manner. In the case of education this is exemplified by higher education claiming a large share of government financé as compared to primary education.

One can easily find that Economic Reforms' has tackled the foreign exchange crisis of 1990-91 very successfully and helped the economy to maintain its pre-reform trend under a healthy macro-economic balance.

Policy Implications on the Human Resource Development

The increasing disparities in the different social indicators and the slowing down of poverty eradication in the India between States and classes, in spite of an accelerated growth, bring into sharp focus the need for consideration of not only the 'quantitative' but also the 'qualitative' aspects of growth. Indeed, the composition of the income growth between sectors, regions, classes, and the production technology and organisation used are all important in determining the impact of any growth process on the major indicators of quality of life like poverty, equity, employment, longivity, health, etc. In the pre-reform period, the Government attempted to ensure many of the 'quality' aspects by use of instruments like licensing procedure, reservation policy, controlled choice of technology, protection against monopolies and against foreign competition and implicit subsidies in several key economic and social activities, public work programmed and the public distribution system on food. Most of these programs have lost their relevance in India's new market-oriented regime, which ask for the implementing of an integrated human development policy, both in the public and private sectors.

In India, the Constitution provides that the responsibility of HRD lies with the States. Only 18 per cent of the total HRD expenditure in 1996-97 was spent by the center. So, it is more important to monitor the rate of growth of such expenditure at the State level. At the center, in the aggregate, HRD grew almost at the same rate as in 1980s, although in 1996-97 it felt drastically from 16.4 per cent per annum to 12 per cent per annum. But in the States, the rate of growth of HRD expenditure came down from 15.9 per cent in the 1980s to 8.2 per cent in 1996-97 over 1995-96. The record of the education sector was almost the same, wherein expenditure on education has been declining since the 1980s, and in terms of real per capita it became almost negative in 1996-97. In health and family welfare, the growth rate declined faster at the State level, although it was comparatively better at the Center. An enquiry into the behaviour of human development expenditure of the Government of India reveals that it lacks any clear-cut focus. Moreover, it is observed that the behavior of human development expenditure of the government and components thereof has witnessed volatility.

The present plan aims at realising the objective of 'growth with equity and distributive justice'. Quite evidently, this focal objective requires emphasis on human development.

Apart from it, government expenditure on social sectors is a causative factor for substantial electoral gains. In view of adverse implications of economic reforms and structural adjustment programs, the government expenditure policy will have to focus more sharply on human development and socio-economic welfare. The worsening scenario of poverty, unemployment, inequality and deprivation is a hard reality with which the government will have to confront heard-on by pressing into service a well though-out strategy of government expenditure for human development.

Towards Human Resource Development Strategy

Keeping in view the enormity of human development concomitant with dismal scenario of government expenditure on it, the following specific policy prescriptions may be offered:

1. The focus of government expenditure should be on removal of poverty, through provision of basic minimum services and social development;
2. The states having dismal level of human development should raise social sector expenditure substantially;
3. The Center should provide more financial resources to state for HRD;
4. Provision of housing, water supply, power, health services, etc. should also make available to the rural poor;
5. Population growth should be checked effectively.

Finally, it must be emphasised here that if inter-state disparities in social development are not addressed by government intervention through appropriately formulated expenditure policy effectively and aptly, India's federal policy may witness burgeoning politico-socio-economic tensions.

Hopes Ahead

Though there has been apprehension in several quarters that the Economic Reforms would undermine our social and economic philosophy, which we adopted after Independence, it has been the declared policy of the government to carry out these reforms while given them a human face. Consequently, we adopted several measures like National Renewal Fund to take care of the labor redundancies, which might occur in the course of economic restructuring. It has been our constant endeavour that social sector development does not suffer in our quest of higher growth efficiency. We introduced several measures of social assistance, took several measures to spread primary education and provide health care to the poor. Because of our conscious policy and all these efforts, our reform measures have not in general adversely affected the conditions of labourers and the poor as happened in several developing countries, particularly Latin America and Sub-Saharan Africa. This is a significant achievement of the Indian system, which has been widely acknowledged both in India and outside. Let us hope that the managers of India's mixed economy boldly confront the emerging challenges of regional imbalances in human development.

Conclusion

In spite of many achievements, we have several daunting problems, which need to be addressed with all our endeavours. Although we have been able to reduce the proportion of people below the poverty line, the magnitude is still very large. The fact that about one-third of our population is still poor, the only about half of the population is illiterate, that many villages do not have access to safe drinking water, and that the productivity of our workforce remains very low in comparison to the international standards. It is incumbent on the Government to take up these responsibilities under an appropriate HRD policy. It is indeed difficult to usher in an appropriate social and economic programme that will not only improve deficiency but also at the same time ensure distributive justice also through selective and often target-oriented expenditure on education, health, sanitation, housing, employment and other welfare programmes. This call for vigorous effort on our part. Many new challenges have emerged in the wake of globalisation and new international economic order. We have to accordingly reorient our strategies and evolve suitable institutions in the wake of the development.

REFERENCES

1. Correa, H. (1963), *The Economics of Human Resources,* Amsterdam, North Holland Publishing Co.
2. Dreze, J. and K. Sen. (1995), India: *Economic Development and Social Opportunity,* Oxford University Press, New Delhi.
3. Goulet, D. (1992), *Development: Creator and Destroyer of Values',* World Development 20 (3), pp. 407-47
4. Government of India, Central Statistical Organisational, Statistical Abstract (various issues).
5. Government of India, Ministry of Finance, Economic Survey (various issues)
6. Guha, Biswajeet (1998), *Human Development in India—A Study of Inter-state Disparity,* Indian Economic Association Conference Volume.
7. Morris, M.D. (1979), *Measuring the Conditions of World's Poor: The Physical Quality of Life Index,* Oxford: Pregamon Press.
8. UNDP, Human Development Report (various issues).

23

Human Resource Development in the Context of Economic Reforms

Dr. P. Gnana Soundari

The Concept

Manpower is not only the most important resource for development, it is also the objective of all developments. The relationship between human resources and the behaviour of economy can be moulded by the social system and the pattern of education.

Human Development report of 1997 describes Human Development as the process of widening people's choices and the level of well-being they achieve are at the core of the notion of human development.

According to F.H. Harbison, human resource are the energies, skills, talent and knowledge of people which are or which potentially can or should be applied to the production of goods or the rendering of useful services.

Alfred Marshall considered the investment in human beings as the most of valuable of all capital. A country that cannot develop the skill and knowledge of its people and put them to effective use will not be able to prosper. Hence, human resource can be thought of as the total knowledge, skills, creative abilities, talents and aptitudes of the workforce as well as the values, attitudes and beliefs of the people in general.

Level of Development

Level of Development means the three essential choices for people are to lead a long and healthy life, to acquire knowledge and to have access to the resources needed for a decent standard of living. Human development does not end there, however other choices highly valued by many people, range from 'political, economic and social freedom to opportunities for being creative and productive and enjoying self respect and guaranteed human rights.

Significance of Human Resources

The human resources are solely responsible for transforming traditional economies into modern and industrial economies. The difference in the level of economic development of the country is largely a reflection of the difference in the quality of their human resources. The key element in this proposition is that of the values, attitudes, general orientation of the people. The socio-economic transformation in the economies is possible with the development of human resources which in turn leads to sustained economic development.

The purpose of this chapter is to get an idea regarding the magnitude of involvement of the Government in the development of social aspects of life and living of the people in India. Social aspects of level of living of people include housing, education and health.

Housing

Housing is one of the factors measures the social status of human beings. While people migrate to urban areas in search of a better life, the poor quality of urban infrastructure and housing forces them into shanties. The rapid increase in population in cities has resulted in the growth of what are referred to as slums and squatter settlements where the living environment is pathetic.

Delhi Slums—The Reality

Delhi has seen a swelling of its population from 2 millions in 1947 to over 13 millions today. The government has been unable to meet the infrastructure and social challenges that have arisen from this growth and shanty towns have emerged as a response. For those living in shanties the outlook is bleak. Records show:

- 1500 shanty colonies in Delhi house over 3 million people;
- The average population density in a shanty town is 3 lakh per sq. km;
- The average dwelling houses 6-8 people;
- The under five mortality rate is 149 per 1000 live births;
- One water pump on average serves 1000 people;
- No latrine facilities, where latrines are provided, the average is one latrine per 27 households;
- 40 per cent of children are severely malnourished in Delhi, about 40,000 children are labourers, 30,000 assists in shops, 30,000 work in teashops and 20,000 in auto-repair shops;
- 75 per cent of men and 90 per cent of women living in shanties are illiterate.

Source: http://www.asha.india.org/slumsreality.asp.

Housing is a major problem in most urban centres in India. By 1997, the total housing shortage in the country was

Table 23.1: Urban Households Living in Slums (2001)

States	*Percentage*
Maharashtra	25.4
Orissa	19.1
Arunachal Pradesh	18.2
Madhya Pradesh	18.1
West Bengal	17.6

Source: India Development Report—2002.

Table 23.2: Selected Indicators of Housing Conditions in Rural and Urban India Based on NSS Enquiries

Indicators	*1973-74*		*1983-84*		*1993-94*		*1999-2000**	
	Rural	*Urban*	*Rural*	*Urban*	*Rural*	*Urban*	*Rural*	*Urban*
Percentage of households living in								
(a) Pucca houses	18.5	—	16.7	57.6	32.3	73.8	37.2	76.7
(b) Kutcha houses	49.1	—	50.8	16.5	31.7	8.3	39.4	8.0
Percentage of households having no build-up latrine	92.4	—	91.4	36.8	85.8	30.6	82.7	27.9
Percentage of households with source of drinking water								
(a) Tap	4.7	67.0	—	—	19.0	70.0	22.0	76.0
(b) Tubewell	7.0	—	—	—	—	—	—	—
(c) Well	65.8	—	—	—	—	—	—	—
Percentage of households having electricity for lighting	6.6	—	—	—	36.5	80.9	46.5	85.8

Source: Man and Development—June 2003—p. 52.

*India 2002, p. 617.

estimated to be 13.66 million units, out of which 7.57 million units would be in the urban areas. More than 90 per cent of this shortage is for the poor and the low-income category.

In India around 20 to 25 per cent of the urban households in the country live in slums, squalor settlements and refugee colonies due to non-availability of affordable habitat in formal settlements.

However, the few studies which considered the social aspects of level of living such as conditions of shelter, drinking water and other related facilities in the household reveals that the picture for India is not so satisfactory. The 49th round of NSS enquiry provides data on housing conditions from which some idea can be made regarding the homeless or near homeless people in India.

Housing is a state subject but the union government is responsible for the formulation of policy with regard to programme and approaches for the effective implementation of social housing schemes, particularly those pertaining to weaker sections of the society. A new housing and habitat policy 1998 had been formulated to address the issues of sustainable development infrastructure and for strong public-private partnership for shelter delivery.

Table 23.3: Population covered with Drinking Water and Sanitation Facilities

Indicator	*Percentage coverage as on March 31st*			
	1985	*1990*	*1995*	*1999 estimated*
Drinking Water Supply				
Rural	56.3	73.9	82.8	98.0
Urban	72.9	83.8	84.3	90.2
Sanitation Facilities				
Rural	0.7	2.4	3.6	9.0
Urban	28.4	49.9	49.9	49.3

Source: Economic Survey (2000-01)

Table 23.4: Construction Agencies

Name of the agency	*Year of Establishment*	*Purpose*	*Achievement*
1	*2*	*3*	*4*
National Buildings Construction Corporation Ltd.	1960	• Provide technology • Develop Real Estate Projects • Project Management • Maintenance contracts.	Paid up capital as on 31st March 2001 Rs. 111.65 crore earned a profile of Rs. 7 crore by in 2000-01
National Capital Region Planning Board	1985	• Development of National Capital Region	• Covered an area of 30242 sq. km which covers Delhi and parts of Haryana, Rajasthan and Uttar Pradesh with a loan, amount of Rs. 1592.93 crore upto 30th June 2001
		• Develop urban slums	* Up to June 2001 Rs. 1528 crore
National Slum Development Programme	1996	Provide adequate and satisfactory water supply sanitation, primary education facility, health care, etc.	Released by the general Govt. benefiting nearly 2.82 crore people since its inception.
Ganga Barrage Project at Kanpur	1999	* to develop housing in UP	Rs. 70.49 was released up to 31st May 2001.

Table 23.4: ***(Contd)***

1	*2*	*3*	*4*
Hindustan Prefab Ltd.	1995	* To serve both as a production unit and a contracting company for the execution of civil works.	—
Integrated Development of small and medium towns scheme	1979	* To provide urban Infrastructure towns upto 5 lakh population.	Up to March 2001 1058 were benefited out of Rs. 444.93 crore
Mega City scheme in Mumbai, Chennai, Kolkata, Hyderabad and Bangalore	1993	Enabling the mega cities to build a Revolving fund for sustained investment in urban infrastructure	Upto March 2001 Rs. 598.95 crore has been released
Urban mapping scheme	during eighth plan	Aerial photography for 50 towns from different states.	38 towns were covered.

The objectives of the policy are to create surpluses in housing stock and facilitate construction of 2 million additional dwelling units each year in pursuance of National Agenda for Governance. It also seeks to ensure that having along with supporting services is treated as a priority sector at par with infrastructure. The central theme of the policy is strong public-private partnerships for tackling housing and infrastructure problems. The Government would provide fiscal concessions, carryout legal and regulatory reforms and create an abling environment.

To overcome housing problem the public investment in the housing sector is required. The Table 23.4 gives details on the agencies incorporated as public sector construction agencies.

Assuming that there will be one house on an average per 4.70 persons, the total homeless population of India was calculated as 112.10 million in the year 1993. Using the norm 4.70 persons per housing unit, the homeless households was calculated as 23.85 million in 1993. The government has to build these number of houses in each year along with the increase in incremental number of houses due to population growth in each year if all the people have to have homes.

Health

Health is important for welfare. As a Gujarati Proverb says the first happiness is health, the second is a full stomach. Without health food cannot be enjoyed and one cannot be healthy without enough food. As Viner (1953) observed the first requirements of high labour productivity under modern conditions are that the masses of the population shall be literate, healthy and sufficiently well-fed to be strong and energetic. To emerge as a wealthy nation, a healthy society is desirable. Social action and public action is particularly important for the health of the poor as they are not able to take care of themselves.

The two aspects of healthy care preventive and curative health measures include life expectancy, mortality, expenditure on health and nutrition programmes. Since 1951, the life expectancy at birth has nearly doubled in 2001, i.e. 62.4 years. The basic indicators are given in Table 23.5.

Table 23.5: Indicators

Year	*Life expectancy at birth (years)*	*Birth rate (per '000)*	*Health Rate (per '000)*	*Infant mortality rate (per '000)*
1951	32.1	39.9	27.4	146
1981		33.9	12.5	105
1991		29.5	9.8	80
2001	62.4	25.8	8.5	68

Source: India Development Report, 2002.

The high infant mortality rate reflects the poor state of public health, inadequate medical attention during pregnancy at birth and poor post-natal care. To reduce infant and child mortality, 100 per cent immunisation supply of safe drinking water and provision of sanitation facilities are necessary. The coverage of these facilities is shown in Table 23.6.

Table 23.6: Sources of High Infant and Child Mortality in Per cent (1998-99)

Children 12-13 months without immunisation	
BCG	28.4
DPT 3 does	44.9
Polio 3 doses	37.2
Measles	49.3
All	58.0
No access to drinking water	
Rural	7.5
Urban	9.8
No sanitation facilities	
Rural	91.9
Urban	50.7
Births not attended by medical professionals	57.5

Source: India Development Report, 2002 p. 109.

The reform period has helped in a little way to improve health care of the people. On September 4th, 2001 the Union Health Minister has announced the New Health Policy which envisages a massive infusion of Public investment to rejuvenate the health care system.

Investment in Health in the various plans is given in Table 23.7.

Table 23.7: Pattern of investment in Health

Plans	*Total Plan Outlay (Rs. in crore)*	*Health outlay*	
		Outlay (Rs. in crore)	*% of outlay*
First Plan (1951-56)	1960	65	3.31
Second Plan (1956-61)	4672	141	3.01
Third Plan (1961-66)	8576	226	2.63
Annual Plan (1966-69)	6625	140	2.12
Fourth Plan (1969-74)	15779	336	2.13
Fifth Plan (1974-79)	39426	761	1.93
Annual Plan (1979-80)	12176	223	1.83
Sixth Plan (1980-85)	109292	2025	1.85
Seventh Plan (1985-90)	218730	3689	1.69
Annual Plan (1990-91)	61518	961	1.56
Annual Plan (1991-92)	65856	1042	1.58
Eighth Plan (1992-97)	412605	8138	1.97
Ninth Plan (1997-01)	635073	15969	2.51

Source: Economic Survey (2001-02).

The trend of investment in various plans highlights that sufficient attention was not paid to health. Of health, family welfare, water supply and sanitation are taken together as a measure to improve the quality of health of the population, then total public expenditure incurred on them was of the order 4.33 per cent of GDP during the first five year plan, it was gradually raised to as level of 5.95 per cent of GDP during the fifth plan and has further improved to 7.1 per cent of GDP during the Eighth plan. There is an urgent need to improve the expenditure on public health services further in order to improve the capabilities of human resources.

Education

The importance of education not only as a component of basic need but also an essential ingredient for human development cannot be overemphasised. It is, therefore, absolutely necessary to take up an assessment of the situation in India with respect to education.

Before 1976, education was the exclusive responsibility of states. In 1976 through 42nd constitutional amendment, education was incorporated in the concurrent list and became a joint responsibility of the centre and the states. The objective of incorporating education in the concurrent list was to facilitate evolution of all-India policies in the field of education. In addition to policy formulation, the Ministry of Human Resources Development shares with the states the responsibility for educational planning.

However, the spread of education in the country has to be increased. The literacy rate for both male and female since 1951 has been provided in Table 23.8.

Table 23.8: Literacy Rate in India ***(in percentage)***

Year	*Persons*	*Male*	*Female*	*Male-Female gap in literacy rate*
1951	18.3	27.2	8.9	18.3
1961	28.3	40.4	15.4	25.1
1971	34.5	46.0	22.0	24.0
1981	43.6	56.4	29.8	26.6
1991	52.2	64.1	39.3	24.8
2001	65.4	75.9	54.2	21.7

Source: India 2001, p. 22.

From a figure of only 18.3 per cent in 1951, it has gone upto 65.4 per cent in 2001. However, the rate among the male

Table 23.9: Plan Expenditure on Different Sectors of Education

(in percentage)

Plan	*Elementary Education*	*Secondary Education*	*Adult Education*	*Higher Education*	*Others*	*Technical Education*	*Total*
First Plan 1951-56	56 (850)	13 (200)	—	9 (140)	9 (140)	13 (200)	100 (1530)
Second Plan 1956-61	35 (950)	19 (510)	—	18 (480)	10 (300)	18 (490)	100 (2730)
Third Plan 1961-66	34 (2010)	18 (1030)	—	15 (870)	12 (730)	21 (1250)	100 (5890)
Annual Plan 1966-69	24 (750)	16 (530)	—	24 (770)	11 (370)	25 (810)	100 (810)
Fourth Plan (1969-74)	30 (2390)	18 (1400)	—	25 (1950)	14 (1060)	13 (1050)	100 (7860)
Fifth Plan (1974-79)	35 (3170)	17 (1560)	—	22 (2050)	14 (1090)	12 (1060)	100 (8940)
Sixth Plan (1980-85)	33 (8360)	21 (5300)	9 (2240)	22 (5590)	4 (1080)	11 (2730)	100 (25300)
Seventh Plan (1985-90)	37 (28490)	24 (18320)	6 (4700)	16 (12010)	3 (1980)	14 (10830)	100 (76330)
Annual Plan (1990-92)	37 (17290)	232 (10530)	9 (4160)	12 (5880)	2 (1180)	17 (8230)	100 (47270)
Eighth Plan (1992-97)	47 (92010)	18 (34980)	9 (18480)	8 (15160)	4 (7510)	14 (27860)	100 (196000)
Ninth Plan (1997-02)	58 (118428)	13 (26035)	3 (6304)	12 (25000)	2 (4314)	12 (23735)	100 (203816)

*Figures in brackets in million of rupees

Source: India 2002-p. 81.

population is considerably high compared to that for females. It is distressing to note that about half the females are still not literate. In order to improve the literacy rate, universalisation of elementary education has been accepted as a national goal. The national policy on education (1986) and the programme of action (1992) envisage free and compulsory education of satisfactory quality for all children upto the age of 14 years. As per the commitment the Government allot 6 per cent of GDP for education sector out of which 50 per cent would be spent on primary education. Table 23.9 shows the plan expenditure on different sectors of education.

Inspite of Centre and State Governments' effort and commitment towards free and compulsory education quite unexpectedly the drop-out rates has been increasing. The major reason for dropping out with percentage has been presented in Table 23.10.

Table 23.10: Main Reason for Dropping Out (between 5-24 age groups)

(in percentage)

Reasons for dropping out	*Rural*	*Urban*	*Percentage to total population*
Child not interested in studies	25.3	22.0	24.4
Unable to Cope	21.5	25.6	22.5
Financial Constraints	12.1	13.3	12.4
Parents not interested in studies	10.2	6.9	9.4
Has to participate in other economic activities	8.2	6.5	7.8
Has to work for wage	4.1	6.9	4.8
Has to attend to domestic duties	4.6	4.3	4.6

Source: Man and Development: June 2003, p. 62.

The data presented in Table 23.10 has clearly depict that our educational system has failed to attract a significant proportion of students of age 5-24 years in continuing their studies at different levels of education. No significant measure have been taken by the government to reduce the financial burden of the weaker sections of society that results in the dropping out and forced labour prematurely.

Another important factor to be noted is that there is quite a proportion of population of age 5-24 years who never enrolled themselves in schools. The reasons for non-enrolment is shown in Table 23.11.

Table 23.11: Percentage of never enrolled persons of age 5-24 years by main reasons for Non-enrolment

Reasons for Non-enrolment	*Age Group*	*Rural*	*Urban*	*% to Total population*
Parents not interested in studies of the wards	6-10	33.8	26.1	33.1
	11-13	34.4	30.6	34.1
	14-17	31.9	26.1	31.3
	18-24	36.2	29.2	35.3
	5-24	32.6	25.6	31.8
Child not interested in studies	6-10	19.8	20.9	19.9
	11-13	18.8	22.1	19.1
	14-17	17.6	19.0	17.7
	18-24	15.0	17.4	15.3
	5-24	17.2	17.9	17.3
Financial constraints	6-10	16.2	21.7	16.8
	11-13	18.9	25.8	19.5
	14-17	18.6	27.1	19.5
	5-24	14.6	19.7	15.2

Source: NSSO 1998-Report No. 439, p. 35.

Reasons given for non-enrolment reveals that the parents not interested in studies of their wards is the main reason towards non-enrolment both for rural and urban areas. Parents hesitation may be due to ignorance and financial problem. It is necessary to educate the parents on importance of education. As a part of educating the target out of school children in the age group of 6-14 years who had remained outside the formal system of schooling the scheme of non-formal education was introduced in 1979-80.

National Committee of State Education Minister recommended a new scheme Sarva Shiksha Abhiyan to pursue universal elementary education in a mission mode. The goals of this new scheme were:

(i) All 6-14 age children enroll in schools by 2003;

(ii) Complete five year primary education by 2007;

(iii) Complete eight years of schooling by 2010.

The media publicity and advocacy plan in being launched for universalisation of elementary education as a part of Sarva Shiksha Abhiyan.

It is now the right time to seriously focus on educating every child with a goal of empowering through quality education. It is not only a duty of the government but also the private sector and Non-Governmental Organisation. It may take long years still to achieve complete literacy in India.

Suggestions for Better Results

Basic Education and better education is to the provided in order to enjoy better results out of every investment on sanitation, health and nutrition.

Technical education and skill-oriented education should be a part of education to every child in order to improve the quality of human resource.

Value-based education should be provided to all from the primary education level to produce committed manpower.

All programmes, projects and schemes undertaken by the centre, state and local governments are to be monitored thoroughly throughout the period.

Public co-operation is to be sought towards the success of all efforts and measures carried on by the government.

Over dependence on government is to be reduced and private and other agencies should come forward to develop human resource.

The development of human resources in India during the Post-reform period is not so satisfactory. The increase in Human Development Index in India from 1995-2000 is only 0.033. By and large the states maintained their relative positions during the reform period. The National Human Development Report 2001 reported that HDI for India has been improving from 0.302 in 1981 to 0.381 in 1991 further to 0.472 in 2001, since HDI is less than 0.500 even in 2001, India continues to be a low HDI country judged by international standards.

In such a situation, India must demonstrate its commitment to full employment. Along with this growth process should promote equitable growth with greater people's participation. This would require heavy investment in the social sector namely health and education so that a better equipped labour force improves productivity and thus can claim legitimately a better share in the fruit of development.

REFERENCES

1. Mahajan V.S., *Economic Reforms and Liberalisation,* Deep and Deep Publication, 1999.
2. India, 2002 Publication Division, Ministry of Information and Boardcasting, Govt. of India.
3. Ruddar Dutt and KPM Sudharam, *Indian Economy,* S. Chand and Company, New Delhi, 2003.
4. *India Development Report*, 2002.
5. *Man and Development*, June 2003.
6. *Human Resource Development and Economic Development,* Ruddar Dutt.

Globalisation and Stress Management

Dr. Vanathi Vembar
Venkatesh Kumar

When India as a newly independent nation set out on the path of rapid economic development within a democratic political framework, it aroused great expectations. Today, 50 years later, the record is a mixed one. India's greatest achievement is in building a working democracy in exceptionally difficult circumstances, thereby making India the largest "free" market in the world. In contrast, its economic achievements have been modest with some distinct disappointments.

India has developed a scientific and technological capability that is impressive in many ways. The record of economic development in India is far less impressive than that of the East Asian countries and also much below its own potential. The Indian economy has grown slowly in the first 35 years of independence and at a more respectable pace during the last 20 years For long-term growth to be sustainable, India will have to do a great deal in the social sectors, especially health and education. Despite being in many ways a strong emerging market, India scores poorly on human development indicators.

With the New Economic Policy of the nineties, India has opened its gates for foreign trade in a wider range of goods. The liberalisation of imports and exports coupled with globalisation has caused a plethora of change at a rapid pace. It has led to multiplicity of work, and mandated large business units to manage the wide assortment of jobs involved in the production and distribution of a single item of goods. Also, the production sector has spawned a host of services like banking, logistics, etc. to take care of operations linked to it. Increasing task complexities have resulted in greater specialisation of job profiles. Such focus at work entails constant updation of skills and knowledge within the area of specialisation since a failure to perform can cost an individual his or her job. All these changes can affect various aspects of one's life related to the job, the organisation or group, and the individual. When one confronts a change in any area of life and if the individual feels that he or she lacks the ability and skill to effectively deal with that situation, one will experience stress.

With the globalisation of the Indian market during the nineties, there has been an increasing awareness about stress. This has led to a spate of studies on stress. In a changing scenario, anyone is liable to develop tension, frustration and anxiety arising from the duties they perform. This is especially true of the job of an executive. Since the executive is responsible for initiating and directing change, he or she has to cope with complexity, set a direction and create a vision for change. Hence, with excessive pressures, executive stress is a workplace reality.

For people to consider an event to be stressful, they must perceive it as threatening and must lack the resources to deal with it effectively (Folkman *et al*, 1986). Thus, stress is essentially an individual phenomenon and must be understood with reference to the characteristics of both the focal individual and his or her environment.

Many people consider stress as an excess of demands over resources. This makes them believe that stress is caused by external factors. But pressures also come from within, from our beliefs, attitudes and expectations about the world around us, from habits and behaviour and from our personality (Atkinson, 1999). Thus, stress can be caused both by external factors like the organisation, the job and the like as well as personal factors that include individual values and the inherent characteristics of the executive.

Therefore, individual characteristics that could cause stress to an individual were taken for assessment. In this study, the following characteristics were identified:

- Job Involvement
- Job Satisfaction
- Physical Health
- Mental Health
- Emotional Intelligence
- Hardiness
- Protestant Work Ethic
- Spousal Support
- Learned Helplessness

Methodology

The sample for the present study was drawn from the service sector. The banking industry was chosen, both public and private sector banks. The respondents, 480 executives, working in banks in Chennai responded to a questionnaire listing the various characteristics of an individual such as job involvement, job satisfaction, physical health, mental health, emotional intelligence, hardiness, protestant work ethic, spousal support and learned helplessness. All these variables were studied with organisational stress as the dependent variable.

Measures

The following Table 24.1, the tools used for the study and the figures in parentheses indicate their respective reliability coefficient (Cronbach's Alpha):

The Organisational stress scale has been developed and standardised by Carol A. Beatty (1996). This scale consist of

Table 24.1: Reliability (Cronbach's alpha) Co-efficient of Instruments used

S. No.	*Scales*	*Coefficient*	*T*	*L. S.*
1.	Organisational Stress	0.85	35.27	0.01
2.	Job Involvement	0.76	25.56	0.01
3.	Job Satisfaction	0.75	24.79	0.01
4.	Physical Health	0.89	42.67	0.01
5.	Mental Health	0.79	28.17	0.01
6.	Emotional Intelligence	0.97	87.23	0.01
7.	Hardiness	0.64	18.21	0.01
8.	Protestant Work Ethic	0.79	28.17	0.01
9.	Spousal Support	0.71	22.04	0.01
10.	Learned Helplessness	0.74	24.05	0.01

24 items, which were to be responded to on a five-point scale. The job involvement scale has been developed and standardised by Lodahl & Kejner (1976). This scale consists of 6 items, which were to be responded to on a five-point scale.

The job satisfaction scale has been developed and standardised by L. Grunberg *et al.* (1998). This construct was measured with a five item index comprising the respondent's satisfaction with four types of benefits (pay, vacation, retirement and medical) as well as a question concerning their global satisfaction (measured with a question 'All in all, how satisfied would you say you are with your job').

The physical health scale has been developed and standardised by Cary. L. Cooper (1988). This scale consists of 12 items, which were to be responded to on a six-point scale.

The mental health scale has been developed and standardised by Goldberg (1972). This scale consists of 12 items, which were to be responded to on a five-point scale.

The emotional intelligence scale has been developed and standardised by Richard Boyatzis et al (1999). This scale consists of 110 items, which were to be responded to on a seven point scale.

The Hardiness scale has been developed and standardised by Emrika Padus (1992). This scale consists of 12 items, which were to be responded to on a four point scale.

The Protestant Work Ethic scale has been developed and standardised by Mirels & Garrett (1971). It has 19 items, which were to be responded to on a seven point scale.

The spousal support scale has been standardised by Carol A. Beatty (1996). This scale consists of 8 items, which were to be responded to on a five point scale.

The learned helplessness scale has been developed and standardised by D.M.Pestonjee and Prathap Reddy (1988). This scale consists of 24 items, which were to be responded to on a six point scale.

Results

In order to find out which among the various characteristics of executives contributed to Organisational Stress in a significant manner, stepwise multiple regression was used.

Table 24.2: Multiple Regression Carried out on the Criterion Variable Organisational Stress by the Predictor Variables among Women and Men Executives

Gender	*Factors*	*R*	*R Square*	*Increment* R^2
Female	Learned Helplessness	.589	.347	.589
	Job Satisfaction	.644	.415	.055
	Mental Health	.667	.445	.023
	Spousal Support	.675	.456	.008
Male	Mental Health	.511	.261	.511
	Learned Helplessness	.585	.342	.074

It is seen from Table 24.2 that the variables, which contributed significantly to organisational stress among women executives, were learned helplessness, job satisfaction, mental health and spousal support. The R^2 value for learned helplessness was 34.7. Job satisfaction increased the R^2 value by 6.8. Next, mental health boosted the R^2 value by 3.0 while Spousal support augmented it by a value of 1.1. All these values were found to be significant at 0.01 level. These four factors of high learned helplessness, low job satisfaction, poor mental health and low spousal support accounted for 45.6 per cent of the total variance.

With regard to the men executives, it was found that mental health and learned helplessness significantly contributed to the prediction of Organisational Stress and comprised 34.2 per cent of the total variance. The R^2 value for mental health was 26.1, while learned helplessness enhanced the R^2 value by 8.1.

The negative beta values revealed that high learned helplessness, low job satisfaction, poor mental health and low spousal support were predictive of Organisational Stress among women executives. For men executives, only two factors, namely, poor mental health and high learned helplessness predicted Organisational Stress. The beta values for both the factors were negative.

Poor mental health was a predictor of Oganisational Stress for both women and men. This can be attributed to the difficulty in realistic appraisal of situations and lack of confidence in the self. Among men executives, mental health accounted for 26.1 per cent of the total variance, while among women it explained only 3.1 per cent.

The job of a woman has comparatively less responsibility and freedom compared to the job of a man. This may possibly be due to the apprehension that a woman still performs the dual role of a homemaker and an office executive. It is assumed that women may not be able to devote necessary attention and time if they are given a vital position and role in the Organisation.

Table 24.3: Details Regarding Contributing Variables to Organisational Stress

Gender	*Factors*	*F Ratio*	*Sig.*	*Beta (Unstd.)*	*Beta (std)*	*T-value*	*Sig.*	*Constant*
Female	Learned Helplessness	112.426	.000	-.525	-.466	-7.878	.000	
	Job Satisfaction	74.716	.000	-.508	-.223	-4.040	.000	
								131.431
	Mental Health	56.221	.000	.-.376	-.223	-3.659	.001	
	Spousal Support	43.729	.000	.173	.108	1.978	.049	
Male	Mental Health	69.181	.000	-.558	-.367	-5.641	.000	
								129.079
	Learned Helplessness	50.761	.000	-.454	-.320	-4.916	.000	

Hence, the tasks a woman may have to perform are less complex. Moreover, the status of a woman in the society is not dependent on the job. This could be the reason for mental health to be a lower predictor of Organisational Stress in women executives than for men executives. However, an optimum appraisal of reality is essential for performance on the job. Therefore, mental health was a common predictor of Organisational Stress among both women and men.

Learned helplessness in women executives accounted for 34.7 per cent of the variance, while among men it was only 8.1 per cent. The deprivation of opportunities for a long time and lack of social support regarding career should explain such a strong predictive power of learned helplessness among women executives. Since the learned helplessness is prevalent in men also, it was a common predictor of Organisational Stress for women and men.

Low job satisfaction was factor that predicted Organisational Stress among women executives, but not in men. This factor justified 3.0 per cent of the total variance. Women are burdened with household chores in addition to work in the organisation. At the office, she may not get the reward and recognition that her efforts warrant, even though she could be as efficient as the men. Therefore, the job experience may not be a pleasurable one and there is less job satisfaction. Such a negative attitude normally generates organisational stress. This finding is in line with the results of the study of Bogg and cooper (1995) and Mehra and Mishra (1999).

Another variable that has a predictive role in Organisational Stress among women executives only was spousal support, which accounted for 1.0 per cent of the total variance. The final say in retaining the job may possibly be dependent on the husband or his family. There could also be no one to assist or partake in household duties.

Implications

From the results of the study it can be discerned that executives in the service sector need to focus more on their personal characteristics such as mental health, learned helplessness, job satisfaction and spousal support. When these factors are taken care of, by/for the executives, the tend to experience lesser organisational stress. Lesser the executives' stress better the performance of the industry. Thus, it is imperative that such factors are also taken into consideration while framing major policies.

REFERENCES

1. Atkinson, J.M. (1999). *Coping with Stress at Work,* New Delhi: Harper Collins India Pvt. Ltd., p. 35.
2. Beatty, C.A. (1996). "The Stress of Managerial and Professional Women: Is the Price too High"? *Journal of OB.* Vol. 17, ISS 3, 1996, pp. 233-251.
3. Bogg, J., & Cooper, C.L. (1995). "Job Satisfaction, Mental Health, and Occupational Stress Among Senior Civil Servants", *Human Relations,* Vol. 48, No. 3, pp. 327-341.
4. Boyatzis, R.E., Goleman, D., Rhee, K. (1999). *Emotional Competence Inventory* with Special Permission from The Hay/ McBer Training and Research Group.
5. Cooper, C.L., Sloan, S.J., & Williams, S. (1988). *Occupational Stress Indicator: Management Guide,* NFER-Nelson, Windsor
6. Embrika, P. (1992). Emotion and Your Health: *The Winning Combination for a Long and Happy Life,* Rajendra Publication House Pvt. Ltd. Bombay, pp. 3-13.
7. Folkman, S., Lazarus, R.S., Dunkel-Schetter, C., DeLongis, A., & Green, R.J. (1986). Dynamics of a Stressful Encounter: Cognitive Appraisal, Coping, and Encounter Outcome, *Journal of Personality and Social Psychology,* 50, pp. 992-1003.
8. Goldberg, D. (1972). *Manual of the General Health Questionnaire,* Windsor: National Foundation for Educational Research, 1978.
9. Grunberg, L., Moore, S., & Greenberg, E.S. (1998). Work Stress and Problem Alcohol Behaviour: A Test of the Spill Over Model, *Journal of Organisational Behaviour,* Vol.19, pp. 487-502.
10. Lodhal, J.M., & Kejner, M. (1965). The Definition and Measurement of Job Involvement, *Journal of Applied Psychology,* Vol. 49, No. 1, pp. 24-33.

11. Mehra, G., & Mishra, P.C. (1999). Integration of Personality as a Moderator Variable, Indian Academy of Applied Psychology, 1999 (Jan-July), Vol. 25, No. 1 and 2., p. 51-55.

12. Mirels, H.L. & Garrett, J.B. (1971). The Protestant ethic as a personality variable, *Journal of consulting and clinical psychology,* Vol. 36, (1), pp. 40-44.

13. Panandiker, Pai, V.A., & Nandy, Ashish. (1999): *Contemporary India,* Tata McGrawHill Publishing Company Limited.

14. Pestonjee, D.M. & Prathap R. (1988). Development of a Psychometric Measure of Learned Helplessness, Working Paper No. 746, May 1988, IIM—Ahmedabad.

25

Redundancy, Redeployment of Manpower and Training Among Various Sectors in and Around the City of Chennai:

A Case Study Approach

Dr. N. Balasubramanian
Prof. G. Shankar

Introduction

The Concept: Redundancy of human power in organisations refers to the state of becoming excess in number or of not being needed for a job any longer. It commonly occurs because of people becoming easily replaceable by machines, technology, processes or even by more cost-efficient employees.

The Context: Mobility of people, technology and even investments have become part of our milieu and the order of the day, according to Kanter, R.M (1995). The era of Jack Welch's General Electric witnessed the system of categorizing employees within the 20:70:10 ratio of high, medium and low performers. Consequentially, the dictum, "Scrape off the rust; Pull out the weed" used frequently by Welch, spread among the employers who did not hesitate to show the pink slip to remove their redundant employees from their rolls. The outsourcing boom has to resulted in bringing its own quota of redundancy of non-core, non-value adding functions within large corporations. Business Process Re-reengineering carried out by Ford by comparing their processes with that of Mazda in Japan, resulted in the elimination of over 50 per cent of jobs in just few months. Extraneous factors such as terrorist attacks and the resultant slow down in the airline industry also resulted in heavy retrenchment. Stock markets have also found to react positively to large scale redundancy and thereby encouraging the trend further.

Emerging Trends Worldwide: Employees too began to have multiple choices in the terms and conditions of their employment. Home working, Job-sharing, Network marketing etc, on the one side alternatives to full time employment. Unemployment allowances, Golden Handshakes and golden parachutes came to be put up as solutions to neutralize the ill effects of sudden unemployment of retirement. Life long employment and organisation-linked growth has given way to short stints of work and swift ascent in the career ladder for talented individuals. Contractual, Part time or freelance working-arrangements have come to stay, thus minimizing the number of core, full time staff members, according to C. Handy (1994) in his reference to Shamrock organisations.

The Research

The objectives of the research included compilation of best practices on tackling redundancy across the sectors of employment and comparison of the relative merits of the practices. The study began with the basic questions about the causes and the consequences and manifestations of the problem of redundancy and the attempts made by organisations to manage them successfully. The researcher interviewed respondents, mainly from the field of Human Resources Management, who have had a minimum experience of at least ten years to their credit. Typical cases of redundancies were listed with the help of secondary data from the web sites and journals like the Human Capital, HRD Newsletter and Indian Management. From among this list, organisations were chosen based on the acceptance of respondents to answer queries on their offorts to manage redundancy.

Analysis of Data

The following passages attempt to objectively analyze the situations as reported by the respondents to the best of their knowledge and accuracy.

***Jobs in the Social Sector*:** In the case of a reputed company manufacturing construction equipment and machinery, a new machine to mix concrete and sprinkle them on roofing slabs is reported to have caused heavy job losses in the labour-intensive process of roof laying. As a result, social evils such as child labour, prostitution, victimless crimes like drinking and drug abuse, maladies like indebtedness and forced labour have been reported to rise significantly. Newspaper reports stated that instances of ex-employees assaulting or abducting their erstwhile employers or their family members have also indicated that unregulated redundancy can be a direct cause for societal disturbances and chaos.

Computer and Information Technology Sector: Human Resource Professionals from the South India-based Information Technology firms in the city of Chennai seem to tell a different story regarding redundancy. IT field has been one of the fastest changing and upgrading sectors in recent times. Skills become obsolete within short periods here. Ironically, problems of redundancy of employees or the prevalence of its negative effects are not prominently reported by any of the HR professionals interviewed by this researcher. Most of the leading IT firms interviewed for this purpose have acknowledged that they provide huge budgetary allocations for upgrading skills, better exposure to international development and more frequent and elaborate appraisals of performance and the maintenance of up-to-date skill inventories of all their staff. Thus, most of the IT firms are found to have successfully averted any large scale skill redundancy, at least among their high performance employees.

Higher Education: Educational sector is currently on the threshold of becoming more self-reliant, techno savvy and sensitive to the changing needs of the industries and commerce. It is therefore found to be in a volatile situation in terms of skill redundancy and related concerns. With practices like televised classrooms, Multi-media kits, and other audio visual aids, programmed instruction methods and e-learning, the importance of lectures as the sole methods of knowledge dissemination is waning in the premier institutions. With education becoming a commodity in the free market economy, even entire courses could be dropped citing lack of demand from students. With the forthcoming implementation of General Agreement of Trade in Services (GATS) from the year 2005 in India, the probability of skill and job redundancy are high. Experts in the field speaking to this researcher stated that multidisciplinary, tailor-made courses, involving creative techniques in the teaching-learning process would be the answer to face stiff competition from global players in the field of higher education. Continuous research and practical hands on experience in the fields of specialisation are envisaged to become mandatory for academicians. However, the present conditions in the sector are found to be far from being satisfactory. Restricted access to knowledge resources, a near total lack of sharing of expertise among co-professionals, slip shod human resource planning and discriminatory practices between the permanent and temporary staff are found to mar progress in the development of Human Resources in most of the institutions interviewed by this researcher.

THE CASES

CASE ONE: The Entry of Highly Paid Professionals and the Dedicated Old-timers

The Organisation: DCF is a reputed name in the travel and tourism industry today. Five years earlier, it had started as a one-table company. All that they had as an office to start with, were a table and a chair with a telephone connection. The office began to function from an unused corner of a leading showroom in the city, being magnanimously allowed to do so by a philanthropic owner of the shop. From that stage, the organisation evolved steadily by expanding its turnover, workforce strength, image and profitability, to become sustainable with a sizable level of capital and assets, including their own office complex. The main cause for this achievement was the enthusiasm, capabilities and sacrifices made by the staff.

DCF caters to what John Naisbitt's *Mega Trends* describe as the *High Touch factors, in the context of renaissance in the arts* throughout the world. The goal of DCF was to promote the concept of heritage tourism in the children, the youth and their parents. The founders, though aspiring businesspersons with a profit motive, firmly believed that India is rich and varied in its culture and heritage and its citizens ought not to be ignorant of its richness and diversity. Their strategy was to organize package tours to places of archaeological, artistic, architectural and ecological significance, besides publishing books and organizing events on various themes on Culture. DCF now has a new, own theme park that attracts people from people from several nations including dignitaries and diplomats.

The Crisis: The problem of redundancy showed up its face during the crucial period of the organisation's growth, which Larry Greiner calls as the stage of *Growth Through Creativity* leading to *Crisis of Leadership*. In the sixth year since inception the founder-owners realised that the organisation is poised for further growth through professionalism and strategic moves. The Economic, Social, Technological and International factors in the environment were conducive for its growth. However, the growth would be possible only if qualified professionals were brought to work with them, as the existing staffs are low-paid, unqualified persons who joined out of desperate need for job. With the recently attained financial stability, they can now afford to pay professionals like Architects Lawyers, Auditors and Computer Engineers and employ them on a full time basis. This would enable them to effectively plan and execute strategies for their growth. It would also boost their organisation's stature in the investors and the customers.

The news about the move by the Chief Executive Officer (CEO) to bring in outside professionals with high pay and perquisites spread like a wildfire. It was rumoured within the existing employees' groups that the CEO's decision would sideline the old time staff. The new professionals would get the coveted rooms, separate infrastructure, more pay and the old timers may be reduced to second class citizens in the very same firm that grew because of their efforts. Ironically, the surplus that is to be used to pay the new managers had been generated out of the sheer hard work, sacrifices and thrift by the old staff.

As if to add insult to injury, fresh rumors spread that the old staff will have to report to the newcomers and act per the latter's direction. It was to much to bear for the old set of staff, who decided to wait and watch if the newcomers could deliver the goods without their support and cooperation. The reality showed that however much qualified they may be, achieving good results depended much on the assistance from the old staff who knew the precedents and had the network of resource persons and bureaucrats within their reach. For example, one of the staff had quick, unhindered access to the top Government officials and CEOs of the collaborating firms while another was familiar with the lower level support staff of various organisation, who would help DCF in getting its requirements processed speedily. Yet another staff was well-informed about the buying behavior pattern of the local population.

Thus, it was an approach-approach conflict for the CEO. If the original plan for growth was pursued without change, there could be massive resignations or non-cooperation from the talented old timers. On the other hand, if DCF chooses to remain in the present contentment, the CEO realised that sooner or later the organisation is likely to be surpassed or taken over by other bigger players in the same sector. It would also be failing in utilizing the opportunity provided by the environment.

The Solution: To resolve the issue, the CEO contemplated a variety of solutions that were complementary to each other, rather than being mutually exclusive. Consultations with an OD consultant lead to the generation of the following possibilities. It was decided to adopt a combination of the suggestions, according to the principle of OD that emphasizes on simultaneously lighting many fires and produce small wins. The solutions included the following measures:

1. ***Structural Adjustments:*** The old timers would be permitted to function as independently as before and would be called to perform the role of collateral team members with the newcomers whenever necessary;

2. ***Equity in Pay:*** Since higher qualifications demand higher pay, the differences could not be entirely eliminated. But the perceived gap was sought to be minimised by a one-time lumpsum reward for the old-timers for their previous services and a seniority-based stock option that would benefit the oldtimers to begin with;

3. ***Parity in abilities:*** Intensive skill-based training programs for short duration and educational opportunities were organised to reduce the gaps in skills and knowledge. The organisation also offered to sponsor its senior staff to register them for courses in Business Administration or Software, depending on their needs, abilities and interests. This is to help to make the two groups more equal in the longer run;

4. ***Communication and Counseling:*** The CEO began to spike rumors by a continuous process of face-to-face transparent communication that would convince the employees of the need to grow and change in order to survive and allay any fears in their minds about their skills of talents becoming redundant.

Results: The sense of security and equity instilled in the oldtimers worked well. They became aware of the real intentions of the CEO and decided to cooperate. Free and frank discussions helped in clarifying points of doubts and gray areas. The newly joining professionals were sensitised about the dynamics existing in the organisation and they accorded due regard to the contributions of the pioneers. Growth through collaboration was thus made possible.

CASE ONE: Business Orientation Versus People Orientation

In a Service Organisation

The Organisation: Amity Mission Hospital is a popular organisation that began approaching redundancy with a pure business approach like many of its counterparts in the manufacturing sector. Over a hundred women permanent labourers employed as sweepers in the prestigious corporate hospital in Chennai faced a threat of job-loss recently. They were categorised as unskilled and were targeted for retrenchment within a period of one year, so that automation could take place. The ownership to the hospital had changed hands two years ago and the new management brought-in shift in the HR policy, from that of paternalism to a pure business approach to managing people. The Head of HR was given a mandate to downsize the workforce by at least one hundred. The previous incumbent in the position was removed because of his reluctance to downsize.

The Issue that Caused Concern: The Chairman of the Hospitals had found that Hospitals in developed nations used huge expensive machines. The machines seemed to have the following distinct advantage over human sweepers.

1. ***Effectiveness:*** The machines can sweep not only the floors but also the walls and the roof simultaneously, while the sweepers can only clean the floor effectively. The machines are similar to the car cleaners at the modern service, where strong and supple bristles clean the surfaces from all sides;

2. ***Speed:*** The machines swiftly sweep the rooms and entail minimal disturbance to the ailing inmates. Hospitals are places where dirt and smell accumulate very fast and need to be cleaned immediately. Human beings even in their best of abilities could not match these machines' speed;

3. ***Legal Constraints:*** While protective labour laws made it difficult to alter the workload, timings, pay and social insurance of the sweepers, the machines were expected

eliminate these 'hassles' and would save labor costs in the future.

The commitment of the workforce had been high and there were seldom any disciplinary problems among the sweepers. A liberal Voluntary Retirement Scheme (VRS) package was introduced involving about Rs. 2 to 3 lakhs as cost-to-company per employee, depending on the years of service put in and the years that remained.

The workers were unionised and resisted the move because of certain genuine fears. First, their average age was 40, which would be a disadvantage to get alternative employment. Second, though the present average salary is about Rupees Two thousand, and sweeper are unskilled and therefore, their experience would not be counted for fixation of salary, even if they get another job. Third, they would be losing out on the Social Security Measures like ESI, Provident Fund etc. Without addressing these fears, the VRS could become a failure.

The organisation's move to downsize also resulted in general criticisms from different quarters. They include:

(a) ***Threat to the Financial Soundness:*** The Management at the top was trying to implement capital intensive and technology intensive processes which is financially risky for the size of the organisation;

(b) ***Employee Morale:*** Showing scant regard for long and sincere service can act as a threat to the morale of even the professional or skilled workforce. Loyalty and commitment among the employees towards the organisation cannot be a one-way path but should be mutual. Highly Skilled employees would tend to switch over to other organisations if they perceive any insecurity of tenure;

(c) ***Social Costs:*** "Poverty anywhere is a threat to prosperity everywhere" says a declaration of global importance. In a country that is populous

the society requires human intensive, employment generating processes rather than labor-saving processes. Social costs of unemployment in large numbers such as crime and unrest could not be overlooked.

The Present Status: Negotiations are on in full swing and a decision is likely to be reached soon that would amicably settle the concerns of all the stakeholders of the organisation. Indications are available that some of the younger employees would be retrained in more skilled jobs and thereby retained. Alternative employment would be the responsibility of the organisation and they would hire a placement consultant for this purpose. However, it is not impossible to visualize the consequences of people-supportive measures as it happened in another organisation depicted in Case Three.

CASE THREE: Insightful Solution to an Individual Problem

The Organisation: Progressive India Management Consultants Private Limited, is well-established, hi-tech, professionally managed group. They were employing about forty employees including five management trainees in their marketing departments. The trainees underwent a three-month induction training process and were about to be put on the job. Their job involved making power point presentations about their services to potential Corporate clients. The employer would give each trainee a laptop computer and the trainee would have to be responsible for its upkeep and safety. Since the cost of the laptop set was quite high, the employer had to get a legal document signed by the candidates and countersigned by their guarantors, before beginning their work, with an undertaking about the ownership of the laptops.

The Problem: All but one of the five trainees could complete the formality. One trainee's family members refused to sign in the document and he was new to the place and could get no others for the purpose.

The trainee was one of the top-ranking recruits in the organisation. Yet, allowing the trainee to continue without the formality it would not only be risky, but also be against the policy of the organisation. Moreover, the others who have duly signed the document might also feel being treated unfairly. In the ultimate analysis, it was a question of making a choice between relaxing rules and retaining a valuable employee and sticking to rules and foregoing the returns on investment in recruitment and training.

The Solution: The Director of Progressive India Management Consultants, a Human Resource Development Specialist himself had to make the final choice. He was thinking of a win-win solution that would not harm or insult anyone. He decided to be firm with the formality and at the same time considerate to the genuineness of the trainee. He made a unique move by seeking employment for his own employee in other firms and could manage to get a couple of offers for the trainee to choose from. The marketing trainee was filled with emotions of joy and sorrow. He was relieved to know that his hard-earned job opportunity is not going to go waste. He was also sad to leave such a caring organisation. He resolved to continue to his loyalty to the first employer and be a life-long well-wisher and a professional associate.

Results: The Director's timely and prudent move did have a salutary effect on the rest of the employees. They seemed to carry home a message that, when they are skillful and committed, their organisation would reciprocate by showing concern and understanding even in the wake of their redundancy and that though job-loss may be inevitable, Insecurity is not a major threat factor in their work-life.

Conclusion

Almost all the organisations studied by the researcher have adopted at least a few creative ways to solve the problem of redundancy, giving due importance to the human resource element of their organisation and their development. In the process of tackling redundancy, these organisations have undergone a significant change in their approach to people. It is also seen that people can no longer seek all-time security in the job, but can only seek security in their ownselves, arising out of one's skill sets, talents and marketable competencies. Redeployment may have to be extended beyond organisations' physical boundaries, involving professional agencies.

Overcoming redundancy as a joint effort seems to have given the organisations greater cohesiveness, motivation and new-found strength and agility. There is however, one common flaw identified through this research study in most of the organisations except those in the IT sector. It is the lack of proactive approach in order to predict and prevent redundancy. Most of the solutions are found to have been on a trial and error basis and were reactive in nature.

Theoretically, managing the issue of redundancy has been found to go through the stages of *Burning, Yearning, Churning, Turning, Learning and Re-turning* in the organisations. *Burning* refers to a marked discomfort with the *status quo* with regard to redundancy while *yearning* refers to a longing or deep desire for change of the situation. *Churning* is the stage in which ideas and opinions of various employees are put together to clarify the exact nature of the redundancy and concretize the strategy to be adopted to counter redundancy. Turning is the phase in which actual implementation of the change takes place. Learning stage is comprised of assessing the aptness of the measures taken and re-turning involves getting ready for the next round of changes.

Approaches to tackle Redundancy: It is stated that redundancy may not be entirely eliminated of avoid with respect to all sectors, but could be creatively overcome in any type of organisation. To tackle redundancy, organisations studied through participant observation tend to adopt any of the following approaches:

(a) *Scientific approach:* The study of the organisation and subsequent intervention by a consultant specialised in Management or Organisation Development;

(b) *Contingency Approach:* Innovative and insightful decisions depending on the merits of the particular cases of redundancy by the Chief functionaries of the firms.

(c) *Participatory Approach:* A process of consultations with employees and elaborate negotiations in which the issue may be jointly debated and decided upon by the employer and the employees.

Suggestions and Recommendations

1. A Skill Audit linked with the Human Resources Information system and the findings of Market surveys should be made mandatory on the lines of laws on Human Resource Accounting that are in vogue in countries like Denmark.

2. Continuous opportunities and encouragement linked with financial backing to acquire and sharpen capabilities required for present and future jobs have to be ensured by organisations.

3. Employers and top management of organisations should be sensitised on the need for retraining and retaining human power rather than the current tendency to follow ad hoc recruitment or separation.

4. Flexible work arrangements have to be implemented on a larger scale and for more levels of employees, especially during lean periods of employment, so as to minimize the hazards of redundancy.

5. A combination of efforts to prevent redundancy would be preferable to dependence on a single-best solution.

6. More successful benchmarks and experiences at sectors other than the ones studied are to be analysed and documented through further research studies.

REFERENCES

1. Kanter, R.M., *World Class,* Simon & Schuster, 1995.

2. Handy, Charles. *The Age of Paradox,* HBS Press, 1994,

3. Greiner, L., ***Evolution and Revolution as Organisations.*** Grow Harvard Business Review: July-August 1972.

4. Naisbitt, John (1992) ***Mega Trends: Ten New Directions Transforming Our Lives,*** Warner Books, New York.

26

Economic Reforms

Its Implications on Trade Unions

S. Pravin

Introduction

This chapter examines the role of organised labour in India in a structural and historical context. It attempts to trace the economic, political and social effects of the trade union movement and its strategies over time. These effects are felt at enterprise—and/or firm-level, industry-level, regional and national level. The effect of changing economic conditions on the evolution of trade unions and bargaining institutions in largely urban labour markets in the post-independence period (1947 onwards) and contemporary issues affecting the organised labour movement in India today are then discussed in this chapter. The evolution of trade unionism (and industrial relations in general) is described in terms of the "four phases of unionism". This corresponds with structural changes in the economy and the effect of these changes is felt on labour markets as well as on the (very broadly defined) industrial relations arena.

Four Phases of Unionism

The first phase (1950 to mid-1960s) corresponds to an era of state planning and import substitution, when public-sector employment and public-sector unionism rose phenomenally. Unions and bargaining structures were highly-centralised; the two main federations were the nationalist Indian National Trade Union Congress and the communist All India Trade Union Congress. State intervention in the determination of wages and working conditions was the norm and "state-dominated pluralism" was the labour regime during this first phase.

The second phase (mid-1960s to 1979) is associated with a period of economic stagnation and political turmoil. Employment slowed down, there were massive inter-union rivalries, and industrial conflict increased. Centralised bargaining institutions started feeling the pressure of dissent from below, and both the Hind Mazdoor Sabha and the Centre of Indian Trade Unions made significant progress in the labour movement. The crisis culminated in the May 1974 railway strike that was followed by the 1975-77 Emergency Regime of Mrs. Indira Gandhi the then Prime Minister. An "involuted" pluralism dominated Indian labour relations during this second phase.

The third phase (1980-1991) corresponds to a period of segmented and uneven economic development. Decentralised bargaining and independent trade unionism enter the stage in a significant way. Two major strikes (the 1980/81 Bangalore public-sector strike and the 1982 Mumbai textile workers strike) marked this phase, and inter-state and inter-regional variations in the nature of labour-management regimes became much wider. In the more profitable economic sectors the unions gained, but in the unorganised and declining sector, workers lost out and unions were left with few strategies.

Finally, *the fourth phase of unionism (1991-2000)* represents the post-economic reform period. The stabilisation and structural adjustment programmes led to demands for increased labour market flexibility, especially employment flexibility. This has led to a recruitment freeze in many public sector sites, and unions in these sectors now have to cope with competition at local level. In non-viable public enterprises, unions are coming to terms with "voluntary" retirement schemes. In the early years of economic reform there were sincere attempts by all parties to engage in tripartite consultations, but there now seem to be several barriers to this form of engagement.

The crucial issues which are particularly relevant to the trade union movement are: the relationship between unionisation and employment; union structure and union density; wages and working conditions; changing patterns of industrial conflict; the (extremely important) issue of inter-state and regional variations in labour regimes and the question of women workers and unionisation (which are analysed).

Two Divergent Views About Unionism

There are two views for the unions as institutions, "two faces of unionism". the "monopoly" versus the "collective voice" view. These lead to a completely divergent analysis of the union as an economic and political institution; the policy implications of the two views are therefore fundamentally incompatible.

The first view analyses unions as large *monopolies* in the labour market whose basic objective is to increase their members' wages above the market level by restricting labour supply. This "wage mark-up" leads to a misallocation of human and capital resources, and is therefore not only economically suboptimal, but may also be socially undesirable in that it leads to greater inequalities within the workforce. In addition, strikes of all kinds impose an easily measurable loss on the economy. Finally, "union work rules", embedded in contract provisions often lower the productivity of both labour and capital by creating inflexibilities at the workplace.

In sharp contrast, the *collective voice* view asserts that unions have positive economic, political and social effects in pluralist democracies. The union's collective voice, determined by a "median voter", provides management with information on workplace and shopfloor issues, acting as a communication channel. This leads to the development and retention of specific skills, improves worker morale, provides conditions that eliminate quitting, and enables the union to pressure management to act fairly and efficiently in its daily operations. It is believed that unionised work environments are more productive than comparable non-unionised environments. Finally, Unions are socially beneficial as they represent the interests of lower income groups and vulnerable sections of society.

Using the above framework, Freeman and Medoff examine union effects on economic efficiency and the distribution of income. They also examine the social nature of the union as an institution of modern industrial society. Questions about economic efficiency usually relate to whether unions enhance productivity through their collective voice or whether they block technological change through "monopoly" routes, such as inflexible contract provisions. These often compel employers to substitute capital for labour and to invest in better "quality" labour. Thugs leads to productivity growth only in the sectors concerned, at the cost of overall employment growth in the economy. Questions relating to income distribution have to do with the effects of unions on non-unionised and unorganised workers. That is, do unions have positive or negative "spillover" effects on unorganised labour markets? Generally speaking, the higher the degree of unionisation in an economy, the greater are the positive spillover effects and the smaller the wage inequalities within the workforce. Finally, the "monopoly" view holds that unions fight for their own selfish interests at the expense of others, and blames their political lobbying for bureaucratic and corrupt practices. The "collective voice" view sees unions as the economic and political institutions of the weaker segments of society.

A Comparative Framework

It is now a truism that economic performance is related to the nature of labour market institutions. Economic performance here means controlling inflation and generating employment, which implies productivity growth. In the world of unions and collective negotiations, the key variables frequently cited as determining economic performance are: the level at which bargaining takes place (plant, firm, industry/ region, nation), and the nature of trade union structures.

While most commentators would agree that labour market flexibility is required for facilitating economic restructuring, heated controversy surrounds the question of how this flexibility is to be achieved. As transition will involve considerable social costs, what is to be the role of the state and the trade union movement in managing this transition?

Where does India fit in this comparative framework? The Indian economy represents a mix of all three bargaining levels and a variety of union structures. In the private corporate sector, plant-level bargaining takes place with enterprise based unions that may or may not be affiliated to parliamentary political parties. In public-sector enterprises, centralised trade union federations affiliated to political parties bargain with the state (as employer) at industry-and/or national-level. Central and state government employees in the service sector (transport, postal services, banking and insurance, police and firefighters, etc.) are usually represented by politically affiliated unions bargaining at national and/or regional level. Most of these centralised bargaining and union structures were stable during the period of planned industrialisation while India pursued a policy of import substitution. However, since the mid-1980s the economy has opened up to greater domestic and international competition, and these structures have come under increasing pressure to decentralize. These pressures have become stronger since the economic liberalisation programme was introduced in 1991, especially in the public sector. As in other countries, the state has gradually retreated from its earlier role of creating permanent employment and regulating union-management bargaining.

With economic liberalisation, competitive forces began to affect the structure of the union movement. In several private enterprises, "independent" rank-and-file led unions came into existence and engaged in informed and militant bargaining, often with multinational employers, securing substantial wage and non-wage gains in the process. More recently, since the liberalisation process officially begin in

1992, many of these centralised party-based unions have united under a common front to resist government attempts at privatisation and decentralisation in the public sector. However, the organised labour movement as a comprehensive organisation continues to face a fractured and segmented constituency, divided by skill, region, industry and ethnicity.

Unionisation and Employment

Over time, average annual growth rates in GDP have outstripped average annual growth rates in employment (Table 26.2) and employment elasticities in major sectors have fallen (Table 26.3). Table 26.1 shows the level of employment in the private and public sectors over the "four phases of unionism". This table clearly shows the following: in the first phase, public sector employment increased sharply and private sector employment increased marginally; during the second phase, public sector employment increased rapidly, whereas private sector employment remained sluggish; during the third phase, employment growth in both sectors sharply tapered off; and during the first few years of the fourth phase, growth in both sectors remained nearly static.

Table 26.1: Employment in the Organised Sector (000, 000s)

Four Phases of Unionisations	*Year (end of March)*	*Employment*		
		Public Sector	*Private Sector*	*Total*
The First Phase (1950 to mid-1960s)	1960	70.5	50.40	120.90
The Second Phase (mid-1960s to 1979)	1979	146.76	72.08	218.84
The Third Phase (1980 to 1991)	1991	190.58	76.75	267.33
The Fourth Phase (1992 to 2000)	2000	195.60	83.79	281.04

Table 26.2: Economic Indicators

Four Phases of Unionisation	*Plans*	*Annual Average Growth Rate*	
		GDP	*Employment*
The First Phase (1950 to mid-1960's	1951-56 (First Five-Year Plan)	3.6	0.39
	1956-61 (Second Five-Year Plan)	4.2	0.85
	1961-66 (Third Five-Year Plan)	2.8	2.03
The Second Phase (mid-1960's to 1979)	1967-69 (Annual Plans)	3.9	2.21
	1969-74 (Fourth Five-Year Plan)	3.3	1.99
	1974-79 (Fifth Five-Year Plan)	4.8	1.84
The Third Phase (1980-1991)	1980-85 (Sixth Five-Year Plan)	5.7	1.73
	1985-90 (Seventh Five-Year Plan)	5.8	1.89
	1990-92 (Annual Plans)	3.4	1.67
The Fourth Plan (1992-2000)	1992-97 (Eighth Five-Year Plan)	5.6	2.14
	1997-2002	6.51	2.49

Declining employment Elasticities imply that more output is attained with less employment. This could be due to the fact that employers are investing in more capital-intensive technologies, and that there has been a considerable amount of labour shedding in the private and public-sector enterprises since the mid-1980s. (Table 26.3) Unions can affect these employment elasticities by resisting technological change that increases the possibility of substituting between capital and labour and by limiting the availability of goods and services that compete with the output of unionised firms. In addition, union bargaining power varies indirectly with

Table 26.3: Employment Elasticities in Major Sectors

Sector	*1972-73 to 1977-78*	*1977-78 to 1983*	*1983 to 1987-88*	*1992 to 1997*
Agriculture	0.66	0.49	0.36	0.50
Mining and Quarrying	0.95	0.67	0.85	0.85
Manufacturing	0.55	0.42	0.26	0.50
Construction	0.35	1.00	1.00	1.00
Electricity, Gas and Water	1.00	0.74	0.48	0.50
Commerce				
Transport, Storage and Communication	0.76	0.92	0.35	0.60
Services	0.80	0.99	0.42	0.70
All Sectors	0.61	0.55	0.38	0.49

labour's share in total costs: unions are more powerful in relatively more capital-intensive firms and industries, as the demand for labour is relatively inelastic compared to labour-intensive sectors. Employers in capital-intensive firms find it much easier to meet union wage demands compared to employers in labour-intensive firms. Finally, it is in the interest of unions to raise the price of other inputs, particularly non-union labour, as this increases the cost of switching from union to non-union labour (see Borjas, 1996, pp. 126-127).

Table 26.4 presents a sectoral distribution of employment in the formal economy. We note two trends: since the third phase, growth in employment in manufacturing, both in the public and private sectors, has remained virtually stagnant; however, during the third phase, employment increased in public services. We also observe the phenomenal growth in employment in services (especially in the public sector) relative to manufacturing. Finally, except in manufacturing, the public sector continued to be the dominant employer in the organised economy. Table 26.5 shows a sector-wise ranking of the number and membership of trade unions that register and submit returns over the four phases of unionism. we observe that: (a) manufacturing leads in the number of unions and membership size; (b) construction lags behind most other sectors.

Table 26.4: Sectoral Distribution of Employment in the Formal Economy

(in 000, 000s)

Year (ending in March)		*1960*	*1979*	*1991*	*1998*
Agriculture and Allied	Public	1.80	4.08	5.6	5.4
	Private	6.70	8.41	8.9	8.8
	Total	8.50	12.49	14.5	14.2
Mining and Quarrying	Public	1.29	7.71	10.0	10.1
	Private	5.50	1.24	1.0	1.0
	Total	6.79	8.95	11.0	11.1
Manufacturing	Public	3.39	14.16	18.5	17.8
	Private	30.20	44.33	44.8	46.3
	Total	33.89	58.49	63.3	64.1
Power, Gas and water Supply	Public	2.24	6.34	9.1	9.4
	Private	0.40	0.34	0.4	0.4
	Total	2.64	6.68	9.5	9.8
Construction	Public	6.03	10.32	11.5	11.7
	Private	2.40	0.83	0.7	0.5
	Total	8.43	11.15	12.2	12.2
Services	Public	55.45	104.14	136	140
	Private	5.20	16.93	20.9	22.3
	Total	60.65	121.07	156.9	162.3

Table 26.5: Sector-wise Number and Membership of Trade Unions Submitting Returns

Sector	*The First Phase (1950 to mid-1960's*				*The Second Phase (mid-1960's to 1979*				*The Third Phase (1980 to 1991)*				*The Fourth Phase (1992 to 2000)*			
	1958-59				*1968*				*1986*				*1992*			
	No. of Unions Submitting Returns		*Membership of Unions (in '000s)*		*No. of Unions Submitting Returns*		*Membership of Unions (in '000s)*		*No. of Unions Submitting Returns*		*Membership of Unions (in '000s)*		*No. of Unions Submitting Returns*		*Membership of Unions (in '000s)*	
	Value	*Rank*	*Value*	*Rank*	*Value*	*Rank*	*Value*	*Rank*	*Value*	*Rank*	*Value*	*Rank*	*Value*	*Rank*	*Value*	*Rank*
Agriculture and Allied Activities	121	VIII	447	III	306	VI	487	III	258	VI	288	VI	381	VI	458	V
Mining and Quarring	123	VII	269	VI	205	VIII	330	VI	142	IX	164	VII	179	IX	154	VII
Manufacturing	2101	I	1203	I	4222	I	2077	I	3141	I	1707	II	3479	I	2014	I
Construction	66	IX	50	IX	117	IX	49	IX	158	VIII	314	V	214	VIII	327	VI
Electricity, Gas and Water	258	VI	87	VIII	269	VII	161	VIII	195	VII	115	IX	286	VII	327	VI
Commerce	602	II	141	V	1016	III	277	VI	456	V	121	VIII	451	V	127	VIII
Transport, Storage and Communication	454	III	583	II	734	IV	1146	II	833	III	2032	I	1201	III	880	III
Services	387	V	106	VII	1106	II	279	V	1605	II	918	III	1808	II	745	VI
Activities not Adequately Described	442	VI	141	V	434	V	194	VII	763	IV	700	IV	1074	VI	958	II

The "monopoly effects" of trade unions, together with inflexible labour laws, have enabled employers to move up their demand curves and have practically frozen employment growth in permanent unionised jobs. Due to union wage mark-ups, employers have increased the capital intensity of production, thereby raising productivity. But this route can only lead to jobless growth, clearly a sub-optimal outcome in a labour surplus economy. Those who oppose this view point out that wage increases took place not because of union power but largely because of an intensification of the labour process resulting from a decline in union power.

Union Structure and Union Density

The number of registered unions increased from 3,766 in 1950/51 to 55,784 in 1993, whereas the average size of those that submitted returns decreased from 577 to 460 during the same period (see Table 26.6). As stated earlier, not all registered trade unions submit returns on their membership. If we assume that the registered unions which submit returns are the large, established politically-affiliated unions with the organisational resources to engage in this process, whereas the registered unions that do not submit returns are the plant-based independent unions, then movements in the fifth column of table 26.6 (percentage of unions submitting returns to total registered unions) makes for an interesting interpretation. It appears that the centralised unions dominated during the first phase, lost ground during the second phase, and then sharply declined during the third phase, dropping to an all-time low of only 12 per cent in 1993. Although this is only one possible reading of the data, several detailed case studies have also pointed to these movements in union structure (Ramswamy, 1988; Davala, 1992).

Wages and Working Conditions

Table 26.7 provides data on the movement of the consumer price index for industrial workers and urban non-manual employees across the four phases of unionism. Table 26.9 provide some data on the movement of nominal (a general index for 12 industries) and real wage rates (in organised manufacturing).

Table 26.6: Number of Registered Unions and Membership of Unions Submitting Returns

Four Phases of Unionisation	*Year*	*Number of Reg. Trade Unions*	*Number of Union Submitting Returns*	*Percentage of Unions Submitting Returns*	*Member of Unions Submitting Returns (in thousands)*			*Average Membership Per Union Submitting Returns*
					Men	*Women*	*Total*	
The First Phase (1950 to mid-1960s)	1960	10811	6588	60.9	3532	391	3923	596
The Second Phase (mid-1960 to 1979)	1979	34430	10021	29.1	6915	559	7474	746
The Third Phase (1980 to 1991)	1991	53535	8418	15.7	5507	594	6100	725
The Fourth Phase (1992-2000)	1998	55784	6806	12.7	2667	467	3134	460

Table 26.7: Index Number of Consumer Prices (1960-61 to 1998)

Four Phases of Unionisation	*Year*	*Index*		*Percentage increase Over Previous Year*	
		Industrial Workers (Base 1982=100)	*Urban Non-Manual Employee*	*Industrial Workers*	*Urban Non-Manual Workers*
The First Phase (1950 to mid-1960s)	1960	20	19	0.56	0.49
The Second Phase (mid-1960s to 1979)	1979-80	67	58	2.2	3.4
The Third Phase (1980-1991)	1990-91	193	161	11.6	11.0
The Four Phase (1992-2000)	1998	296	231	8.9	5.7

Standard neoclassical economic theory would argue that increased global trade raises the earnings of unskilled workers relative to those of skilled workers in a country such as India, which has unlimited supplies of the former. This implies that India's exports are largely unskilled labour-intensive products. Nambiar et al. (1999) found that wage disparity for the period 1980/81 to 1992/93 increased but only marginally. In addition, they found that the disparity rises from less skill-intensive to more skill-intensive sectors. To the extent that the union voice reduces earnings inequality within the unionised workforce, employers, especially in the private sector, have "manufactured consent" with the unions in setting up ingenious pay incentive systems.

Industrial conflict

Even though union density is very low by international standards, India loses more days every year as a result of strikes and lockouts than almost any other country (ILO, 1997/98, pp. 253-254). This raises the classic question of whether conflict reflects union power or union weakness? It certainly indicates that the basic premise of industrial pluralism, the regulation of conflict, has not been achieved.

The answer to this question in India depends on whether workers resist strikes or whether employers are on the offensive during lockouts. Table 26.8 presents some time series conflict data. We note that during the third and fourth phase, the number of lockouts rose whereas the number of strikes decreased. The sample applies to the number of workdays lost and the number of workers involved. Until 1989 industrial conflict occurred mainly in the private sector in terms of number of disputes, workdays and wages lost, and lost production, although the actual number of workers involved in disputes was higher in the public sector in the early 1980s. Since 1990, however, industrial disputes in both sectors have increased significantly (Venkataratnam, 1996).

Inter-state Variations

One critical reason why labour law reform has been continually debated but ultimately shelved, is the lack of a

Table 26.8: Industrial Conflict (1950-1998)

Four Phases of Unionisation		*The first Phase (1950 to mid-1960*	*The Second Phase (mid-1960s to 1979)*	*The Third Phase (1980 to 1991)*	*The Fourth Phase (1992 to 2000)*
	Year	*1960*	*1979*	*1991*	*1998*
Number of Disputes	Strikes	1240	2709	1278	903
	Lockouts	117	339	532	402
	Total	1357	3048	1810	1305
No. of Workers involved in Disputes (000's)	Strikes	432	2714	872	653
	Lockouts	80	159	470	328
	Total	512	2873	1342	981
No. of Work days lost in Disputes (000's)	Strikes	2969	35804	12428	5652
	Lockouts	1950	8050	14000	11381
	Total	4919	43854	26428	17033

Table 26.9: Index Number of Wage Rate (Base 1063-65 = 100)

Phases of Unionisation	*Year*	*General Index for Twelve Industries*
The Second Phase (mid-1960's to 1979)	1979	376.6
The Third Phase (1980-1991)	1991	1304.9
The Fourth Phase (1992-2000)	2000	2086.7

consensus within the labour movement and across different state governments. Since economic liberalisation, every state government has attempted to attract national and international capital. This has involved significant media costs, and many states have even hired international consultants to draw up economic renewal agendas. A vital consideration in this post-liberalisation discourse has been the question of work ethic and comparative union militancy.

The number and membership of registered unions that submit returns according to the four phases of unionism. Although the data are sketchy, some trends can be discerned: (a) the more industrial states of Maharashtra and Tamil Nadu have maintained their high rankings through the four phases; (b) West Bengal ranks high during the first two phases, but we could not find comparable data for the following two phases; and (c) Gujarat is doing well during the fourth phase, no doubt reflecting the rise of unions affiliated to the Bharatiya Janata Party.

Women Workers and Unionisation

The percentage of women members in trade unions that submit returns rose from 7.3 per cent in 1951-52 to 10.3 per cent in 1985; in 1992 it was 11.6 per cent (see Table 26.5). Detailed information on the extent of unionisation among women workers is not available, although there are rich case studies of specific sectors/industries where women workers form a substantial section of the workforce.

There is considerable controversy on whether there has been an increasing "feminisation" of the workforce over the last decade, especially since the liberalisation process began. Deshpande and Deshpande (1992, p. 1998) assessed the short-run impact of liberalisation on female employment and participation. They found that: (a) in urban areas, both male and female participation rates increased after liberalisation; (b) gender-based wage differentials widened among regular wage/salaried rural and urban workers; (c) women workers were increasingly taking to self-employment and to the informal sectors as their proportion in manufacturing declined even though women's share in the urban workforce rose slightly.

Although in several countries globalisation has led to feminisation of the manufacturing workforce, Banerjee (1997) argues that in India the reverse has taken place: women's opportunities in the secondary sectors have fallen drastically in all states. However, there has been a slight increase in work opportunities for rural women in agriculture and some gains were made in the tertiary sector. According to Banerjee (1997, p. 433), it would be unrealistic to expect a "mechanical reproduction of international trends in a country the size of India". Women workers account for only 17 per cent of the manufacturing workforce that in turn is only 13 per cent of the total workforce. She goes on to suggest that even if the entire export sector (commodities) were staffed by women, "it is doubtful that this would result in a ferminisation of the Indian manufacturing workforce as a whole".

Given that a substantial section of women workers in India today are engaged as "homeworkers" in several industries (such as bangle makers, cobblers, dye makers, flower workers, kite makers, lace makers, leather workers, etc.), it is encouraging that the Indian trade union movement, under the leadership of the Self-Employed Women's Association (SEWA) has taken a lead in drafting an ILO convention on homeworkers.

The Major Findings Are:

- In both the public and private sectors, employment in industry has substantially declined, especially since the economic reforms; however, employment in public sector services has increased since the third phase of unionism. The trend in most industries is to reduce permanent employment and to use more contract, temporary and casual workers;
- Trade unions have performed well in profitable industries, mainly in private (often multinational) enterprises, but also in some public sector firms with decentralised bargaining structures. However, they lack new strategies in the older and declining sectors of production where industry-wise bargaining structures are typically the norm. Whereas workers and unions in non-

viable public enterprises are facing closure and an uncertain future, centralised unions representing employees in public services remain strong due to the monopolistic nature of their product markers;

- The number of plant-based independent and unaffiliated trade unions has risen, which may have caused a decline in the power of centralised affiliated unions, especially in the private sector;
- Women workers are largely concentrated in the self-employed and unorganised sectors with little representation in trade unions. Non-governmental organisations have made considerable efforts to organize women in these vulnerable occupations.

Conclusion

The role of trade unions, should concentrate on the unionisation of informal sector workers. Given the low levels of unionizaiton in India (relative to comparable countries), and given that a large proportion of workers are employed in the informal sector (a trend which is likely to intensify with the economic reforms currently underway), the trade union movement has to make a determined effort to organize informal sector workers. This calls for concerted action on the part of the centralised trade union federations in alliance with other social movements and non-governmental organisations. It is only through this kind of extensive mobilisation that "public action" can be triggered to "level-up" the labour market institutions of vulnerable sections of the workforce.

The organised labour movement will have to come to terms with global competition, technology, new industrial organisation and structural/demographic changes in the workforce. The earlier, relatively insulated, systems for regulating employment will have to give way to more market-sensitive and flexible systems, ultimately even in the public sphere. Unions, especially in the service sector, will have to become sensitive to consumer needs. In the private sector, trade unions have adapted their structures in response to the decentralisation of industrial relations, but these adjustments are painful and difficult in the public sector. There is no other way but to increase membership, which means organizing vulnerable workers in the informal sector. This is the most obvious way for unions to win broader community support. Finally, trade unions can only gain by cooperating and working together. Perhaps the new millennium will witness a series of mergers leading to a united and independent labour movement.

REFERENCES

1. Banerjee, N. (1997) "How Real is the Bogey of Fermentation?", *The Indian Journal of Labour Economics,* Vol. 40, July-Sept.
2. Borjas, G. (1996) *Labour Economics* (Singapore, McGraw-Hill).
3. Davala, S. (ed.) (1992) *Employment and Unionisation in Indian Industry.* (New Delhi).
4. Deshpande, S: Deshapnde, L.K. (1992): "New Economic Policy and Female Employment", in *Economic and Political Weekly,* Vol. 27 (Oct.).
5. ILO (1997-98) World Labour Report, Industrial Relations, Democracy and Social Stability (Geneva, ILO).
6. Mazumdar, D. (1997) "Labour Markets, Trade Patterns and Workers Living Standard", in *Economic and Political Weekly,* Vol. 32, (1-14 March).
7. Nambiar, R.G, Mungekar, B.L. and Tadas, G.A. (1999) "Is Import Liberalisation Hurting Domestic Industry and Employment?", in *Economic and Political Weekly,* Vol. 34, (13-19 Feb.).
8. Ramasamy, E.A. (1988) *Worker Consciousness and Trade Union Response* (New Delhi, Oxford University Press).
9. Sen. A. (1996) "Economic Reforms, Employment and Poverty; Trends and Options", in *Economic and Political Weekly,* Vol. 31, (Sept.).
10. Venkataratnam, C.S. (1996) "Industrial Relations in India", Paper Presented to a Seminar on "Labour Market and Industrial Relations in South Asia: Emerging Issues and Policy Options" (New Delhi, India International Centre, 18-20 Sept.).

Transformation of Local Human Resources to Cope with Economic Liberalisation and Globalisation

Dr. Samwel Kakuko Lopoyetum

Globalisation and Modern Business Management

Globalisation means adoption and presentation of global outlook for the business strategies and management orientation aiming at enhancing global reach and facing competitiveness, incorporating world-wide manufacturing systems, marketing policies, financial flows, logistical system/approach. In the era of globalisation executives and managers must be trained in worldwide operations and they are recruited from many countries (usually obtained at low cost and investments returns are high). For examples: Honda, Casio, MacDonalds (serving food around the world), IBM corp, Unilever, General Motors, Royal Dutch/Shell Groups, Exxon, Ford Motor Company, Toyota (Japan), British Petroleum, Mobil, General Electronics, etc.

Changing Globalisation Approach from Ethnocentric to Geocentric Orientation

In the earlier days, International Business and Management was conducted with an Ethnocentric outlook meaning that the operations are based on the parent organisations, whereas the Polycentric attitude is based on the notion that is the foreign subsidiaries, staffed by local nationals shall be given great deal of managerial freedom with the assumptions that they have best understanding and knowledge of the local environment but Regio-centric orientations favours the staffing on a regional basis and the Modern Multinational Corporations (MNCs) has this type of approach. They view total organisation as an interdependent system operating in many overseas countries having collaborations with Communication flowing in both direction. They have international outlook with key staffing position filled by managers of different nationalities and goes beyond narrow nationalistic viewpoint.

The combination of the terminologies Globalisation, Business and Management field leads to the adoptions of Global Management functions and principles (Internationalisations of management function and principles) i.e., Globalisation of POSTCORB. In fact, top International firms such as IBM Corporation, Oracle Corporation have already announced plans to move white collar jobs and staff to India.

It is estimated that, by the end of 2004, one out of 10 jobs in the USA information-technology sector will shift or move to India. The offshore outsourcing ramps up and dislocation of IT jobs in the USA would lead to potential loss of talent knowledge and organisational performance, loss of intellectual asset, etc. in developed countries such as USA. One out of every ten jobs within US-based IT vendors, IT service providers will move to the emerging markets and one of every 20 IT jobs within user enterprise. India, is the worlds top beneficiary of Business Process Outsourcing (BPO) among large companies (according to Diane Morello, President and Director, Gartner) and part of the reasons are cost, low Billings rates, fiscal soundness, the quality, the value and process advantages. The need to enhance capacity building and operational performance of emerging organisations plus the promotion of Indigenous micro-enterprises would be essential to attract the best skills and professionals shifting from developed world particularly in the ERA of Globalisation.

Rural Industrial Villages in the Global Modern Business Management and Human Resource Management

We need to promote industrial adaptation of rural villages at a factor Rate and faster modes and faster modes to cope-up with Globalisation. We are living in a *"global village dealing with Global Business and management"*. Several decades ago, *Marshall McLuhan* prognosticated that, the advancement in technology and communication technology would transform the World into a Global Village and today we are all citizen of the Global Village. It needs global strategies and approaches when we are dealing with management and business strategies. The geographical and psychological distance has been reduced tremendously such that you can take breakfast at Gandhigram Rural University and take lunch in Singapore, easily take supper in Tokyo (Japan) and relax your mind at midnight in New York city (USA). Can you imagine this scenario!!!. An international executive or officer (manager) or international chief executive officer (ICEO) can supervise a corporate office located at Madras in the morning and supervise another office at Singapore in the evening and take major decision on Business and Management in the corporate office headquartered in New York next day!!. We can refer this phenomenon as feasible and practical movement of Human resources and manpower in Globalisation era therefore the Globalisation of world economy and management is emerging swiftly. In other words, there is extreme Globalisation, of Trade, Commerce, Business, Industries, Manufacturing and almost everything on earth including electronic transfer of money within the shortest time possible!!. But there should be proper development and growth of Human resource and personnel systems in Developing countries like *India and Kenya* at a micro-level to meet the faster rate of Globalisation. Developing countries need to develop new theories of Human resources management and personnel practices in order to meet the new emerging global perspective of Modern Business Management, Industries and Commerce. If the nineteenth Century belonged primarily to Europe, and Twentieth Century primarily to the North America, then the Twenty First Century could as well belong to Asia and Africa.

In the era of Globalisation, open market economy and Economic Liberalisation Distance is no longer a problem. Distance barriers has been reduced (space and time) due to advancement of Science and Technology. The Technology such as Microwaves Telephone, Cellular tech, Data voice mail, pagers (Message services), satellite phone and communication system (Mobile Terminals) have really reduced this world into a global village of Business, Industry and Commerce.

In the era of LPGs, I would advocate for the globalisation with local touch (micro-level approaches) and Transformation of Local Human Resources to directly face Globalisation and economic liberalisations and many changes happening within the country itself. No changes can be brought to the country from outside the country. We need to achieve Afro-Asian Collaboration & Cooperation to Dominate the World Economy by 2050. In order to achieve this mission and dreams we need global brands produced at African village level and Asian village level. For this to succeed, we need local transformation of Human Resources, personnel, and manpower to meet the emerging challenges and seize the opportunities created by Globalisations. This can only be achieved by globalisation of national economy and trade and Commerce through local touch (micro-level transformation approach) and upgradation of technology, modernisation of traditional Industries and economy. Unless we experience substantial changes within the local, regional, state and national levels, it is not possible to achieve the vision of 2050 (as stated above). Africa and Asia may not enter into Globalisation process of the world economy if local transformational approach (micro-level approaches) are abandoned. We must all work hard and strive hard to achieve this noble vision and mission. The most important problem facing Indian and African economy is how to transform the indigenous Business/Trade/Commerce/management/into a Global business? The process of transformation of local Human resources would take two fashions viz: (1) Internal changes within the organisation itself i.e. Development of Dynamic Organisations and Management and R&D. (2) Coping up with the external changes. Pre-requisites for creating and enhancing the level of Globalisation of Human Resource and Personnel system: (1) Enhancing and Creating new infrastructure (2) Business Planning and Marketing (3) Organisation must respond to Globalisations and Economic Liberalisations (EL) (4) Indigenous Organisational initiative to open doors for internationalisation and R&D (5) To inculcate the habit of Penetrating the web of patents (6) Attracting and retaining Qualified professionals (7) Protection of Intellectual Property Right (IPR) (8) Export (Indirect & Direct Exporting) (9) Merger and acquisitions (M&As) (10) Strategic alliance and International collaborations.

Evolving New Pattern of Modern Business Managements and Human Resources

The need to evolve new pattern of modern Business Management in the LPGs era is highly imperative in areas such as (1) Concern for high quality of products (intangible and Tangible products) and manufacturing process. (2) Use of Information Technology (IT) and advanced communication technology. (3) Efficiency and effectiveness in their production operations. (4) Inculcating Self-Confidence and Effective leadership. (5) Use of modern management strategies and planning. (6) Professionalisation of management process and modernisation of machines (7) Quality upgradation. (8) Necessary Financial support measures. (10) Promotion and development of new enterprises (11) Provision of high quality inputs and technical assistance/knowledge. (12) Minimisation of all types of risks. Moreover, in a country like India with growing unemployment and Educated Unemployed youth problems, there is an imperative need to manufacture and promote industrial co-operatives, tiny and small industries, Medium scale industries Agricultural and non-agricultural enterprises, farm and profitable non-farm activities. The prevalence of educated unemployed youth, can be involved in the modern management culture and the spirit will eventually grow. In areas such as IT and computerisation young and energetic youthful people can enter into profitable entrepreneurship. All these can only be possible through (1) Continuos Education and Training (2) Consultancy and Expertisation (3) Motivation and encouragement (4) Development of effective management skills and

Development programmes (5) Creation of awareness (6) Use of entrepreneurship development programemems (EDPs) through reputed institutions and centres for entrepreneur development (CED for example, CED centre located at Gandhigram rural university. It is offering suitable Entrepreneurship skills, Training and Education programmes to rural youths and Self-Help Groups (SHGs). The performance analysis of the CED centre located at Gandhigram Rural University is analysed in this paper as a case study: *A Case Analysis of Centre of Entrepreneurship Development-GRI.*

Establishment; CED was registered as society under the Tamil Nadu Government Society Act and is open of the centres of Gandhigram Rural Institute Extending its outreach Programems to the entrepreneurial community.

Objectives: The major objectives of this centre are (1) To serve as a national Centre for conducting a variety of Training Programems Like; Entrepreneurship Awareness Camp [EAC], Entrepreneurship Development Programmes [EDP}, Training for Entrepreneur Development Trainers [EDT], Training for Small Enterprise Management Assistants [SEMA] (2) To develop methods and models suited to rural enterprises. (3) To develop entrepreneurial resource materials for CED and for the benefit of other institutions and agencies. (4) To carry out consultancy and Information services to Entrepreneurs (5) To carry out entrepreneurial follow-up service programmes.

Target Groups. The target groups are: Rural Women and Men, Rural Artisans, Educated Unemployed Youth, Students from Collages/Universities, Ex-servicemen Disabled persons, Women Self-help Groups [SHGs]. Outreach Programes of CED; The Centre for Entrepreneurship Development are made up of 32 key areas, (See table 27.1).

Other Key Activities

The following are some of the other activities of CED; (1) Formation of Alumini Enterpreneurs Forum (2) CED-Tailoring centre for women (3) Linkages with government agencies/Banks /NGOs/Other CEDs in the state, district-level, KVKs, Departments of GRI/Gandhigram Trust, etc.

Table 27.1: Centre for Entrepreneurship Development

Sl. No.	*Nature of programmes (1998-2002)*	*No. of programmes*
1.	EDP Training Programmes	9
2.	Skill Development Training Programme for Rural Artisans (Potters, Carpenters, Blacksmiths]	4
3.	Seminars Organised	9
4.	Workshop Conducted	1
5.	Business Meet Organised	9
	Total Programmes	32
	Total Beneficiaries	1277

Comprehensive Business Profile and Projects Documents maintained by the CED are: Herbal Agri. Business, Peper Bag Manufacturing, Bakery, Food Processing, Micro-Enterprises for Women, Production and Marketing of Food Items, Fur Doll Manufacturing, Coir Industry, Women Entrepreneuurs Case Analysis.

Table 27.2: Growth Development and Achievement: 1998-2002

Sl. No.	*Nature of Programme*	*Period*	*Beneficiaries*	*Number*
1	*2*	*3*	*4*	*5*
1.	Women EDP Training Programme Sponsored by DIC, Dindigul (1998-99 & 1999-2000)	8 weeks	Women	80
2.	EDP Training Programme for Holy Cross College B.S. Economics Students (8.2.99 to 22.2.99 sponsored by the Holy Cross College, Tiruchirapally.	20 days	College Students	45
3.	PMRY Training Programme (1999) Sponsored by D.I.C. Dindigul.	10 days	Men and Women	32
4.	EDP Training Programme for Ex-Servicemen on Poultry Farming-Broiler, sponsored by the Directorate of Ex-service-men's Welfare, Dindigul (15.4.99 to 25.5.99).	40 days	Ex-servicemen	08

(*Contd.*)

1	*2*	*3*	*4*	*5*
5.	Summer EDP Training Programme (May-June 99) Officered by CED, GRI, 2000-2001.	2 months	Enterprising Women, House-wife, School and College Students	141
6.	Computer Training Programme for Ex-Service-men, Dindigul, Sponsored by the Directorate of Ex-service-men's Welfare, Dindigul (1999).	12 weeks	Ex-Servicemen	03
7.	Regular EDP Training Programme in 20 Trades (1999) on going Programme of CED, GRI.	12 months	College Students, Future Generation Entrepreneurs	45
8.	Week-end EDP Training Programme for Students of GRI (1999) on going Programme of CED, GRI	30 days	GRI students	60
9.	EDP Training Programme for Ex-Servicemen (T.V. Mechanism), Dindigul (2002)	10 weeks	Ex-Servicemen	08

Table 27.3: Skill Development Training Programme for Rural Artisans: 1998-2002

Sl. No.	*Nature of Programme*	*Period*	*Beneficiaries*	*Number*
1.	Skill Development Training Programme for Potters-Sponsored by Department of A.C.E. and Extn, GRI, funded by NCRI (2002)	15 days	Potters	15
2.	Skill Development Training Programme for Carpenters-Sponsored by dept. of ACE and Extn. GRI, funded by NCRI (2001).	15 days	Carpenters	15
3.	Skill Development Training Programme for Blacksmiths—Sponsored by dept. of ACE and Extn. GRI, funded by NCRI (2001).	15 Days	Blacksmiths	15
4.	Skill Development Training Programme in Tailoring and Embroidering sponsored by CED (2002).	1 month	Women	13

Funds Generated

The Centre for Entrepreneurship Development has generated funds to the tune of Rs. 42,551 between the period March 1998 and March 2002 after meeting out the expenses of the centre.

Table 27.4: Details of Fund Generations

Sl. No.	*Year (As on March)*	*Funds Generated*
1.	1998-99	350
2.	1999-2000	17,502
3.	2000-2001	54,365
4.	2001-2002	42,551

The Impact of the CED and Training Programmes

(i) Ex-Servicemen (2 nos.) have started their enterprises. Assembling and servicing of Electronic goods (Batlagund) and another Ex-Serviceman has established a poultry unit (Sempatti).

(ii) Rural Artisans are self-employed (Chinnalapatti, Nadupatti).

(iii) Women Trainees have become entrepreneurs of Tailoring Units (Dindigul).

(iv) Rural youth, trained in Electronics trade has established a service centre (Thirupur).

(v) Developed entrepreneurial culture among the potential rural entrepreneurs.

(vi) Motivated the student Community to start enterprises (Trichy, Holycross college students).

(vii) Motivated the WSHS to start Micro Enterprises.

Proposed Activities for the X Plan Period

(i) Conducting Seminar on Entrepreneurial opportunities for GRI student community—2002.

(ii) Conducting Orientation Training Programme in Entrepreneurship to Technical, Management and other students: District-wise, in Tamil Nadu.

(iii) EDP-Training Programme—PRA Approach to Women Self-Help Groups in Tamil Nadu.

(iv) Workshop on SHGs and Alleviation of Poverty.

(v) Workshop on marketing opportunities and strategies for the products of WSHGs.

(vi) Creation of Women Entreprenerur's Cell.

(vii) Identification of Business Opportunities in the districts of Tamil Nadu.

(viii) Preparation of project profile in Innovative Business-natural dye, Herbal Agri-Business, and Recycling of waste materials.

Targeting the right groups such as technical employees, young engineers, traders, artisans/craftsman. In fact, Tamil Nadu state is among the leading states in turning over qualified engineers and technicians. These engineers can start self-employment and income generating enterprises. They can create internet enterpreneurship, website creation, youth clubs for promoting and developing profitable enterprises, Cooperative companies, Manufacturing Organisations, Business and marketing organisations etc.,

Constraints in Coping-up with Changes in Modern Business Management in Globalisation era

1. Insufficient industrial and market information. 2. Inadequate technological knowledge and skills. 3. Ineffective and insufficient infrastructure development. 4. Lack of start-up capital and low base capital. 5. Lack of business planning skills and knowledge. 6. Lack of capital for expansion and modernisation. 7. Illiteracy (men and women). 8. Inadequate infrastructure facilities, i.e. industrial sheds. 9. Lack of managerial skill to start and manage the enterprise. 10. Lack of risk taking ability. 11. Not sure of sustained support from Government and other agencies. 12. They are economically and politically weak. 13. Low access to business services, i.e. computer services, information processing services, R&D,

marketing services, human development services, etc. 14. Constraints of quality of human resources and personnel 15. Low lobbying capacity, 16. Most of the Small Scale and Medium scale industries are affected by globalisation and liberalisation policies, including unilateral liberalisation. 17. Business and Trade are affected by Multilateral trading rules under agreements of world training (WTO). 18. Affected by liberalisation of services/infrastructure (exogenous forces influencing the Indian economic and management system).

Strategies and Methods of Harvesting Local Manpower and Transformation of the Local Human Resources to Face Economic Liberalisation and Globalisation

They are given under this paragraph. There must be sufficient, efficient and effective local human resource planning in the country. Utilisation of the Educated unemployed youth should be taken into account in manpower planning. While carrying out identification process, it must suit the local needs and must be motivated. Suitable persons must be identified and production of quality local human resources in highly essential. They can form "educated unemployed youth cooperatives energies can be utilised and employed. Therefore, cooperative why is the best way to transform the local human resources into viable and profitable units. Local Human Resources is the total knowledge and skills, creative and innovative ability, talents, aptitable of organisation the.

Strategies for Enhancing and Developing Global Management Through Local (Micro-level) Approach

A number of strategies have been attempted to ensure that Indian managers are made competent in the liberalised and globalised economy. These stratgies will enhance and develop management and Administration of organisations/ Enterprises in the long-run. The entire process can be started by managing the eight 'Ms' effectively and efficiently.

Managing the Eight *M's* for Effective and Efficient Enterprises Development

While managing the Organisational enterprises the eight *M's* must be managed properly. The eight *M's* are:

(a) Men (b) Materials (c) Machine (d) Methods (e) Milieu (environment (c) Measurement (g) Money (h) Markets. In order to manage these *M's* the following are essential pre-requisites and inputs: (1) The entrepreneur must have the following characteristics viz., initiative and independence, industries, co-operation, ability to learn, ability to work, team spirit, leadership skill, communication skills and negotiation skills, capacity to analyse, commitment and conviction, risk taking, hopeful, about future and search for new environment and high personal efficiency, morality, time management, business acumen, self-confidence and perseverance, quick decision making. 2. A strategy to develop members interest in industrial entrepreneurship and promote self-awareness in organisational members. 3. Expand the role of support organisations. 4. Access to adequate funds and financial support (low rate of interest). 5. Developing business planning and managerial capacity. 6. Improving marketing and management. 7. Development of technological capabilities. 8. Modernisation of machines and equipments. 9. Better policy support. 10. Adoption of management development programmes and provision of consultancy services. 11. Provision of training and education in co-operative entrepreneurships. 12. Undertaking research and development (product and processes development). 13. Business and economic diversification. 14. Balance business and cultural practices. If all these factors are addressed in the most honest and appropriate manner with political support, the process of transformation of business and management at the micro-level into macro-level and globalisation can be made possible in the era of open market economy and globalised environment.

REFERENCES

1. Egerstorm, et al, (1996), Seizing Control; *"The International Market Power of Cooperative"*, Lone Dalc Press, Rochester.
2. Gerrity Robert, (1991), *"Globalisation, Vital Speeches of the Day 58"*, (No. VI) 52-58.
3. Kennedy Tracey, (1997), *"U.S. Cooperative Extend Farmers Reach Into Global Markets"*; Age Exporter; 12-13.

4. Seipel, et al, (1997) *"Cooperatives in a Changing Global Food System; Washington"*, DC USA Department of Agriculture, Rural Business Cooperative Service.

5. Lancy Lobo, (2002), *Globalisation; Hindu Nationalism and Christians in India,* Rawat Publications, Jaipur/New Delhi.

6. Ninan Koshy (Ed), (2002), *Globalisation; The Imperial Thrust of Modernity,* Vikas Adhyayam Kendra Publications, Malad West Bombay.

7. Louis Kraar, (March 1989), *"Your Rivals Can Be Your Allies"*, Fortune pp. 66-76.

8. George, V, Priovolos, (Sept. 1988), *"Small Businesses Can Benefit from European Economic Changes if they Take Precautions"* Marketing News p. 6.

9. Nan Stone, (May-June 1989), *"The Globalisation of Europe; An interview with Wisse Dekker"* Harvard Business Review pp. 90-95.

10. Benard Avishai, (July-August 1991), *"A European Platform for Global Competition; An Interview with VW's Carl Hahn"*, Harvard Business Review, pp. 103-113.

11. Alex Miller and Gregory G. Dess, (1996), *"Strategic Management"* Published by International Edition, North America.

12. Batra G.S. and Bhatia B.S. (1997), *"Strategic Management of Cooperative Banking in Punjab in M.C. Garg"*, (Ed.) Cooperative Credit and Banking in Punjab, New Delhi: Deep and Dep Publications: 149.

13. Guha S.K., Thakurta (March 2001), *"Strategic Management in Project Planning"*, The Management Account Vol. 36, No. 3, p. 185.

14. Jhon L. Thompson, (1990), *"Strategic Management—Awareness and Change"*, London: Chapman & Hall.

15. John, M. Riley, (2002), *"Stakeholders in Rural Development, Critical Collaboration in State and NGO Partnership"*, New Delhi: Sage Publications.

16. Michael. A., et al, (2001), *"Strategic Management—Competitiveness and Globalisation"*, Published by an International Thomson Company, New York.

17. Rastogi T.N. (March 2002), *"Changing Scenario of Management Discipline in the 21st Century"* The Indian Journal of Public Administration Vol. XLVI, No. 1, p. 149.

18. Ricky W. Griffin., (1997), *"Management"*, Published by Laxman Chand Arya, New Delhi.

19. Samwel Kakuko Lopoyetum, Veluraj. R. (April 2003), *"Fundamental Management Dimensions of Cooperatives: An Analysis of Major Imperative Issues"*, India Cooperative Review Vol. 40, No. 4, pp. 239-247.

20. Srinivasan, R. (2002), *"Strategic Management"* the Indian Context Publication by Prentice-Hall of India (Pvt.), New Delhi.

21. Subburaj, B., Samwel Kakuko Lopoyetum, Velanganni. S. (June 2003), *"Strength and Weakness of Cooperative—An Introspection in the Era of open market economic system"*, Tamil Nadu Journal of Cooperation, Vol. 3, No. 8, pp. 27-30.

22. Subburaj. B., Ravichandran, K., Samwel Kakuko Lopoyetum; (Feb. 2003), *"Appropriatesness of Management Strategies; Are they Myth to Cooperatives'*, The Cooperator, Vol. 40, No. 8, pp. 338-340.

23. Thompson and Strickland, (2001), *"Strategic Management—Concepts and Cases"*, New Delhi: Tata McGraw Hill.

24. Heinz Weihrich and Harold Koontz, (1993), *"Management—Global Perspective"*, (Inter Edition), MacGraw Hill Inc, New Delhi.

28

Economic Reforms and HRD in India—Achievements and Future Strategy

S Natchathira Jothi
M. Jeyakani

Prof. Len Nadler in American Society of Training of Development Conference first used the term Human Resource Development (HRD) during 1969. The concept of HRD includes all the activities and processes undertaken to promote the intellectual, moral, psychological, social, cultural and economic development of the individuals. It helps the human beings to acquire the maximum level of potential and assist them to become a vital resource for the society. HRD attempts to identify the hidden or special or unique qualities in people, to develop their competencies and to bring about changes in the whole system. These steps may improve the skills of the human beings and prepare them to meet emerging challenges more confidently. It ensures the achievement of individual, organisational and social goals. It assists the people to understand their roles better. It not only increases the skill of the people but also improves their capabilities in utilizing other resources better. This will result in increase in productivity, production and national income. By converting the people in to skilled labour, HRD helps the country to improve the standard of living of the people and to solve the problems like poverty, unemployment, etc.

Human resource is the real wealth of the Nation. Acceding to Prof. Alfred Marshall, the most valuable of all capital is that invested in human beings. Economic reforms introduced in our country successfully solved one of its objectives of setting right the Balance of Payment Crisis. It still attempts to take structural changes in the economy. The major drawback of economic reforms in our country is the reduction in employment opportunities and employment generation. People thought that liberalisation and globalisation might bring in foreign investment and improve employment opportunities. But actually due to economic reforms and withdrawal of protection and subsidies many public sector enterprises reduce their staff strength. Ban on recruitment in Government departments, closure of many private sector units due to their inability to face competition from Multinational Companies (MNCs) etc. leads to deceleration in employment generation. In such circumstances Economists feel that only HRD can make people more competent to face the challenges posed by in our country MNCs. This chapter attempts to study the HRD Programmes in Economic Reforms Era in our country.

HRD in India

HRD programmes gain importance in our country since such programmes could help the country to convert the excess population in to a reservoir of skilled labourers. Achieving higher growth with social justice is the major objective of Indian Economic Policy. National Human Development Report declared that the three dimensions of well-being are longevity, education and command over resources.

Human development efforts were taken even during early 80s in our country. Increase in expenditure on education is one of the essential measures for HRD. Perusal of data exhibited in Table 28.1 shows a gradual and steady increase in the Gross Domestic Product (GDP) during the period 1981-1997. During the same period the total expenditure on education and training also increased to Rs. 51,683 crore in 1997 from Rs. 4436 crore during 1981.

To analyse the growth rates of GDP and the total expenditure on Education and Training, *Semi-log Growth*

Table 28.1: Educational Expenditure in India (Rs. Crore)

Year	*Total Education and Training Expenditure*	*% change in Total Education and Training Expenditure*	*Gross Domestic Product*	*% change in Gross Domestic Product*	*Education expenditure as % of GDP*
1981	4436	—	143256	—	3.10
1982	5736	29.31	158761	10.82	3.61
1983	6229	8.59	185779	17.02	3.35
1984	7456	19.70	207109	11.48	3.60
1985	8713	16.86	232370	12.20	3.75
1986	9749	8.79	258225	11.13	3.67
1987	11798	24.46	292232	13.17	4.04
1988	14070	19.26	349021	19.43	4.03
1989	17950	27.58	408662	17.09	4.39
1990	20491	14.16	477814	16.92	4.29
1991	22349	9.07	552768	15.69	4.04
1992	25030	12.00	630772	14.11	3.97
1993	28280	12.98	732874	16.19	3.86
1994	32606	15.30	868019	18.44	3.76
1995	38178	17.09	1006286	15.93	3.79
1996	44695	17.07	1149215	14.20	3.89
1997	51683	15.63	1426670	24.14	3.62

Source: Prof. Ruddar Datt, Second Generation Reforms: Need for Changing Growth Strategy, IEA Conference Volume, 2000, p. 179.

Equation of the $Ln = a + bt + v$ was used. To analyse the changes in the growth rates during Post-Reform Period over Pre-Reform Period, two periods, namely, Period I (1981-1990) and Period II (1991-1997) were considered.

Table 28.2: The estimated results of the Semi-Log Growth Equation

	Total Expenditure on Education and Training		*Gross Domestic Product*	
	Period I	*Period II*	*Period I*	*Period II*
Constant	8.249	8.423	11.703	11.484
Regression	0.166*	0.142*	0.132*	0.156*
Coefficient	(31.976)	(39.488)	(37.593)	(35.849)
CGR	18.057	15.258	14.111	16.883
R^2	0.992	0.997	0.994	0.996

Figures in Parentheses represent *t*-values.

* represents the regression coefficient is significant at 1 per cent level.

CGR denotes Compound Growth Rates.

The estimated compound growth rates of GDP and the total expenditure on education and training are presented in Table 28.2. From the estimated results, it is evident that the CGR of total expenditure on education and training has declined from 18.057 per cent per annum during the period I (1981-1990) to 15.258 per cent during the period II (1991-1997). But, the CGR of GDP has raised to 16.883 per cent in period II from 14.111 per cent in period I. The value of the Goodness of Fit (R^2) ranges between 0.992 and 0.997, which indicates the fitted regression, is the best fit.

Human Development Indicators

Life expectancy, Literacy level, Infant Mortality Rate, Death rate, Birth Rate, etc. are some of the indicators of Human Development (HD). The Table 28.3 shows the details about these aspects during the reforms era.

Table 28.3 highlights the data related to few selected indicators of HD in our country, in few forward and few backward states of our country. Data reveals wide disparities among different States. Kerala and Tamil Nadu shown that even with low levels of economic development it is possible

Table 28.3: Selected Indicators of Human Development

	Life Expectancy at birth (Years)	*Literacy Rate (2001)*			*IMR*	*Death Rate*	*Birth Rate*
	1991-95	*Male*	*Female*	*Total*	*1997 (Per Thousands*		
Forward States							
1. Punjab	67.2	75.6	63.6	69.9	51	7.4	23.4
2. Maharashtra	64.8	86.0	68.1	77.1	47	7.3	23.1
3. Kerala	72.9	94.2	87.9	90.9	12	6.2	17.9
4. Tamil Nadu	63.3	82.3	64.6	73.5	53	8.0	19.0
5. Gujarat	61.0	80.5	58.6	70.0	62	7.6	25.6
Backward States							
1. Rajasthan	59.1	76.5	44.3	61.0	85	8.9	32.1
2. Bihar	59.3	60.3	33.6	47.5	71	10.0	31.7
3. M. Pradesh	54.7	76.8	50.3	64.1	94	11.0	31.9
All India	**60.3**	**76.0**	**54.3**	**65.4**	**71**	**8.9**	**17.2**

Source: Economic Survey (1999-2000), and Census of India (2001).

to achieve higher levels of HD. Few states like M.P., Bihar, Rajasthan have poor record in literacy level (especially in female literacy), life expectancy, etc.

According to the Human Development Report, 2000, during the year 1998, India occupied 128th position among 174 countries, in terms of Human Development Index (HDI). India's position was 58th among 85 countries under the classification based on Human Poverty Index. Under the Gender Related Development Index, it was 108th among 143 countries. According to Census 2001, population of India is 102.7 crore persons. There was an increase in population density from 267 persons per sq. km. during 1991 to 324 persons per sq. km. during the year 2001. Number of female per 1000 males was 933 during 2001 when compared to the figure of 927 during 1991. There is an improvement in life expectancy also. It has increased from 59.4 in 1995-97 to 67.6 years during 1999-2000. All these figures provide empirical evidence to the fact that the HD situation has been improving in our country. Moreover, during reform era, there was tremendous improvement in information, communication technology, which can open path for knowledge, based growth of individuals. Growth in communication facilities during the economic reforms can also improve health and education of the people.

Economic reforms, in few other ways, acts as a hindrance to the human resource development. Globalisation and liberalisation leads to large-scale movement of skilled labourers from our country to U.S.A. Europe and other western countries. Reforms become a dangerous threat to unskilled labourers working in private sector in our country, since many private companies started adopting modern technologies to compete with Multinational Companies. This results in retrenchment of more unskilled or semi-skilled employees. It may not be possible for the government to invest huge amount to convert these people into skilled labourers. In spite of these drawbacks, the contribution of economic reforms to human resource development is significant in our country and one can say that there was an improvement in HRD during the era of economic reforms.

Policy Implications and Conclusion

In the era of economic reforms, successful and meaningful HRD only can enhance employment opportunities for the people living in our country. To compete with MNCs, our enterprises require skilled personnel. Moreover, in an overpopulated country like India, unless people are developed as skilled workforce, they may become heavy burden to the society. It seems growth in HRD is inadequate in our country. Government may change its policy and invest more in education, especially higher and professional education. More funds are required for providing basic amenities to the people to improve their health. Even today crores of people in our country do not have protected drinking water. In many places, especially in rural India, sanitary conditions are very poor and inadequate. Adequate measures are required to protect and develop women and child labourers. Only sincere efforts from the Government can protect and develop the human resource, which is considered to be the real wealth of the Nation.

REFERENCES

1. Dr. Basanta Kumar (2000), *HRD,* Mohit Publications, New Delhi.
2. Kohli, V. and Gautham, V. (1988), *HRD and Planning Process in India,* Vikas Publishing Co., New Delhi.
3. Murali Krishna. P (1998), HRD, Discovery Publishing House, New Delhi.
4. Gupta, K.R. (ed.) (2000), Issues in Indian Economy, Atlantic Publishers & Distributors, New Delhi.
5. Prof. S.L.N. Simha, UNDP-HD Report, 1999, *Southern Economists,* Vol. 38, No. 7, August 1, 1999.

Economic Reforms and Human Resource Development in India

S. Kanagasabai

To get together is the beginning
To stay together is the progress
To work together is the success

Human Resource Development has been assigned a key role in India's development strategy. The meaning of development has shifted from economic improvement to improvement of human resource. Sound long-term development of social sectors such as education and health is vital for sustaining higher rates of overall economic growth. Economic development of an economy depends on the quality of its people. Efficient utilisation of the resources of the country greatly depends on the conditions of labour force employed in production.

People are available as factors of production to work in combination with other factors. As consumers, human beings make demand on the national product of the economy. The size of the population therefore, is a crucial determinant of economic development. A large population may not necessarily contribute to economic development. In fact, a large fast rising population may find itself in a situation described by economists as over population.

Demographic Problems in India

India's population has crossed the one billion mark on May 11, 2000 at 5.05 a.m. This distinction is not a moment for celebration, rather it is a matter of serious concern to realise and act upon how to tackle the problems relating to growing population at the fast speed. This essentially calls for to address and explore the avenues and strategies for meetings the challenges of housing, education, health, etc.

Therefore, it is essential to address this problem in detail. In this chapter an attempt is made to outline the demographic scenario with other selected countries in Globe, and also to assess the India's performance on various population related issues. This chapter is divided in to Four parts:

- Theoretical Framework on Human Resources;
- Comparative social indicators profile among selected countries in the Globe;
- Vital statistics of India and Tamil Nadu;
- Need for Paradigm shift.

Theoretical Framework on Demographic Issues

The subject of population has been the main issue of debate right from the ancient time all over the world. The ancient scholars and philosophers such as Plato and Aristotle realize the importance and the issue of population. Godwin and Candorecet are the exponents of the utopian thought during ancient days. They thought that higher or larger population of a state will lead to bad laws, corrupt Government, evil rulers, greedy employers, made men selfish, biased, evil and caused social degradation or deterioration leading to misery and strongly contended to limit the size of the population of a Country or State to avoid these trends and consequences.

T.R. Mathus believed in the dictum that *"Mans ability to reproduce is greater than his ability to produce"*. He believed that the need for food and passion for sexes were antagonistic. It was easy for population to increase limitlessly but not food as the land through which is grown in finite and limited.

The theory of demographic transition formulated by Frank Notestein views economic growth as a sufficient condition for a decline in fertility.

Optimum theory of population was developed by Edwin Cannon of London School of Economics. According to Dalton, optimum population is that which gives the maximum income per head. The optimum varies from time to time.

Trends of Population Growth in the World

Trends of population growth among the world largest countries in 2003 and 2050 (projected) is given in Tables 29.1 and 29.2.

Table 29.1: World Largest Countries in 2003

Rank	*Country*	*Population in Millions*
1.	China	1289
2.	India	1069
3.	USA	292
4.	Indonesia	220
5.	Brazil	176
6.	Pakistan	149
7.	Bangladesh	147
8.	Russia	146
9.	Nigeria	134
10.	Japan	128
11.	Mexico	105
12.	Germany	83
13.	Philippines	82
14.	Vietnam	72
15.	Egypt	71
16.	Turkey	71
17.	Ethiopia	71
18.	Iran	67
19.	Thailand	63
20.	France	60

Source: The directory for global population information.

Table 29.2: World Largest Countries in 2050 (Projected)

Rank	*Country*	*Population in Millions*
1.	India	1628
2.	China	1391
3.	USA	422
4.	Pakistan	349
5.	Indonesia	316
6.	Nigeria	307
7.	Bangladesh	255
8.	Brazil	221
9.	Congo. Dem. Rop. of	181
10.	Ethiopia	173
11.	Mexico	153
12.	Philippines	133
13.	Egypt	127
14.	Russia	119
15.	Vietnam	117
16.	Japan	101
17.	Turkey	98
18.	Iran	95
19.	Sudan	84
20.	Uganda	82

Source: The directory for global population information.

It is seen from the Table 29.1, India is the second largest country in the world with the total population enumerated in the 2001 census at about 102.7 crore. This forms about 15 per cent of the total population of the world. In other words, every sixth person on the earth is Indian. India, on the other hand, has got only 2.4 per cent of the total area in the world. China with about 20 per cent of the worlds population has about 7 per cent of the total area, the USA maintains only 6 per cent of the total world population on about 7 per cent of the total area, Russia has 5 per cent of the population and 12 per cent of the land area.

Table 29.3: Comparison of Social Indicator Performances Among Selected Countries

	Indices	*India*	*Singapore*	*China*	*Pakistan*	*Srilanka*	*South Africa*	*Mexico*	*USA*	*Japan*
(a)	Public Expenditure on health as per cent of GDP (1990-98)	0.6	1.1	2.0	0.9	1.4	3.2	2.8	6.5	5.9
(b)	Percentage of population with access to improved water service (1990-96)	81	100	90	60	46	70	83	NA	96
(c)	Percentage of population with access to sanitation (1990-96)	16	100	21	30	52	46	66	NA	100
(d)	Infant mortality rate per 1000 live births (1988)	70	4	31	91	16	51	30	7	4
(e)	Life expectancy at birth (in years)	62.9	77.3	70.1	64.4	73.3	53.2	72.3	76.8	80.0
(f)	Doctors per lakh of population (1992-95)	48	147	115	52	23	59	85	245	177
(g)	Per cent of infants with low birth-weight (1990-97)	33	7	9	25	25	NA	7	7	7
(h)	Tuberculosis per one lakh people in 1997	118.3	57.5	33.7	3.1	35.7	242.7	25.0	6.4	33.6
(i)	Daily per capita supply of calories (1997)	2496	—	2897	2476	2302	2990	3097	3699	2932
(j)	Adult literacy rate 1998	55.7	91.8	82.8	44.0	91.1	84.6	90.8	99.0	99.0
(k)	Youth literacy rate 1998	70.9	99.7	97.2	61.4	96.5	90.8	96.6	—	—

Source: Reserve Bank of India Bulletin, December 2000, Annexure-1, pp. 1305-1306.

It would thus be seen that India has been seriously handicapped in that a large proportion of the world's population is found Jampacked in a small area. Table 29.2 explains the projected population of the world largest countries in 2050.

India in the Global Context (Economic Reform Period)

Table 29.3 gives a cursory look at social indices which help us to understand where India stands with respect to Pears as well as developed countries. Nine countries are assumed to be fairly representative of geographical distribution of countries on the globe, differences in the level of income, sizes of the economy and of our neighbouring countries.

General comparison of social indicates performances during the reform periods are explained in the Table 29.3.

- An important social indicator in any country is the literacy of its people. In 1998, the adult literacy rate in our country was 55.7 per cent only and better than Pakistan (44%) but for below Sri Lanka (91.1%) and China (82.8%). The picture is same with respect to youth literacy, which was 71 per cent as against 96.5 per cent in Sri Lanka and 87.2 per cent in China.
- Besides education, health is a basic necessity of life. Though 81 per cent of our people during 1990-96 had access to safe water sources, we were better off only in comparison to three countries. And in sanitation, with just 16 per cent of the people having access to it, were worse off as compared to all these countries in the group.
- 70 infants out of every 1000 died in India in 1998. Similarly in 1998, only one country had a lower life expectancy than India (63 years).
- Out of the every one lakh Indians, 118.3 suffered from tuberculosis in 1997, overshadowed by South Africa (242.7) only.

- During 1990-97, 33 per cent of the infants were born underweight. Our record is worse than Pakistan and Sri Lanka where it was 25 per cent.
- In 1997, two countries supplied fewer calories daily to each of their people than the supply of 2496 calories by India. We spent only 0.60 per cent of GDP on health services in 1990-98 than other countries have spent.
- During 1992-95, there were 48 doctors available to every lakh Indians, better than Sri Lanka only.

The World Bank prepares a composite index called Human Development Index (HDI) to measure the average achievement in basic human development. The index comprises, per capita GDP index, Education Index, and Life Expectancy Index considered to be the basic essentials of life. In 1998, only one country in our group was worse than our position in the first two subindices, and only one other in 1998 in the third index. Not surprisingly India's HDI ranking out of 174 countries in 1998 was 128th.

Overall, we rank rather low in human development and high in human deprivation. The end product of all economic policy is social well being, and admittedly the long term prospects for economic growth also depend crucially on the social well being. The social indicators in regard to our country do not give us too much of comfort.

Literacy levels are low and the picture regard to health and sanitation is not encouraging, and it is unfortunate that we spent in this area a much lower proportion of GDP than others.

Population Growth in India: 1901-2001

India's population has grown over the years. This can be seen from Table 29.4.

The history of population growth in India divides itself into four natural phases:

Table 29.4: Population Growth in India; 1901-2001

Census Years	*Population*	*Absolute*	*Per cent*	*Average Annual Exponential Growth Rate (per cent)*
1901	23,83,96,327	—	—	—
1911	25,20,93,390	1,36,97,063	5.75	0.56
1921	25,13,21,213	-7,72,177	-0.31	-0.03
1931	27,89,77,238	2,76,56,025	11.00	1.04
1941	31,86,60,580	3,96,83,342	14.22	1.33
1951	36,10,88,090	4,24,27,510	13.31	1.25
1961	43,92,34,771	7,81,46,681	21.64	1.96
1971	54,81,59,652	10,89,24,881	24.80	2.20
1981	68,33,29,097	13,51,69,445	24.66	2.22
1991	84,33,87,888	16,30,58,791	23.86	2.14
2001	1,02,70,15,247	18,06,27,359	21.34	1.93

Source: Various Census Reports GOI.

They are:

1901-1921 : Stagnant population

1921-1951 : Steady growth

1951-1981 : Rapid high growth

1981-2001 : High growth with definite signs of slowing down.

In India, several policy initiatives have been taken up from time to time in this direction to deal with various aspects of delivery of health care and family welfare for stabilizing population growth. One of the important lessons gained so far is that the policies and programmes could not reach up to the expected mark. Therefore it is essential to address this problem in an effective manner.

Health Transition in Tamil Nadu

Health transition comprises three components, namely, demographic, transition, epidemiological transition and health care transition. Of these, demographic transition is the most dominant. Demographic transition in India is not confined to Tamil Nadu; all the states are in the process. Tamil Nadu stands ahead of national average (next to Kerala).

Table 29.5: Census Population in Tamil Nadu

Census Year	*Total Population (in lakhs)*	*Growth Rate (% Decennial)*	*Sex Ratio Females (Per 1000 Males)*	*Density of of Population*	*Percentage Population to Total Population*
1901	192.5	—	1044	148	—
1911	209.0	8.57	1042	161	—
1921	216.3	3.47	1029	166	—
1931	234.7	8.52	1027	180	—
1941	262.7	11.91	1012	202	—
1951	301.2	14.66	1007	232	24.35
1961	336.9	11.85	992	259	26.69
1971	412.0	22.30	978	317	30.26
1981	484.1	17.50	977	372	32.95
1991	558.6	15.39	974	429	34.20
2001	621.11	11.19	986	478	43.86

Source: Various Reports, GOI.

The above table presents data on the population growth in Tamil Nadu from 1901 to 2001. During the period 1901-1931 the population grew less than the growth rate of 10 per cent. While in the subsequent decades, 1931 to 2001, it grow at more than 11 per cent per decade. This spurt in the growth rate after 1951 can be largely attributed to the National/State level programmes of public health and socio-economic development undertaken after independence that contributed for large declines in the mortality levels. The State Tamil Nadu experienced a sharp decrease in the sex ratio with regard to density of population in Tamil Nadu, a further sharp rise in their growth rates from 1951 to 2001.

The growth rate of Tamil Nadu population, today appears to be high, but still there are several of other states with even higher growth rates in India.

Table 29.6: Vital Statistics of India and Tamil Nadu

Year	*Crude Birth Rate*		*Crude Death Rate*		*Infant Mortality Rate*	
	Tamil Nadu	*India*	*Tamil Nadu*	*India*	*Tamil Nadu*	*India*
1971	31.4	36.9	14.4	14.9	—	—
1981	28.0	33.9	11.8	12.5	—	—
1990	21.6	30.2	8.5	9.7	59	80
1991	20.8	29.5	8.8	9.8	57	80
1992	20.7	29.2	8.4	10.1	58	79
1993	19.5	28.7	8.2	9.3	57	74
1994	19.2	28.7	8.0	9.3	59	74
1995	20.3	28.3	7.9	9.0	56	74
1996	19.2	27.4	7.9	8.9	53	72
1997	19.0	27.2	8.0	8.9	53	71
1998	19.2	26.4	8.4	9.0	53	72

Source: Family Welfare Programmes, Department Circulation, Tamil Nadu, 2000, p. 24.

Tamil Nadu has apparently centered the demographic transition (especially 1991 onwards) characterised by low death rate and declining death rate leading to a slow down in the growth rate of population. Thus, as 1998, birth rate in Tamil Nadu was estimated as 19.2 (per 1000 population) as against 26.4 for all India.

The crude death rate of Tamil Nadu in 1997 was 8.0 (per 1000 population) compared to national average of 088.9 per 1000 population. The infant mortality rate of Tamil Nadu in 1998 was estimated as 53 (per 1000 infants) as against 72 for all India.

It is noteworthy to mention that the vial statistics in Tamil Nadu (Birth Rate, Death Rate and IMR) have been significantly lower than in India's National Average.

Conclusion

Man is a social animal. He wants to live along with his fellow human begins and share his happiness and suffering with them. Ever since the existence of human life on earth, man is able to lead on organised life for the development of his personality and to lead a peaceful and happy life. Demographic transition is a global phenomenon. With rapid population growth, the number of now entrants to the labour force in India increases each year. Unemployment increases the country finds it difficult to provide jobs for all the new entrants. Rapid growing population requires large investments for the provision of social infrastructure and takes away resources directly from productive assets. Therefore, the need of the hour is to bring population under control through family planning/welfare programemS which will facilitate to reach Human Resource Development in India. This is what the paradigm shift is needed today.

REFERENCES

1. *Reserve Bank of India Bulletin,* Vol. LIV, No. 12, December, 2000.
2. *Planning Commission* (Health Nutrition and Family Welfare Division), Government of India, New Delhi, Part I, Part II and Part III, Population and Human and Social Development, July 2000.
3. Fred Singer, S., *Is there an Optimum Population?* McGraw Hill Book Company, A Population Council Book, New York, 1971.
4. Krishna Reddy, MM, *Marriage Population and Society,* Kanishka Publishers and Distributors, New Delhi, 2000.
5. Krishna Reddy, M.M., *Health and Family Welfare, Public Policy and People Participation in India,* Kanishka Publishers and Distributors, New Delhi, 2000.
6. Digumarti [illegible]skara Rao and Digumarti Pushpalatha Rao, *International Encyclopaedia of Women-14, Women and Family Health,* Discovery Publishing House, New Delhi, 1999.
7. Kanagasabai, C.S., *Economics of HRD,* Rasee Publications, Theni District, January 2003.

8. *Family Welfare Programme, Tamil Nadu 2000,* Booklet Published by Department of Family Programme, Chennai.

9. Kunhikannan, T.R. and Aravindhan, T.P., *Charges in the Health Status of Kerala 1987-1997,* KRPLLD, Centre for Development Studies, Tiruvananthapuram, June 2000.

10. Singh, S.K., PRI's in Health Case Future Strategies, *Kurukshetra,* October 2000, pp. 48-54.

11. Family Welfare Programme in Tamil Nadu Year book 1999-2000, Directory of Family Welfare, Chennai-6.

30

Redundancy, Redeployment of Manpower and Training in Banking Industries

Dr. S. Hasan Banu

Introduction

Liberalisation of the economy has had contradictory effects on employment and labour. It is now recognised that poor employment generation has been a major casualty of the Indian neo-liberal economic reform process. Liberalisation of the economy and its movements towards globalisation has brought in new challenges for the Indian business and more particularly to the banking sector due to structural changes in financial markets.

The year 2000-01 in a way happens to be a landmark year in the year of Indian Banking. In early 2000 National Productivity Council, New Delhi submitted its report on productivity norms for "Banking Industry". In its findings, it mentioned that existing manpower surplus varied from 0 per cent to 51 per cent in respect of branches it had studied. The study also found out that many of the activities are carried out which are unproductive and not related to normal listed element of different. This was a conformation of already existing belief in the Industry circle that there exists substantial surplus manpower and considers its redeployment.[1]

The committee noted that the economic reforms set in motion in 1990 have unleashed market forces and competition, which affect all sectors of the economy including banking sector.

At present, banks are facing two major challenges—management of assets or precisely *Non-Performing Assets and Management of Human Resources* (NPA and HRA). Banking, being service Industry reform process will not be complete without reforming human resources area. The HRM in banks is a very complex issue. Therefore, reforming this area is going to be a major challenge before public sector banks in the coming years.

Redundancy, Redeployment in Banks

The human resource, which is one of the valuable assets of an organisation, does not find a place in the balance sheet but of late the concept of valuing the human resource as an asset is gaining ground. The Public Sector Banks are now at the crossroads. For Today's and Tomorrow's Banking, Public Sector Banks need more young Hybrid bankers having adequate knowledge in general banking, retail banking, marketing specialised banking technology and peoples skills. Growing competition and even changing technology are changing business profile of the banks.

An overhauling of the entire human resource in banks, keeping a holistic view of HRM is essentially required for working towards the survival and success of the public sector banks. As per the recommendation of the HRM committee the Govt. of India permitted of the Indian Banks Association to circulate the Voluntary Retirement Scheme (VRS) to public sector banks for implementation as per their individual manpower planning.

Prior to implementation of VRS 43 per cent of employees in PSBs were in 46 +age group and only 12 per cent in the 25-35 age group. This pattern has serious implications for the banks with reference to mobility, training development of skills and succession plans for higher-level positions and introduction of new skills.[2]

The manpower planning exercise was carried out at the corporate level before implementation VRS. The surplus was estimated after providing for the needs across all the branches and contouring offices, equitably. Surplus employees were identified as one of the main reasons for low profitability of public sector banks.

The manpower planning should also address several important issues like:

(i) Recruitment plans to avoid in expected shortage, etc;

(ii) Identification of training needs to avoid skills shortage;

(iii) Characteristics or skill profile of the human resources that are required both in the short term and long term; and

(iv) Policy changes, if any, to attract, retain and develop and human resources in the organisation.

Post-VRS

The role of Human Resource Development is very vital under the changed scenario in the Public Sector Banks should consider the gradual shift from *"Traditional Banking"* to newer activities were there is good potential to deploy skills and talents optimally. The Public Sector Banks are obviously having their *strengths and weakness, opportunities and threats* existence and survival by transforming their weakness into strengths and converting threats into opportunities.

Generally speaking, VRS means, the surplus of a large number of workforce at one go, and in the natural process it takes away certain degree of specialised skills and talents of the organisation. VRS posts a severe challenge to the organisation as a whole, as there will serious implication of immediate as well as fine placement process and also training and as the remaining workforce, their performance monitoring and appraisal and also ensure proper elevation.

VRS is having ramification as well as strong challenges for the entire process of Human Resources Management, in any organisation and if managed. Efficiently and effectively with required prudence, can deliver the desired results.

The public sector banks in India aimed at considerable right sizing of workforce at the bottom level than at the upper level, but the outcome of the VRS process did not bring the desired result. Experience shows that employees at the upper level and experience opt for VRS more in number than the other segment of workforce.[3]

The table below shows the total number of employees, number of VRS optees and their percentage.

Table 30.1: Bank Employees Response to VRS Offer

Bank	*Total Strength*	*VRS Optees*	*Percentage*
State Bank of India	2,37,000	35,000	13.89
Allahabad Bank	22,345	1,571	7.03
Andhra Bank	14,603	1,758	12.04
Bank of Baroda	47,054	3,200	6.80
Bank of Maharashtra	16,098	2,700	16.77
Bank of India	51,962	7,700	14.82
Canara Bank	55,363	8,600	15.53
Dena Bank	14,412	3,710	25.74
Indian Bank	25,935	3,710	25.74
Indian Overseas Bank	28,008	3,944	14.08
Oriental Bank	14,398	800	5.56
Punjab National Bank	65,705	5,800	8.83
Punjab & Sind Bank	12,192	2,000	16.40
Syndicate Bank	33,883	7,157	21.12
UCO Bank	31,223	5,479	17.55
Union Bank of India	30,834	4,303	13.96
United Bank of India	21,316	3,000	14.07
Vijaya Bank	13,646	2,400	17.59

Source: IBA Bulletin Special Issue, March 2002.

The above table shows that in almost all the banks, percentage of VRS optees is quite noteworthy. Experience in the post-VRS scenario shows that the flight of skilled personnel is quite large in number and interestingly the shift was from the Public Sector Banks to Private Sector Banks in many of the cases. Thus, the retention of the best talents in the post-VRS scenario has become a major challenge for the Public Sector Banks as a whole.

Some of the significant challenges to the public sector banks due to VRS:

- Loss of skills and talents to the banks due to large scale exist at a time;
- Dearth of skills and talents amongst the remaining workforce in the organisation and the problem of filing the necessary gaps;
- Psychological insecurity of the remaining workforce in the organised action in the changed scenario;
- Ambiguity about future prospects in the organisation.

Role of Training

In the post-VRS scenario, development of Human Resource is of permanent importance. As a matter of fact, time and again the experts have stressed on the importance of development of Human Resources for the success of any organisation. Dr. Bimal Jalam, RBI Governor, Emphasised this point very seriously in his speech at the Bank Economist's conference held in New Delhi, during January 15-17, 2001.[4]

The Principals conference, organised at NIBM in the year 1989, attended by the General Manager, Deputy General Managers (P) and the principals of the Training Establishments identified certain important areas to be attended immediately to make the training systems more effective and conductive to the needs of the banking industry.

Most important among them are:

- Active involvement of Top management in the training Programmes;

- Professional faculty at the training establishment.

Vijaya Bank will spend Rs. 50 crore in creating training facilities of its employees. The bank has purchased 10.9 acres of land in Bangalore for this purpose. It should consist modern classroom features. The Vijaya Bank felt that a training facility exclusively for itself would be necessary.[5]

- Quality of the training programmes
- Identification of training needs
- Post-training placements
- Autonomy for the training systems.

Training Strategy

A bank employee is expected to be adopted at various aspects of law, administration, management, banking technology, communication, public relations, credit appraisal and various deposit investment scheme.

The challenge before the banks is not only produce such employees of multi-skills and applications but re-skill them on continuous basis.

Problems in Re-skilling

Banks are facing problems in re-skilling their employees with the required knowledge and skills due to some intrinsic factors. These are as follows:

- The training programmes have hither to been somewhat routine and stereotyped;
- The training system is lacking capabilities and capacities to undertake such re-skilling programme;
- Many banks do not have a centralised database of their skill profile and they do not undertake skill mapping. This is a major handicap for undertaking effective re-skilling programme;
- The existing HRM policies of the banks give preference to seniority over the skills in the

promotion process and also there is no placement policy for skilled personal.

Recommendation for Overcoming the Post-VRS Challenges—Training

- Banks should immediately create a centralised personnel database/inventory covering age profile, skill profile, training profile, job profile, etc. of all categories of employees and determine the skills and training gaps.
- In the public sector banks many posts have become redundant due to the changed business process mechanisation and new business requirement. It has become necessary to rationalize all the posts in subordinates, clerical and officer cadres.
- A scientific job and role analysis should be undertaken to redefine various posts in all cadres in order to achieve improvement in efficiency and utilisation of manpower.
- Banks should start immediately renegotiation with the concerned recognised unions, wherever required for effective redeployment of the workmen staff.
- Onsite learning and online training are some innovative training system. It reduces the travelling cost, and also helpful to the employees to get more time for customised learning.
- Offering training over the Internet also helps employees to have access to training facilities at the workplace itself.
- While reviewing the training strategy, banks should critically study the adequacy and impact of training on qualitative change in banking operations.

- Training should be devised for the development of the Individual as well as of the organisation in an integrated manner;
- Banks should revamp their training system with reference to the following aspects.

Conclusion

The Human Resource Management has got a very vital role to play. Training Programmes should ensure the necessary role-played in this regard, in the process of effective Human Resource Development. Banks to function effectively in the changed situation need "Effective Bankers" and "Efficient Bankers" only to deliver the goods.

In the process the services of "Software Professionals" are to be utilised more extensively.

Training is thus to be used as the most effective tool in bringing the necessary change is the most vital factors of production, namely, the "Human Resources".

REFERENCES

1. V.P. Shetty, "Voluntary Retirement in Banking Industry". *IBA Bulletin Special Issue,* March 2002 p. 36.
2. Ibid, p. 37.
3. Dr. Bani Prasad Bhattachariya, "Post VRS Scenario. Human Resource Development Role of Training." *IBA Bulletin Special Issue,* March 2002. p. 96.
4. Ibid, p. 97.
5. *Business Line,* dated Oct. 4, 2003, p. 10.
6. Banambar Sahoo, "Re-skilling in Banks", *IBA Bulletin Special Issue,* 2003, p. 127.
7. *Business Line,* Various Issues.

31

Human Resource Development in the Context of Economic Reforms in India

Dr. S. Karuppaiyan

The development of human resources which mainly comes under social sector, includes education, health, sanitation, housing, family welfare, water supply, social welfare, nutrition, rural employment, minimum basic services, increases the productivity of the economy and acts as an important factor in economic development. It is both a means as well as an end to economic development. It was only in the early sixties that the importance of skill and abilities of man in accelerating the process of development was clearly identified and acknowledged.

Marlaine Lockheed, an education specialist at the World Bank pointed out "Increasing the labour forces average primary schooling by even one year can increase output substantially." So education considers as an instrument for the progress of the entire country. Primary education in particular leads to better family health, lower fertility and slower population growth. Minimum education enables every citizen in raising his standard of living, understand the technological change and adopt the modern techniques in his respective area.

The Nobel Laurate Amartya Sen exhorted that without education and health care we can not have participatory economic growth. Human beings are not only the instrument of production, but also ends in human development. Investment in human beings by providing education, skills and better health improved their capabilities to contribute more to the process of GDP growth. Even the provision of adequate food by cutting down under-nutrition and mal-nutrition also help to raise productivity. Besides, the need for shelter was also considered as a basic input to improve the capacity of human beings to raise the life expectancy and also their lifetime earnings.

This chapter focuses its attention on the Indian Government's efforts for the development of human resources such as education, health, family welfare, housing sanitation, drinking water, food after introducing Economic Reforms in India, on the achievements made so far and also on the existing disparities and gaps in human resource development under social sectors development in India. In India expenditure on education is financed by the Central Government, State Governments, and local bodies in addition to endowments, donations and voluntary contributions. The economic reforms, which began in the early 1990s in India still remain much in controversy because in sensitive areas such as social sector development, labour, financial services, agriculture, the pace has been static, leaving the nation poor. Economic Development cloning modules transplanted in the closed laboratories of WB, IMF and WTO that are replicated in India over the past ten years have created syndrome in the sustainable growth of social sectors.

The Central Government expenditure on social sectors comprising education, health and family welfare, water supply, sanitation, housing, social welfare, nutrition, rural employment and minimum basic services as a ratio to total expenditure increased from 7.7 per cent in 1990-91 to 11.4 per cent in 1999-2000. It is generally assumed that the Government focusing increasingly on the social sector by way of enhancing the sector's budgetary allocation each year. In fact, the Government spending on the social sector and rural development in percentage terms has been stagnating since

1996-97. While the Budget Estimate (BE) presented each year has remained more or less static with only negligible increase during certain years in between, the decline in the Revised Estimate (RE) on social sector has been steady.

For comparison purpose, the BE for social sector has been steady. For comparison purpose the BE for social sector during 1993-94 was 1.09 per cent of the GDP and in the RE it increased to 1.17 per cent of GDP. In 1996-97, while the BE was 1.2 per cent of GDP, it became 1.07 per cent of GDP in the RE. In the subsequent year, the social sector spending was 1.21 per cent of GDP in the BE which reduced to 1.09 per cent of GDP in the RE. Again during the financial year, 1998-99, the RE reduced to 1.09 per cent of GDP from the BE of 1.18 per cent. In other words, speaking in terms of money, the RE has been a decrease from the BE by Rs. 1,707 crore in 1996-97 Rs. 1948 crore in 1997-98, Rs. 1,601, crore in 1998-99 and Rs. 1,782 crore in 1999-2000.

Percolation Effect

There are wider inter-state variations in indicators of social development. The Percolation effect is pseudo in its actualities. It has been observed that generally, High income (per capita Net Domestic product above Rs. 7500) states (Tamil Nadu, Karnataka, Andhra Pradesh, Kerala and West Bengal) show better performance in the development as compared to low-income (below Rs. 6000) States. (Madhya Pradesh, Rajasthan, Uttar Pradesh, Orissa and Bihar). Kerala is far ahead of all other states in India in the matter of social development. On the other hand, Haryana, in spite of a high income state, is comparatively backward in social development. Andhra Pradesh, a middle income state shows poor performance in the matter of literacy rates. It has to be stated that per capita expenditure on health and education is low in Andhra Pradesh. The share of development expenditures in total state government spending has gone down sharply over the years and that of the non-development expenditure has increased from 4.2 per cent during 1990-95 to 5.6 per cent in 1999-2000. The amount spent on social development expenditure has also declined as a proportion of GDP from 6.6 per cent during 1985-90 (pre-reform period) and 5.8 per cent during 1990-1995 and 5.5 per cent during 1999-2000.

Though 53 years passed after independence, the condition of basic services in rural areas remains very unsatisfactory. In this context, is has to be mentioned that 40 per cent of our villages do not have primary schools; that 4.5 lakh villages have drinking water problems: that there is a shortage of 140 lakh rural dwelling units; and that the rural health infrastructures suffer from large deficiencies. The latest National Family Health survey for 1998-99 shows that almost half the children under three years of age and more than one-third of the women and three-fourth of the children are anaemic. Out of 13 million girls born every year, 25 per cent do not live to see their 15th year in India.

In respect of food aspects, Indian food economy shows a paradoxical situation. It is estimated that a large number of people are clearly below the minimum prescribed nutrition levels, as worked out by the National Institute of Nutrition (NIN) and other bodies. Studies put the number of malnourished children in India at nearly 40 per cent of the global population. Besides, it is stated that about 80 per cent of the rural and 70 per cent of the urban households consume less than the recommended levels of 2,400 kilo calories and 2,100 kilo calories respectively in the country.

Education

Human capital is more important than financial capital. Education is considered as an index of development. The National Policy on Education (1986) has stipulated the Government to spend at least 6 per cent of the GDP on education. But actual figure was very dismal. There has been serious deterioration in per pupil expenditure in education in all sectors of education. In the sphere of elementary education, the annual average growth rate of expenditure slumped from 6.9 per cent to 1.22 per cent during 1990-96. In secondary education, there was zero growth rate per pupil expenditure and in University education, this growth rate became negative to the extent of 4.4 per cent in the post-reform period. The Centrally Sponsored Schemes (CSS) in the social sector also show declining trends. For instance, the share of education under CSS expenditure, which was 12.1 per cent in 1991 declined to 8 per cent in 1997-98. The actual expenditure on education in 1996-97 was only 3.4 per cent down from 3.6 per cent in 1992 showing discrepancy against the stipulation of National Policy to spend 6 per cent of GDP on education. The number of States which showed lower stagnating education expenditure rose considerably between 1985-90 and 1990-95.

The available statistical data on literacy rates in Asian countries show that the countries which had succeeded market based reforms had achieved remarkable literacy level even before the reforms were initiated. For example, in 1980, the literacy rates in South Korea (93%), Hong Kong (90%), Thailand (83%) and China (69%) were far ahead of India (36%). With reforms, what changes were effected in India on educational sector. For this, a study on the statistical data reveals that there is only a quantitative expansion in the number of educational institutions which is the largest in the common wealth and second largest in the world. Further, there was a significant decrease in the drop outs also. But the adult literacy rate was only 62 per cent in 1997 with 38 per cent still remaining illiterates. Rural-urban differentials also prevail in literacy attainment level.

Accessibility of education to a particular class can be used as a symbol to decide the status of that class. After four decades the literacy rate of women in 1991 has been increased to 39.29 per cent. In 1993-94, only 55.2 per cent of girls who are in the age group of 11-13 years could go to school. Further, drop out rate is relatively higher among female children. It is 39.05 per cent in 1993-94 and at the stage of secondary education it is as high as 74.54 per cent. The observation as to the University level education shows that, the number of female students per every 100 male students is 64.7 per cent in arts, 49.1 per cent in Science, 36.5 per cent in Commerce, 12.5 per cent in technical courses including engineering and 57.5 per cent in medicine. This clearly indicates the prevalence of disparities between male-female education's. In spite of the introduction of programmes like compulsory free primary education, formal and informal education, subsidy, mid-day meal scheme, girls are far behind in the sphere of education.

In these conditions, withdrawal of Government from the education on the name of liberalisation policies and economic reforms resulted in the entry of trends in educational institutions which made the education costly. Consequently, education became inaccessible to common man in general and woman in particular in India. Further, liberalisation policies ultimately resulting in the privatisation and commercialisation of education. Consequently, a mushroom growth is taking place in regard to number of private educational institutions which charge heavy fee which can be afforded by upper middle income group and above. Thus, education is being made inaccessible to the people who belong to middle and lower in income groups in the country.

Health

The World Health Organisation (WHO) defines health as a state of complete physical, mental and social well-being and not merely the absence of disease. The study of the profile of health sector in India reveals that there has been a decline trend in the health care system mainly on account of the countrys' failure to use justly its resources to provide basic health care to the majority of its population. Though there has been a marked expansion in infrastructure for health sector yet it fails to match the growth of population, which neutralizes the improvement in health sector in India. The factors that influence the performance of health sector has been the proportionate declining share of investment on health as compared to total plan out lay and also lack of political will to priorities, this sector in the planning process. Allocation for health sector as a percentage of plan outlays declined from 3.3 in the First Plan to 1 on the 1997-98 Annual Plans. In the 7th and 8th Plan it averaged just 1.7 per cent.

Further there is wide gap between per capita expenditure on health for rural and urban health services. Spending on urban health has been 3.4 per cent higher than on rural health across the states. The problems persist in provision of basic amenities also despite 5 decades of planned era which include:

- 44 per cent of households in rural areas do not have access to safe drinking water;
- 15 per cent of the habitations get less than 10 liters of water per day;
- 69 per cent of households are not electrified;
- 91 per cent of the households in the rural areas do not have toilets.

Though various health parameters such as infant morality rate, prenatal morality rate, life expectancy and death rate have improved over the years, they are still far lower than the world average.

Housing

Provision of shelter is another major component of human resource development. The total rural household shortage as per 1991 census was 13.72 million. Of these 3.41 million were without shelter and 10.31 million were living in kutcha unserviceable houses. In addition, an estimated 10.75 million houses would be required on account of population growth during the period 1991-2002. It has also been estimated that 5.7 million units have been added to rural housing through the ongoing programmes of Indira Awas Yojna (IAY), State Government, HUDCO and self-help systems. Thus, the net housing shortage between 1997 and 2002 is 18.77 million of which 8.46 million are very old houses and 10.31 million are kutcha unserviceable houses in India.

Drinking Water and Sanitation

The water supply and sanitation are important basic needs of the people in both the rural and urban areas, which enhance their productive efficiency (*Economic Survey,* 1997-98). Various reports show that the water in the country has been declining at the alarming rate every year. Further, it is also very clear that most of the facilities of sanitation and drinking water are concentrated only in the urban areas, and the rural people are still not able to access these facilities. Further, the following facts and figures reveal the disturbing trends and complexities of economic reforms.

Nearly 320 million of our people (36%) are living under Below Poverty Line (BPL). How the additional 65 million unproductive mouths are to be fed, clothed and sheltered, with already existing population explosion. In this context, it is necessary to state that nearly 300 millions are illiterate, 1,75,000 villages do not have potable water, 40 per cent of Indian villages are without proper roads, 1.8 lakh villages are without primary school within 1 km range.

Thus, the cumulative effects of all these trends are reflected in the standard of living and Human Development Index (HDI) indicators. Logically analysing the gap is widening between the have and have nots in India.

The problem with the Indian economy under economic reforms is that those who have the money do not need the goods to be produced since they already possess them. And those who need those goods do not have the money to buy them. The emergence of unrivalled supremacy of the 'market forces, have already created islands of prosperity impoverishing the vast deserts of backwardness in India.

Further, evidences indicate that the economic reforms in India appear to have had an adverse effect on social sector expenditure made by the Centre and States. In the State budgets, there has been decline of the social sector, which includes education, health, water supply, sanitation, housing, SC/ST/OBC welfare, social security, nutrition etc., from 39.32 per cent during the pre-reform period to 33.95 per cent in the post-reform period. Except for SC/ST welfare expenditure on all other sub-sector under social service revealed a declining trend. As a percentage of GDP, development expenditure by the centre was 11.5 per cent during 1985-90 but declined to 8.5 per cent in 1991 to 1997. Social sector expenditure was only around 2 per cent of GDP in the country.

Conclusion

The World Education Forum summit held in Dakar, Senegal 2000 on "Education for All by 2015" points out that "human capital—education and skills—is a critical weapon in the war against poverty. If poor countries are to achieve faster economic growth—a necessary condition for reducing poverty—they will need better educated work forces".

The observation and facts in the preceding pages show the declining trend and disparities prevalent under social sector in human resources in the context of economic reforms in India. Under the above circumstances we have a moral obligation to do at least as well as for our successor generation as our predecessors did for us. It implies that as to arise the importance of human development at the grassroot level, (a) required amount of investment should be made in the education and health of today's population so as not to create a social debt for future generations (b) current consumption can not be financed for long and ever by incurring economic debts that other should pay (c) resources must be used in ways that do not create ecological debts by over-exploiting the carrying and productive capacity of the earth. Thus proper attention and investment in social sector with special reference to human resource development by Government by neo-political class with ethical values in the political front along with development efforts and active community participation in implementation of social sector programmes which also a pre-condition, is the need of the hour for the successful and wonderful human resource development in India.

REFERENCES

1. Alain Mingat and Carolyn Winter, "Education for All by 2015"; *Finance and Development*. A Quarterly Publication of International Monetary Fund. Vol. 39, No. 1 March 2002.

2. Ambiga Devi, P. Jaya Sudha, M., 'New Economic Reforms and Social Sector Development with Special Reference to Education". *Peninsular Economist; Revaluation of Economic Reforms in India...*, Journal of the Association of Economists of Tamil Nadu. Vol. XIV No. I 2001-02.

3. Jagdish Gandhi, P., "Humanising Development the 21st Century Perspectives". *Peninsular Economist—Social Sector in the Context of Globalisation.* Journal of the Association of Economists of Tamil Nadu, Vol. XIII, No. 12000-01.

4. Jyothi Rani, T., Girija Rani, H., *"Impact of Liberalisation Policies on the Status of Women—A View-point Globalisation and Liberalisation—New-Developments"* (Ed.). Deep & Deep Publication Pvt., Ltd., New Delhi. 1999.

5. Kala Rani Rengasamy, "Economic Reforms and Neglected Sectors" *Peninsular Economists—Revaluation of Economic Reforms.* Journal of the Association of Economists of Tamil Nadu. Vol. XIV No. I, 2001-02.

6. Lakshminan. S., "Social Sector Reforms", *Peninsular Economists—Revaluation of Economic Reforms in India,* Journal of Association of Economists of Tamil Nadu, Vol. XIV, No. I 2001-02.

7. Lalitha, N. Seethalakshmi, M., "Social Sector in the Context of Economic Reforms—Ground Realities" *Peninsular Economist. Social Sector in the Context of Globalisation,* Journal of the Association of Economists of Tamil Nadu, Vol. XIII, No. I, 2000-01.

8. Natarajan, R., "Impact of L.P.G. on Social Sector"; *Peninsular Economists—Social Sector in the Context of Globalisation...,* Journals of the Association of Economists of Tamil Nadu, Vol. XII No. I, 2000-01.

9. Pandmanabhan, C.B., "Sustainable Human Development (Environment)," *Peninsular Economist—Sustainable Development, Food Security,* Journal of the Association of Economists of Tamil Nadu and Pondicherry, Vol. XI No. 1, 1988-89.

10. Subhulakshmi, B., "Educational Infrastructure in India. An Evaluation of Its Development;". *Peninsular Economist—Special Issue Infrastructure and Development,* Journal of the Association of Economists of Tamil Nadu and Pondicherry, Vol. X, No. 2; 1998-99.

32

Employment in Small Scale Industries During Post-Reforms Period—Opportunities and Challenges

A. Chandraprabha

Introduction

Small Scale Industries have been playing a vital role in our economy for the past four decades by witnessing a thorough transformation on individuals initiatives of small scale units into a mass people's movement. Small scale industries constitute a larger proportion of the industrial sector in India. It accounts for 50 per cent of the industrial production in the country and 80 per cent of the employment. Even with regard to exports SSI is responsible for 24 per ccnt and considering only non-traditional items, as much as 40 per cent of the total exports.

Small Sector Industrial Policy

India's Small Scale Industry Policy has been widely known phenomena. The relative merits of less capital intensity and more labour absorption capacity among others have entered the sector to the policy makers as an instrument to achieve a variety of economic objectives such as employment generation, production of mass consumption goods, balanced regional development and equitable distribution of income.

The SSIs have a lot to offer in the generation of employment opportunities. But here again the Government fails to perform its supporting role.

The new industrial policy was introduced in July 1991 having three important facts. The first dealing with deregulation, decontrol delicensing and debureaucratisation, the second emphasizing on profit maximisation and making the sector competition oriented for future development and lastly opening up the Indian economy for globalisation with a view to promote export-led development in the country.

The real growth of output of the SSI sector in 1991-92 might be less than 2 per cent. The growth of the sector in 1991-92 was in spite of a number of constraints like import restrictions affecting the availability of requisite raw materials and credit squeeze and a rise in the interest rates leading to severe erosion of the liquidity position of the SSI units.

Though there is lack of reliable data for the SSI, more particularly for the traditional group of industries, the products of the sector. Needless to comment that the cottage and small scale industries play a significant role in the sphere of national income of the country.

Employment Generation

This sector has a high potentiality of employment orientation. They are not capital-intensive rather labour-intensive. Labour investment ratio in their case is very high. The most important single argument advocated in favour of these industries since a long compass of time is that they are capable to create a large volume of employment for the people relevant particularly for India where the problem of unemployment and under-employment are rampant on a mass scale which is also characterised by the feature of lack of resources.

In such a grave and contrast situation, i.e. labour—abundant and capital—scarce economy. It is argued that the development of this sector is the only alternative strategy which are labour-intensive and the level of employment can be enlarged by a smaller dose of capital. In 1991, 130 lakhs people were employed in this sector rose to 167 lakhs in 1997 registering 78 per cent growth over the period.

Creation of Self Employment

The development of this sector provides an advantage of self-employment among the people as it is an open secret that the problem of unemployment is hampering rapid growth of the country and such burning problem of unemployment is a serious cause of all economic and political distribution on the society.

In such a situation, the importance of the development of cottage and small scale industries is greater whether the scope of self-employment exists. Therefore, these industries offer larger avenues for self-employment.

Table 32.1: Industrial Investment through IEMs and LOTs

Year	*IEM Number*	*Proposed Invest-ment (Rs. in crores)*	*Proposed employ-ment*	*Number (0005)*	*LOT proposed investment (Rs. in crore)*	*Proposed Employ-ment*
1991*	3084	76310	759	195	2071	34
1992	4860	115872	923	620	13994	97
1993	4456	63976	703	528	12845	100
1994	4664	88771	829	546	17937	130
1995	6502	125509	1114	355	14265	91
1996	4825	73278	696	522	29932	181
1997	3873	53379	522	321	9528	96
1998*	2530	51011	446	144	3273	27
(1997)**	(3590)	(46668)	(492)	(294)	(9012)	(91)
Total	34794	647106	6002	3231	103845	756

*August to December

**January—November.

Note: Total may not tally because of rounding off an annual basis.

Source: Economic Survey, 1998-99.

Cumulative foreign investment approved in the process amounted to Rs. 1,75,032 crore and actual inflow (Rs. 51,558 crore) constitutes 29.5 per cent of the approved amount.

Table 32.2: Total Foreign Technology Agreements and Direct Approvals

Year	*No. of FICS Approved*	*No. of FIDs approved*	*Amount Approved (Rs. in crores)*	*Actual inflow (Rs. in crores)*
1991	661	289	534	351
1992	828	692	3888	675
1993	691	786	8859	1787
1994	792	1062	14190	3829
1995	982	1355	32070	6820
1996	744	1559	36150	10389
1997	660	1665	54891	16425
1998*	516	989	24454	11821
(1999)**	(533)	(1317)	(46658)	(10296)
Total	5874	8396	175032**	51558

*upto October

** includes 57 proposals for GDR/FCCB involving Rs. 18,729 crores.

Note: Total may not tally because of rounding off an annual basis.

Source: Economic Survey 1998-99.

Table 32.3: Employment of Small Scale Industries in India

Year	*Employment (in lakhs)*
1991-92	130.51
1992-93	134.06
1993-94	139.38
1994-95	146.56
1995-96	152.61
1996-97	160.00
1997-98	167.20
1998-99	171.58

Source: Government of India, Planning Commission, and Ninth Five Year Plan.

The importance of Rural Industries is to provide employment opportunities, it is a source of such income, helps to distribute the workforce, possible to raise the living standards of weaker section are to various social illiteracy poverty etc.

This table explains that employment opportunities in Small Scale industries in India during New Economic Policy period. The number of employment has been increased from 119.60 lakhs 1989-90 to 171.58 lakhs in 1998-99 are to the adoption of new economic policy in India.

Exports and Production in Small Scale Sector

The annual growth of production of the small scale sector of 10.9 per cent is much higher than the growth rate of industrial production, in the large sector obviously, the growth rate of the Small Scale Sector has been faster both in terms of output and employment (Datt, 1997).

Table 32.4: Exports and Production in Small Scale Sector

Year	*Production (Rs. crores)*	*Exports (Rs. crores)*
1973-74	7,200	393
1977-78	14,300	845
1980-81	28,060	1,643
1985-86	61,228	2,769
1987-88	87,300	4,373
1990-91	1,55,340	9,100
1991-92	1,78,700	13,627
1992-93	2,09,300	17,785
1993-94	2,41,648	22,764
1994-95	2,93,990	28,000

Source: All India report on Functions and Activities (1992-93), Small Industries Development Organisations (SIDO), Department of Small Scale Industry, Government of India pp. 4-6.

It is generally recognised, that the healthy expansion of cottage and Small Scale industries depends upon a number of factors, like the provision of raw materials, cheap power, technological advancements and organised marketing of products.

Problem of the Industry

They face several difficulties and problems in the way of their structural development which are as under:

Shortage of Resources

The first and the foremost problem is with regard to the availability of resources.

Problem of Raw Materials

This problem has also affected the health of this sector.

Problem of Marketing

It is impossible for this sector to maintain the tastes and preferences of the consumers of the world particularly in the age of liberalisation and globalisation.

Problem of Sickness

Another major problem faced by this sector is the magnitude of sickness of large number of units both registered and unregistered.

Problem of Old Methods of Production

Knowledge for the use of new technology is also an obstacle caused by illiteracy among the producers of this sector.

Competition trom Large Scale Industries

An important problem of this sector is related to the extent of competition from large scale industries.

There is a need for promoting non-agriculture's employment in rural areas. While the potential of crop production to generate employment is likely to be low, the potential of allied sectors such as dairy, poultry, pisciculture and sericulture to generate rural employment is high.

Suggestive Policy Prescriptions

Here, an attempt has been made to suggest a list of policy prescriptions to wipe out the problems of this sector.

1. Financing of resources is not the duty of the bank only but they should be vigilant for its recovery.
2. Due to inadequate financial and managerial resources quite often small units find it difficult to market their product.
3. Attempt should be made to provide cheap power facilities to this sector.
4. There must be a provision for industrial education and training for the entrepreneurs of this sector.
5. For all purposes, the facility of advisory assistance should be given to them for rapid development of this sector.

Conclusion

Under the new SSI policy measures for promoting and strengthening SSIs, there is a significant of the overall strategy for a SSI development. It may be too early to judge the sufficiency of the strategy to bring out the desired outcome.

REFERENCES

1. B.N.P. Singh, *Industrial Development Under Structural Adjustment Programems"* Deep & Deep Publications Pvt. Ltd., New Delhi, pp. 202-250.
2. A. Chandraprabha, *"Impact of New Economic Policy on Small Scale Industries"* (ed.) M. Soundarapandian *"Impact of New Economic Policy, Rural Industries Under Liberalisation"* Volume I, Concept Publishing Company, New Delhi-59, pp. 150-153, 186-189.
3. B. Shyamala, *"An Education of New Economic Policy on SSI,"* Small Scale Industries, Vol. 2, pp. 10-11.
4. R.P. Singh, *"New Economic Policy and Perspective to Rural Development,"* National Institute of Rural Development, Hyderabad, pp. 250-254.